$3.00

BEHIND THE STEEL WALL

Arvid Fredborg

is a young Swedish journalist who for two years ending last summer was Berlin correspondent for *Svenska Dagbladet,* a leading Stockholm daily. Fredborg earned the displeasure of the Nazis by his sturdy refusal to accept their version of the news, and by circumventing in various ways the tight censorship. His unpopularity grew steadily in official circles, until he was finally warned by friends to leave the country.

Behind the Steel Wall, which Fredborg wrote from private notes immediately after quitting Germany, was published in Stockholm on September 22. It was received there with sensational excitement (Viking first heard of the book through Associated Press dispatches reporting the enthusiasm) and sold in two months the total, unprecedented for Sweden, of 46,000 copies.

A copy of the book was sent to Viking by air, and a staff of translators was engaged to prepare an English text. This version, after careful editing, was rushed to press, and a large first printing was run off late in 1943, for publication in January.

BEHIND THE STEEL WALL

BEHIND
THE STEEL WALL

ᒧᒪᒧᒪᒧᒪᒧᒪᒧᒪᒧᒪᒧᒪᒧᒪᒧᒪᒧᒪᒧᒪᒧᒪ

A SWEDISH JOURNALIST IN BERLIN

1941-43

BY ARVID FREDBORG

NEW YORK · THE VIKING PRESS · 1944

Bakom Stålvallen

Behind the Steel Wall

TO MY WIFE

ｎｎｎｎ CONTENTS ｎｎｎｎ

⊓⊔⊓⊔⊓⊔⊓⊔ **MAPS** ⊓⊔⊓⊔⊓⊔⊓⊔

BEHIND THE STEEL WALL

A JOURNALIST
IN THE THIRD REICH

The Foreign Press in Berlin

ANY journalist who wants to become acquainted with conditions in Germany today regards it as a great privilege to be assigned to Berlin. Better than any other class of foreigners, the neutral correspondents are able to observe the daily changes and that indefinite something best called atmosphere, which is more clearly expressed in the faces and gestures of high officials than it is in what they say. But to survive as a journalist in the Third Reich one has to be something of a tightrope dancer. What the job requires in the way of mental and physical resistance can hardly be imagined by anyone who has never tried it. Each word sent out by cable or telephone has to be carefully chosen, for one rash phrase can lead to a permanent fall from grace.

Swedish journalists perhaps encounter greater difficulties than any others, except the Swiss, since they have to prepare as accurate a picture as possible of the true situation for a public ignorant of censorship and its practical effects. They hope—but they cannot be sure—that the public at home has learned to read between the lines of their dispatches. Most of the Swedes in Berlin have tried to judge the situation independently of preconceived opinions. But this objectivity is exactly what the Germans do not want. By "objective" they mean at best the suppression of every detail that is unfavorable to Germany and Nazism; at worst they mean outright German propaganda. It thus becomes the duty of every newspaperman from a neutral country not only to resist every attempt to make him a tool for Nazism, but also to learn, in spite of the daily joust with German propaganda, what is really going on.

There is a continual battle between the Nazis, who want to conceal what is happening, and the newspapermen, who want to know everything of importance, even if the facts cannot be published. Sometimes one side wins and sometimes the other. It is not often, however, that Dr. Goebbels succeeds in leading the foreign correspondents completely astray. They usually obtain a fairly clear picture of actual events—sometimes with the aid of hints inadvertently dropped by the German propagandists themselves. After a few months in Berlin, you learn how to read the official statements not only for the story they set forth—which may be false—but also as a revelation of what those in power wish to convey and what they wish to conceal. Conclusions reached in this way often correspond surprisingly well with the facts when they later come to light.

"Dependable sources in the Wilhelmstrasse"; "trustworthy informants"; "well-informed circles in the German capital"—do expressions like these sound familiar? Why do Berlin correspondents use them so often? What are their actual working conditions and where do they get the news they send home?

All foreign journalists in Berlin are accredited to the Press Section of the German Government, which is attached to the Ministry of Propaganda. From the Ministry they receive an authorization which, among other things, entitles the holder to listen to foreign radio broadcasts. About a year ago, a few journalists from occupied countries lost this right. Among them were some Quislings, who might have been corrupted, the Germans thought, by listening to the broadcasts from London. Naturally they continued to do so anyway.

Foreign correspondents in Berlin are also accredited to the Foreign Office, which is often referred to as "AA," the initials standing for its German name of *Auswärtiges Amt*. The Propaganda Ministry, which is called "Promi" for short, attends to all practical details. In addition to the usual ration cards, for example, the foreign newspapermen get an extra card covering meat, butter and bread for one person. They also receive special tobacco cards, allowing them the magnificent ration of twenty cigarettes a day.

Clothes and shoes are provided through special order blanks. There are in Berlin a certain number of shoemakers who work for foreigners and consequently get better leather than the rest. Promi also arranges for invitations to official events and for railroad tickets. To those with the proper credentials, it grants permission to telephone abroad; without such permission, no correspondent could do his work in Berlin. Those who have cars and a license to use them receive a gasoline allowance, also through the mediation of Promi. When I left Berlin, the allowance was 50 liters—about 14 gallons—a month, although some favored Axis correspondents were given more.

The Press and the Ministry of Propaganda

The Foreign Press Section of the Propaganda Ministry is divided into departments for different countries or groups of countries, each under the direction of a specialist known as a *Referent*. He must not only keep an eye on the correspondents representing his special area but also help them get pictures and provide them with information on various topics. Each specialist is assisted by readers, who report what is happening day by day in the press of the countries to which they are assigned. He also has the help of DNB (the German News Bureau) and of German embassies in various countries. From one source or another, he receives translations of the most important news dispatches that have been telephoned from Berlin.

The real contact between the foreign press and the Ministry of Propaganda is established through two daily press conferences. The 12:30 conference takes place in the room of the Foreign Press Chief at the Propaganda Ministry, where the correspondents are packed together like herrings. For the 5:30 conference, Dr. Goebbels' theater auditorium is available. Once a week the latest newsreel is shown there.

Originally the Foreign Press Section of the Propaganda Ministry was directed by Professor Karl Boehmer, who was highly regarded by all correspondents because of his kindly manner and his efforts to give them something, at least, that was of value as news. He also enjoyed the confidence of his chief, Dr. Goebbels, who used to say that in Karl Boehmer Germany had found the right man to deal with representatives of the foreign press. Boehmer succeeded in combining loyalty to his superior with a sense of fair play toward his subordinates. Now and then he might take a stand when he felt that the police had gone too far. Some years ago a Dutch newspaperman named Max Blokzijl enjoyed a certain popularity in Berlin; he was generally considered as having anti-Nazi sympathies. A few journalists suspected that something was wrong, but they had no proof. Meeting some of my older colleagues one day, Boehmer in one way or another let them understand that there was a journalist in Berlin who seemed to be dependable, but who was actually a Gestapo agent sent to spy on his comrades. No name was mentioned, but all present felt that the man in question must be Blokzijl. Later, when the Germans invaded Holland, a new man stepped forward suddenly as Mussert's pro-German Chief of Propaganda and radio announcer. It was Dr. Max Blokzijl.

Boehmer's story illustrates the rivalry between two ministries and the life-and-death struggle in high Nazi circles. He had one weakness that caused his downfall: he liked to drink, and when he drank he liked to talk. This was an opportunity for his rivals in the Foreign Office, who kept organizing little plots against him. They would see to it that Boehmer had plenty to drink; then one of them would come over to the Propaganda Ministry to ask him dangerous questions. Boehmer would answer them in no uncertain terms—even if they had to do with Ribbentrop himself.

The trick was tried once more in the spring of 1941 at a reception in the Bulgarian Legation. This time it worked so well that everybody was frightened. Boehmer happened to betray the fact that the war against Russia was to start on June 22. In Germany such an indiscretion is punished as high treason. Fortunately for Hitler's plans, so many dates for the invasion of Russia had been whispered already that nobody seems to have taken his statement very seriously. I don't know whether the Bulgarians ever passed Boehmer's information on to the Russians. Judging by what happened afterwards, they must have kept quiet.

The fight for Boehmer's life was long and hard. Hitler himself is supposed to have wanted him out of the way as quickly as possible. In this case, however, one must give Dr. Goebbels some credit, for he did everything to save his best man. After long negotiations Boehmer was given a sentence of two years in prison. In 1942 he was released and offered the chance to rehabilitate himself as a private in his old regiment on the eastern front (he had once been a lieutenant in the reserve). He availed himself of this chance. Private Boehmer fought with such bravery that everybody was filled with admiration and his return to official favor seemed assured. At that moment, however, he was seriously wounded and died in a hospital in Cracow.

The correspondents were invited to hear a funeral oration for Boehmer at the Ministry of Propaganda. Some time later Dr. Dietrich, Hitler's press chief, gave a dinner at which Paul Schmidt of the Foreign Office was also obliged to be present. On this occasion,

Dietrich unexpectedly paid tribute to Boehmer's memory. Everybody rose to his feet, even Schmidt, although he was the last to do so. Shortly afterwards he made some excuse to leave the table and did not return. All eyes followed him as he left, since he was generally considered to be the organizer of the plot against Boehmer.

It was Dr. Ernst Brauweiler who succeeded him as chief of the Foreign Press Section. He was an old Nazi provincial editor, bureaucratic and lacking imagination. The two daily conferences at the Ministry of Propaganda at once became dull and colorless. Brauweiler never dared to take responsibility or give out information. At the most he would promise to find out—and a few days later he might let us have the requested information, which by then was no longer news.

Boehmer had charming manners and spoke with ease and an ironic sense of humor. Brauweiler was stuffy. When faced with a difficult question, he would become as obstinate as an army mule; sometimes he would answer with a direct insult. Conscious of his own shortcomings, he tried to assert himself by being rude. Schmidt of the Foreign Office was delighted at the change, because it lowered the prestige of the rival ministry.

Dr. Wilhelm Skippert, a brilliant lawyer, is Brauweiler's first assistant. He works silently and without fuss. Many assume, because of his discretion, that he is the most important of the many Gestapo agents in the Ministry.

The specialists in charge of various countries were frequently changed as the war went on and more and more men were drafted. Scandinavia and Finland had at first been assigned to Dr. Gerhard Kuhlman, one of the most modest men in Berlin. He alternately blushed and turned pale when he talked with us, and always seemed to be afraid that we would ask some question he was not prepared to answer. When he had to reprimand someone, you might think that Kuhlman himself was the culprit. Incidentally he had studied in Sweden, written an interesting treatise on the Stockholm press, and learned to speak Swedish fluently.

Dr. Zuhlsdorff, originally in charge of Spain, Portugal and Latin America, took over Scandinavia when Dr. Kuhlman went into the army. Zuhlsdorff is a small man, domineering and sure of himself, but ignorant of everything that concerns either Sweden or the other northern countries. He is very slow at his work, despite his energy, and he cannot understand that a journalist regards news as something to be written today instead of tomorrow. Recently

Zuhlsdorff was drafted in his turn and replaced by another faithful Party member.

Many other changes took place. The Americans in their day were assigned to Dr. Froehlich, a grim Gestapo type; the Japanese still have the privilege of working with Dr. Schaefer, a man who speaks Japanese perfectly. In the Propaganda Ministry there was, and still is, a man whom nobody quite understands. He is Rolf Hoffman, publisher of *Die Deutsche Stimme* in Munich, a tall man with bushy black hair and affected manners. He appears naïve and even stupid and was no success as a publisher. Many thought it strange that he was not in the army and, what was more, that he had his own office and a private secretary. I sometimes wondered if Hoffman was as stupid as he looked. It was a public secret that he was the tool of Martin Bormann who, since Hess's flight to England, has become the Führer's right-hand man.

Dr. Giese, who takes care of passports, visas and other practical matters, is the most popular of all the staff members at Promi. He is like a father to the foreign correspondents, and sometimes he had to stand for a great deal from his unruly children; but he took everything in his stride, showed a keen sense of humor, and always did his best to straighten things out. He never forced his opinion on us as did the other Nazis. Fond of schnapps and beer, he usually managed to find one or the other for a company of tired and thirsty newspapermen.

Major Martin Sommerfeldt (he was a Captain when I first came to Berlin) usually serves as the spokesman for the General Staff. He too is liked by nearly all the members of the foreign press. He comes from Schleswig and, in civilian life, was a partner in the publishing house of Mittler & Sohn; therefore he understands the problems of the press. Because of his easygoing manners and his sense of humor, he seems more human than the rest. After serving for several years as Goering's press chief in the Prussian Department of the Interior, he was forced to resign for some unknown reason. He was, however, ordered back into public life when the Germans had to find a reasonable and trustworthy interpreter of military affairs.

Major Sommerfeldt has tried his best to please the foreign correspondents as well as his own superiors, but his initiative has been more and more curtailed. By the spring of 1943, he had nothing to do but hand out his mimeographed military comments, just as others handed out the political comments. The situation was not to his liking, any more than it was to ours. But all he could do was to echo headquarters, and each day the echo became emptier of facts.

The Foreign Correspondents and the Foreign Office

The Press Section of the Foreign Office is organized in separate divisions for the different countries, with a special bureau for the foreign press as a whole. The chief is Dr. Paul Schmidt, a plump little man whose career has been remarkable in many respects. After winning his spurs as a Nazi student leader, Schmidt attached himself to the group around the rising star of foreign policy, Joachim von Ribbentrop. When Ribbentrop became Foreign Secretary, he made Schmidt, then only 28 years old, the head of his Press Section. Schmidt continued to advance rapidly, until he reached the titular rank of First-class Envoy (or Ambassador), although he has never been sent abroad to represent his country, except on special missions to the vassal states. Still, as envoy to the foreign press, he is among the chief spokesmen for the Nazi regime, besides being Ribbentrop's right-hand man.

First-class Envoy Schmidt is in constant touch with the press and speaks at most of the official functions. He conducts the press conferences at one o'clock in the Foreign Office. It is not difficult to understand why Schmidt is appreciated in high government circles. Intelligent, quick-thinking and witty, biting in his replies, wholly without moral scruples, he tells you anything that will best serve Ribbentrop's purpose at the moment. Everything he says is taken down by a stenographer for the benefit of his chief and even of Hitler himself. The result is that Schmidt always speaks with both a visible and an invisible audience in mind.

He is a born actor and this is one of the reasons for his success. Even his bitterest enemies are forced to acknowledge his complete self-control, which makes him master of almost any situation, no matter how difficult. Less impressive are his theatrical rantings and his bursts of false indignation. His emotions run the gamut as he mournfully shakes his head at the stupidity of Churchill or Roosevelt and then roars out his rage at the infamy of the opponents. But when he tries to move his audience to tears, his attempts seem false and ridiculous, considering that in private life he is a thoroughgoing cynic and does not try to hide it. Everybody knows that Schmidt would defend *another* German regime with the same quavering fervor—that is, if he were allowed to keep his job. In fact, his cynicism is one of his strongest weapons. Having no scruples, he often gets the upper hand of those who hesitate to use the same means. The plot against Boehmer was only one example.

Schmidt has a not too secret dream: to succeed Ribbentrop. Well-informed people say that he has already taken a few discreet steps to hasten developments leading in that direction.

Dr. Schmidt can sometimes be charming, but most of the time he is ruthless and overbearing; that is the chief reason for his general unpopularity. The way he treats women is incredible. Once he was introduced to some German ladies belonging to distinguished families. He told these representatives of the *ancien régime*, which he hates: "Your time is past, ladies. Mine is coming." At the Press Club in the Fasanenstrasse, Schmidt has issued an ultimatum: every woman who enters the building must greet him before he deigns to acknowledge her presence.

His deputy, Baron Gustav Braun von Stumm, is a man of a wholly different type, an aristocrat from southern Germany who has accepted Nazism and stayed on at the Foreign Office as a monocled souvenir of times gone by. He is an expert in political history with a thorough knowledge of most European countries, acquired during his years of service abroad. Again in contrast to Schmidt, Braun von Stumm is a good linguist and enjoys speaking French. A man of his background and philosophy of life must often have winced at the bullying ways of the Nazis, but he has never dared to oppose them, and sometimes in his fear of not being thought sufficiently faithful, he has copied their brusque manners. Braun von Stumm lacks the oratorical talent of his chief. His speeches are tedious and uninteresting, and most people think he is just dull. But he has suffered deeply during this war. His son Egbert was killed in Russia, another son was crippled at the same front, and the third lost his life in an accident. A short time ago his charming and graceful Italian wife died suddenly. She was one of the few real ladies in the mixed society of the Wilhelmstrasse.

Some Berlin journalists are allowed to attend the press conferences at the Foreign Office. Dr. Karl Megerle, who is often there, has been used by Ribbentrop's ministry as its mouthpiece in the press. He is extremely cordial in his personal contacts and looks not unlike a scholar; it is hard to realize that he can wield so sharp a pen.

Dr. Rudolf Fischer, publisher of the *Süd-Ost-Echo,* can also be seen at these conferences. He is the well-known "Rufi," with the sharp nose, the yellow skin and the shiny pate. Once he was one of the most brilliant journalists in Vienna; now he is merely one of Schmidt's yes-men, graciously permitted by his master to live in an apartment above the Press Club in the Fasanenstrasse. Officially he still publishes the *Süd-Ost-Echo,* getting a good salary, but his position is not easy. It is possible that somebody else writes many of the articles signed "F.F."—the initials he adopted long ago—for they no longer sound like Rufi's work, being dull and orthodox Nazi propaganda. Fischer himself is an extremely intelligent man, known and feared for his cynicism. He is supposed to have made many remarks of the sort that would have landed most people in concentration camps. Doubtless he is useful to the Nazis because of his other skillful "indiscretions," which sound as if they were slips of the tongue, but which are really intended to mislead the foreign correspondents.

First Secretary Emil Rasche once towered above the rank and file both physically and officially. A tall man with a huge belly, he was chief of the Foreign Section of the Press Department. Rasche disappeared some months ago, the official story being that he had returned to his post on a newspaper in western Germany. He was missed by the correspondents, because he knew how to make each of them feel that he was a special friend. He could always be easily persuaded to come along home for a nightcap and many correspondents were flattered by this sign of confidence. And yet we were never quite sure of him. His eyes strayed here and there, sometimes with an expression that was hard to reconcile with his friendly manners. There was good reason for us to be on our guard with him. Afterwards we learned that Rasche was one of the most trusted Gestapo agents in the Ministry and that he had shown no mercy to his bosom friends.

We worked in the big Bundesratsaal of the Foreign Office, where Bismarck once presided over the Congress of Berlin. Nothing much has changed there since Bismarck's time. The walls are still covered with brown paneling, there are dark green curtains at the windows, and from the ceiling hang two magnificent crystal chandeliers. Dr. Schmidt and Braun von Stumm (one or both of them), together with a representative of the Propaganda Ministry and the most important specialists, preside at an enormous table in the middle of the room. Behind them stand any German journalists who have been invited to the conference. Newspapermen from all over the world sit on the opposite side, while the Italians occupy one end of the table. As long as the Americans were in Berlin, Louis P. Lochner and Pierre J. Huss used to sit directly opposite Schmidt. The Quislings kept behind their German masters or sat at the other end of the table, opposite the Italians.

The conferences were opened by Schmidt or Braun von Stumm with the same words: *Meine Herren, ich bitte um Ihre Fragen*— "Gentlemen, I am ready for your questions." There would be many women present, but the phrase as a rule was only *Meine Herren*. The next step would be for one of the Quislings to raise a question prepared in advance for the occasion. Long and dreary dissertations would follow. While the speaker worked himself up into a frenzy by insulting Churchill, Roosevelt or Stalin, the stenographer looked at the ceiling, the smoke became dense, and the correspondents made curlicues in their notebooks. Once I walked slowly around the table to see what they were doing. Some were drawing caricatures of those present, others were making a list of their appointments for the day, others were straightening out their accounts, and one correspondent was writing a letter.

Once in a while a stimulating question brought us back to life. In the old days it was usually our Lithuanian colleague who was inquisitive; later he was sent home for being troublesome. The correspondent for a big Swiss paper often helped him. During my first year in Berlin, our questions were fairly lively, and it was only the Italian and Japanese correspondents who remained silent, under instructions from their embassies. During the second year, however, the Swedes rarely asked questions. This fact attracted attention, and everything was done to make them talk. Sweden would be mentioned time and again. At the end of several conferences, Schmidt said, "No more questions—not even by the Swedes?" but we remained silent. The reason was that we had already burned our fingers. Almost any vital question was embarrassing to the Germans, and during 1942 the tone of both Schmidt and Braun von Stumm became so insulting that we could do only one of two things, either answer back and be told to leave the room or else leave voluntarily. We preferred to remain silent and not to provoke insults that we were not in a position to answer. Schmidt frequently voiced his opinion about the "low intellectual standard" of the foreign press and said that he was thinking of discontinuing the press conferences for that reason. The Swedes were rather flattered.

The material given to us at the press conferences didn't make much sense, and it was a desperately hopeless job to try and squeeze out anything with news value. Even under pressure from Schmidt, we refused to quote his comments. Finally we explained that our newspapers simply wouldn't print most of the material, but this scarcely made us more popular. The evident friendship and cooperation among all Swedish journalists did not improve matters. And yet this unity in our small group is one of the few pleasant memories of my stay in Berlin. Our group also included the non-Quisling newspapermen from other northern countries, all held together by personal friendship and meeting now and then informally. The Germans were far from pleased, especially on the evening when a group of Finnish journalists joined us, after giving the slip to their German chaperons.

Sources of Information for the Foreign Press

As late as 1941, a foreign correspondent could give his paper a fairly accurate picture of Germany and its policies. There were, of course, many restrictions on our work, but in retrospect they seem not unreasonable. We were not allowed to mention anything about the visits and travels of foreign statesmen, about the tours of leading German officials, about the weather, about the air raids or about the relations between Germany and her allies, unless we had special permission to do so. After Pearl Harbor, the situation changed for the worse. The Germans no longer had to be considerate to the Americans, and the remaining neutral journalists were given less information to send home.

We got most of our news from German newspapers published in the Reich and in the occupied countries. It was not long, however, before we were forbidden to quote from the latter. As other sources dried up the German home press became more and more important to foreign correspondents. Unfortunately the German press was printing less and less of what actually happened. German newspapers speak with one voice. The provincial press is particularly stereotyped because of the so-called *Kopfblatt* system, by which a provincial paper receives all its political material from a larger paper and is obliged to publish it unchanged.

The one real distinction among German newspapers is whether

or not they belong to the Party press. If they are owned by the Nazis, directly or indirectly, their standards are likely to be extremely low. But they are also likely to have a better chance for survival than papers still in private ownership. If some newspaper is to be sacrificed as an economy measure, it is most certainly never the Party organ.

The most important of these organs is the official *Völkischer Beobachter*, the old mouthpiece of the Party, once edited by Alfred Rosenberg; the chief editor is now Wilhelm Weiss. It is a dull and uninteresting paper, badly put together, with a very inadequate news coverage. It has no foreign news service worth mentioning. The editor does not object to printing stories that are old even to the German public, whose choice in reading matter is not very great. Nobody is surprised to find in the *Völkischer Beobachter* year-old stories by soldiers at the front, or news articles that have been published in the provinces weeks before. Special editions are published in several big cities, and the Vienna edition is actually better than the one printed in Berlin. The *Angriff*, Dr. Goebbels' old paper and now the organ of the Labor Front, is slightly better than the leading Party organ. Its principal feature is the editorials by Labor Minister Ley, which often contain bad news for the home front.

Among the privately owned newspapers, the *Frankfurter Zeitung* is or was outstanding. Politically, of course, it has been as restricted as the other newspapers, but the editor managed to maintain standards that the rest of the German press had been forced to abandon long ago. For this reason, the *Frankfurter Zeitung* has been subjected to fierce attacks from the Party, which views the efforts of the editor, Dr. Rudolf Kircher, as a disguised criticism of its own mediocre journalism. For a long time Dr. Goebbels held a protecting hand over the paper, not because he liked it, but because he wanted something to display abroad. Many articles in the *Frankfurter Zeitung* which surprised the world by their frankness were written mainly for foreign consumption. The business section was admirable, and the *Frankfurter Zeitung* was almost the only German paper with cultural interests. Well-informed people explained that the editorial staff was so old that it couldn't be drafted, but one must give the old gentlemen credit for having done an excellent job. Today, however, all that is an old story. A statement from Berlin announced that the old and dignified "FZ" would cease publication on August 31, 1943.

The *Deutsche Allgemeine Zeitung*, edited by Dr. Karl Silex, is another newspaper that has done its best to retain the old tradition, though with limited success. The legal advertisements and the personals clearly reveal its character. "DAZ," as it is usually called, is the organ of the German aristocracy. It was through this paper that the former Crown Prince made public the death of his son Wilhelm in the spring of 1941. The notice was signed "Wilhelm, Crown Prince of Prussia."

The special organ of the German Foreign Office is the *Berliner Börsenzeitung*, which carries political articles by Dr. Karl Megerle. The *Börsenzeitung* pays special attention to financial news and is still the organ of the business community.

The *Essener Nationalzeitung* is one of the better papers speaking for the Nazis, though it does not directly belong to the Party press. Under the protection of Marshal Goering, it originally had an unusually homogeneous staff of young, talented and enthusiastic editors. It succeeded in maintaining a fairly high standard and had excellent foreign correspondents, especially in Ankara and elsewhere in the Near East.

The *Hamburger Fremdenblatt* is worth mentioning if only because Dr. Adolf Halfeld is on its staff. He often writes about Scandinavian questions and usually expresses a balanced outlook. The *Kölnische Zeitung* still has some importance. The *Münchener Neueste Nachrichten* is well informed about the Balkans and Italy. There is, however, not much to say about the rest of the German press. Papers that used to be interesting are now dull editorially, dull typographically and carry no news.

Newspapers are published by the Germans in the occupied countries, all with the stereotyped name *Deutsche Zeitung*, the *German Times—in the Netherlands, in Norway, in the East*, etc. These papers were fairly well edited in the beginning, especially the *Danube Times*. After a few weeks, however, they received strict orders not to publish anything that would interest the foreign correspondents in Berlin. We might as well have canceled our subscriptions.

Outside of the German press, a principal source of news was official announcements, usually given out at a press conference. These had to be treated as statements "by the spokesman for the Wilhelmstrasse," or "from the proper authorities" or "made in military circles." There were also off-the-record statements by officials in the ministries that could be used, but with caution, under cover of some such phrase as "in well-informed circles in Berlin."

Finally we come to Dienst aus Deutschland, a news service bureau, that supplied us with comments on the events of the day and other information which, though not strictly official, was distributed with the assent of the Wilhelmstrasse. Dienst aus Deutschland has made one blunder after another, despite the great caution with which it operates. There was many an evening when officials had to telephone and ask us to suppress one or more of the items they themselves had given us earlier in the day. The "DaD," as we called it, has often been used by German propagandists to circulate rumors without making themselves officially responsible. It was very difficult for the foreign correspondents to decide whether DaD was telling us the truth or whether we were being used to spread a lie. As a rule we published the information anyhow, but tried to make the reader understand what type of news we thought it was.

The *Stammtisch* is an institution that makes the life of a Berlin journalist somewhat easier.[1] One such group was founded years ago by some of the older journalists, under the informal leadership of Erich Schneyder, who was then chief Berlin editor of the *Essener Nationalzeitung*, and it has lasted until today, despite attacks from various quarters. It meets with its invited guests every Thursday evening in Dr. Goebbels' Foreign Club to hear a lecture of some kind, under Schneyder's chairmanship. Then follows the sort of general discussion that Germans call an *Eiertanz*, a dancing on eggs, which is not a bad phrase to describe its nature. The lectures are often extremely interesting, as the speaker may be a minister or some other important person. We were allowed to use for publication any information gathered during such an evening, unless strict orders to the contrary had been issued beforehand.

Dr. Schmidt's *Stammtisch* was a different matter entirely. This

---

[1] *Louis P. Lochner wrote a little treatise on the* Stammtisch *in his recent book,* What about Germany? *He said in part, "The* Stammtisch *is an institution indigenous to Germany only. It is usually a table in some restaurant reserved for the same people who come there day after day, usually night after night, to sip their mug of beer or their glass of wine, and to discuss the world in general and their own little problems in particular. Every village has its* Stammtisch; *no sizable saloon or restaurant in the city is without it. It is a 'Dutch treat' affair. Before the Nazis assumed power, every political party in Germany had its* Stammtisch *in every stronghold."—Tr.*

group met every Tuesday at Ribbentrop's Foreign Press Club in the Fasanenstrasse, and its chief purpose was to counteract Schneyder's group, which in turn represented Goebbels. Schmidt had his own reasons for inviting people to his meetings. He said himself that the members of his *Stammtisch* were the cream of the foreign correspondents in Berlin. This cream consisted of practically every Rumanian, Bulgarian, Slovakian and Croatian newspaperman in town. Only one Hungarian was a member and even he had dropped out before I left Berlin. There were very few Danes or Swedes.

Lectures were given at Schmidt's *Stammtisch*, too, but more often there was merely a discussion of some subject that Schmidt had selected. From reports that reached me, I gathered that Schmidt liked to talk about Sweden, a country for which he seemed to feel an unhappy and spiteful love. I also gathered that the discussions in general were more restricted than at Schneyder's, and the audience often spent the evening listening to long dissertations by Schmidt himself, who was obviously in need of "getting things out of his system." Some of the things said on Tuesdays in the Fasanenstrasse were intended as discreet warnings and reprimands for the members of various embassies in Berlin. At other times it was difficult to discover any sensible reason for the indiscretions committed, except that a people systematically gagged, as in the Third Reich, has a purely physical need for talking to foreigners.

Very little of what was said at Schmidt's *Stammtisch* was suitable for publication. The guests were asked to be discreet, but that was more than could humanly be expected, and the next day everything of interest had become common property on the great news exchange. It is impossible to keep anything secret when 60 foreign journalists know it already.

The Press Association and the Clubs for Correspondents

Correspondents for the press of several countries are greatly helped by their embassies in Berlin. Even the Swedes have received such help, although there is no use concealing the general opinion that the conduct of the Press Section of the Swedish Embassy leaves much to be desired, and the fact that all complaints have so far been ignored.

But the Swedes as well as other correspondents have received much support from the Foreign Press Association. Its membership includes most of the authentic foreign journalists in the German capital. So far as possible, paid agents of the Propaganda Ministry or the Foreign Office with newspaper credentials have been excluded. Unfortunately the percentage of more or less suspect individuals has become greater and greater, and it is now hard to draw the line.

The Scandinavians have tried to hold their ranks intact, and happily there are no Nazis among the Swedes. The Norwegian and Danish Quislings are kept at a distance. When one of the worst of their type, an Icelander named Hoyer who claimed to represent several newspapers in Denmark, sought admission to the Association, he was turned down. This man, incidentally, was one of the very few who ostentatiously used the "Heil Hitler" greeting.

The Press Association is probably the only corporation in all Germany that has a democratic election by secret ballot. It is the only one that conducts an election campaign in the full light of publicity. The election early in 1942 was especially heated. The Swede, Bertil Svahnström, who had been president in 1941, was a candidate for re-election. Reich Press Chief Dietrich ordered the Axis journalists to vote for an Italian. After the Americans left Berlin, the neutrals were a minority in the Association. But they were all present and, as the voting was secret, Svahnström was re-elected with a large majority. Then Dietrich chose another way out. He began in a flagrant manner to harass Svahnström, and also let it be known that inasmuch as the Association had not had sense enough to elect a president with Dietrich's confidence, it would feel his wrath.

Finally Svahnström decided to resign, and immediately the Association returned to good favor. But it did not become conformist, because many of the journalists from the Axis nations, including the new president himself, had too much regard for professional integrity. The Japanese, who comprised a strong group, were not intimidated, nor did they have reason for submitting to Dietrich's pressure. The Foreign Press Association could therefore keep its traditions intact, despite certain necessary concessions.

From the material standpoint the Association meant a great deal to its members. Most prized, perhaps, was the pound of Danish butter that every member received each week. When you had to do without that you understood what the fat shortage meant to the German people. A comparison of German with Danish butter was startling. Another important advantage accruing from membership in the Association was that one could buy marks at a cheaper rate through the German Gold Discount Bank.

Both of these privileges depended, of course, on the good will of the German authorities. Every attack against the Association was preceded by a "shortage" of butter, or a rumor that the cheap marks would be withheld. But in general, the Nazis had every reason for keeping foreign newspapermen in a good humor. I have already stated that many of them were paid directly by the Propaganda Ministry. Another method was the payment of various expenses, such as telephone bills. Many of the neutrals had to wage a steady battle to resist "favors" of various kinds. Promi had formulated a definite program for bribing them. Outside of Berlin, for example, there was a magnificent estate called Julianenhof which was maintained for the benefit of journalists. Correspondents from various countries were invited there frequently, and the Quislings could stay on, week after week. It was seldom that German officials invited foreign correspondents to their homes, even though the ministries were provided with extra food coupons. Instead, luncheons and dinners were given at the two press clubs—Dr. Goebbels' German Foreign Club on the Leipziger Platz, where we were entertained by officials of the Propaganda Ministry, and Ribbentrop's Foreign Press Club in the Fasanenstrasse, where we met representatives of the Foreign Office.

Goebbels' club occupied the old Bleichröder Palace. The first floor was set aside for Germans with political pull who wanted a little better food than they could find in ordinary restaurants; while the second, third and fourth floors were at the disposal of foreign correspondents and employees of the Propaganda Ministry. The appointments were magnificent, but somehow coldly impersonal. The food was considerably better than at public restaurants, but the service was bad. In every room there were loud-speakers used for paging guests, but also, we suspected, serving other purposes. We felt that everything said in the club could be overheard. Newspapers, telephones and a radio were found up in the workroom. Adjoining it was a bar which for a long time was very well supplied.

The Foreign Press Club in the Fasanenstrasse had taken over the quarters of the German-English Society—the tableware still bore the society's emblem—and as a result it was comfortably and tastefully furnished. It was immeasurably more homelike there and since the service was excellent—all the staff were formerly servants in German legations abroad—and the food good, the Scandinavians preferred the Fasanenstrasse to Dr. Goebbels' club. Even those who had their own households went there on Saturdays, when parties were planned. But one had to guard against being too partial, for the fact was observed immediately by "the other side," that is to say, the Propaganda Ministry.

Censorship and Surveillance

The competition between the Foreign Office and Promi proved the salvation of many correspondents. Anyone who was in bad standing on the left side of the Wilhelmstrasse could automatically reckon with sympathy on the other. Frequently this situation saved us from penalties that otherwise would have been inescapable.

There is no advance censorship, a fact which the Nazis have widely advertised. They have found a better system of controlling dispatches to the neutral press. By tightening the rules that govern the conduct of correspondents and later making them responsible for what appears in their newspapers, the Nazis force them to observe the German propaganda line, and furthermore to present that propaganda in such a manner that it will be read by people at home. This is what they refer to with great pride as untrammeled reporting, *die freie Berichterstattung*.

It must be acknowledged that Press Chief Dietrich's system has some advantages for the correspondents; primarily it saves time. Freedom of movement, however, is limited to a degree that is hard to imagine. Freedom of expression simply doesn't exist. The correspondent must have a distinct feeling for every nuance of the political situation; what was still permissible yesterday may be forbidden tomorrow. Working within such narrow limits, one tries to stay as close as possible to the borderline of what can be safely said, and this is often a ticklish business. Outsiders sometimes asked us whether it was necessary to hew so close to the line and take so many risks. We answered that it *was* necessary, partly because it was the only way to write anything of interest, and partly to keep the Nazis from imposing even tighter restrictions. Had any great number of foreign correspondents set voluntary limitations on what they wrote, the Germans would certainly have drawn the border tighter, following the line of least resistance.

The day after publication, every word written by the Swedish correspondents in Germany is weighed at the German Embassy in Stockholm and at the ministries in Berlin. That is when you have to be the right side of the invisible but dangerous line. Sometimes you are able to clear up a difficulty by claiming that the editors in Stockholm have condensed the articles too much or that you were misunderstood because of a poor telephone connection—all the Swedish correspondents use the telephone. (Postal censorship at the Propaganda Ministry works rather fast, as a matter of fact, but it is still only in exceptional cases that one can send articles home by mail.) On the other hand, nobody can keep from having scenes with the German officials. It might be on account of a news story obtained in great haste and perhaps formulated as you spoke over the telephone; it might also be on account of bad judgment. No one can avoid mistakes.

Certain types of dispatches would have passed unnoticed if they had not been picked up by Allied propagandists. It was a doubtful pleasure to hear the London or Moscow radio announce: "*Svenska Dagbladet's* Berlin correspondent writes. . . ." The next day you were certain to be reprimanded by one of the specialists. I might add that the quotations from your articles made by the British, American or Russian radio were sometimes anything but accurate.

If you overstep the boundary, the whole machinery is set in motion. Generally the Propaganda Ministry handles the penalties, but, at Schmidt's request, the specialists at the Foreign Ministry can also deliver scoldings when necessary. If it is a minor offense the punishment may be a lecture by telephone from some minor official at Promi. In more serious cases you are summoned to his office and must listen while the master speaks, feeling all the time like a naughty schoolboy. In still graver cases you pay a personal visit to Dr. Brauweiler, who announces the imposition of some more drastic penalty. As a rule, it will fall under one of five general heads:

1. A written warning.
2. Denial of telephone privileges for varying periods.
3. A strong suggestion that you had better leave the country.
4. Expulsion within 48 to 72 hours.
5. Seizure and arrest for high treason or espionage.

There are other punishments—for example, you may be excluded

from press conferences, the press clubs, etc.—but in the main these
are what the foreign correspondent must reckon with if he over-
steps the invisible boundary between the permissible and the forbidden. The penalties are often anything but just. Offenses are
graded both according to the nationality of the culprit and the
influence possessed by the newspaper he works for. Consideration
is given to his own political opinions and his personal relations
with the officials sitting in judgment.

Foreign journalists in Berlin are supervised and spied upon in a
flagrant fashion. This in itself is hardly worth mentioning. But
despite the custom, you find yourself shaken time after time—as
when you discover that people who pretended to be your friends
and colleagues were actually tools of the Gestapo and *agents
provocateurs.*

Gradually the Berlin correspondent learned to divide the foreign
journalists into three groups. The first included the professional
police spies like Dr. Max Blokzijl. There was also a Greek prize
fighter who exposed himself by his clumsiness, and there were
many others. It was a game to talk long and earnestly with them,
apparently laying one's heart bare, without uttering a word of
consequence. The second group included the great majority of
correspondents after the Americans left Berlin. They did not serve
the Gestapo directly, but because of personal reasons, political
opinions or special circumstances they were not dependable. As
a rule you could speak to them frankly without fearing the consequences, but you always had to guard against going too far.
The third group was composed of journalists from various countries all over Europe who were bound together by personal friend-
ships or mutual interests and could depend on one another.

It was often impossible for an outsider to realize how matters
stood. On the surface you were on equally good terms with all
the journalists—except, of course, with the Quislings. A conversation among three persons would continue without a break, even
after a fourth joined in. And yet it would suddenly assume another
character, though nobody betrayed that fact by his words or his
facial expression. No one had greater use than the journalists for
the quick glance over the shoulder that was known as "the German look." We developed an instinct for secrecy that would have
done honor to Cesare Borgia.

But it was not only through our "colleagues" that the surveillance was maintained; it also had a purely police character. You were shadowed, you had your home watched and your telephone tapped. As a rule the tapping was sporadic rather than continuous, though it might last for weeks at a time. It was relatively easy to detect, because voices became fainter at the other end of the line. Often mysterious things would happen to the telephone. Once I lifted up the receiver and, to my amazement, heard a military conversation between a general and a colonel of the High Command. Another time I found myself cut in on two officials who were apparently in charge of the tapping.

Telephones in Berlin could be used as dictographs, even when the receiver was down. Knowing this, we used to pull out the plug, when there was a plug; otherwise we covered the telephone with a heavy cloth. Even then we couldn't be certain of privacy, because there might still be a concealed microphone. Once the Propaganda Ministry committed a blunder. An expert from Siemens was permitted to give a lecture on modern technical progress. He mentioned among other things a new membrane that made it possible to detect the slightest sound. We learned from his talk that a small microphone could be installed anywhere: in the flue of an open fireplace, in a chandelier; wall plugs are especially convenient. Afterwards we began thinking of what he said and searched our dwellings. In our apartment on the Jerusalemerstrasse—yes, it is still called Jerusalem Street—at about eight o'clock every evening, my wife noticed a clicking sound as if someone were turning a switch. The apartment was owned by a Frenchman and had recently been occupied by two American newspapermen. An intensive search revealed an outlet in the wall that had no connection with the lighting system. Behind the outlet there was a small turntable and two mysterious black screws with a very thin record at their points. We replaced them and found a patch to cover the hole.

We began to feel like characters in a Nick Carter story; the secret enemy was on our trail. Diplomats in Berlin had even more reason for being frightened, especially if they lived in newly built legations. In at least two of these buildings, experts of the countries involved discovered that every conversation could be heard by the Gestapo. If Sweden builds a new embassy, the work should be done by Swedish artisans and engineers.

Time after time journalists have received suggestions that would hardly have been possible if their conversations had not been overheard. For instance a colleague from southeast Europe had amused himself by writing an article as he would have liked to publish it. To share the joke, he read the article to a colleague. The next day he was summoned by one of his good friends among the German officials and grilled regarding his activities the previous day at a certain hour. He answered that he had taken a few drinks and enjoyed himself harmlessly. The official pressed a button. In came a man with a phonograph and, after a moment's pause, the journalist heard his own article read by himself. That was in the days when they still used records; they now use steel tape.

Despite the strict surveillance, it was still possible for foreign journalists to mingle with people of many different types, but exceptional caution was necessary. Time after time people would appear with exciting but dubious information; they were sometimes police spies acting as *agents provocateurs*. After meeting them once or twice, most of us learned to hold our tongues.

We could, however, acquire a good understanding of the average mind by talking with the man-in-the-street. If you gave him a few cigarettes or a pat of butter his tongue would loosen, and often he needed no stimulus. During 1942 and 1943, the average Berliner became remarkably voluble; it was amazing what he would say to a foreigner he had met a few moments before. "Swede" and "*Svenska Dagbladet*" were reassuring words. When I parked my car in some quarter of the city that was strange to me and had to look at the map to find directions, men and women on the street would stop and whisper, "Go to so-and-so if you want to learn something."

You had no difficulty getting in touch with the anti-Nazi opposition; its members saw to that. Early in the morning, or better still, in the evening after dark, one or another of them would tap at my door. He would come just before eight o'clock, when the street entrance was locked for the night, and it might be ten or eleven before he disappeared, quietly and cautiously.

Those who wished to familiarize themselves with the situation in the rural areas could take short trips. The Swedish journalists received a 50 per cent rebate on one railroad journey each month, but then you had to report to Dr. Giese, who recorded the purpose and date of the trip. This was both a discreet and an effective control. But if you wished to take a train trip and return late the same evening without taking advantage of the rebate and without reporting to the police, as was required in the case of overnight journeys, it was possible to visit the countryfolk, at least in Brandenburg. Both there and even more in Mecklenburg, the neighboring province to the Northwest, you encountered people who had been evacuated from western Germany. They were quartered everywhere and they weren't exactly cheerful; evacuation had proved to be a psychological burden for both the "hosts" and the "guests." It isn't hard to imagine the domestic tragedy that would occur if the children of the guests broke dishes that couldn't be replaced in wartime; the strain sometimes proved too much for patriotism or hospitality.

Every foreign journalist had his special informants, who bartered information for cigarettes, chocolates or coffee. At their offices the correspondents usually had a few packages of cigarettes or a tin of coffee to be used as stimulants when necessary. There were few Germans who refused these bribes, even when I first came to Berlin, and there were fewer still as time went on.

Farewell to the Third Reich

During the spring of 1943, my position in Berlin became increasingly difficult. From the beginning I had, for some reason, been unpopular at both the Foreign Office and the Propaganda Ministry, but now this disfavor was changing to something worse. When official functions were held, they "forgot" to send me an invitation. This had no practical effect, for I naturally learned what happened anyway, but it was one little symptom, a warning of what was in store.

A more stringent watch was being kept on all my movements. From my balcony I could see strangers spying from empty windows in the neighborhood. I had more and more trouble with my telephone, although constant listening-in for several years should have dashed any hopes the authorities might have had that I would say anything careless over it. Several times I was unable to make an outgoing call. Once I had to run out to a public booth in the middle of the night and call the service department in order to get a late connection to Stockholm.

Another suspicious sign was that there were no longer any complaints. Earlier, at regular intervals, there had been jabs from the Propaganda Ministry or the Foreign Office; now there was the stillness of the grave. I began to get the feeling that a dossier on my case had already been prepared.

Good friends passed on warnings to me: "Don't carry the game too far," they said. Impatiently I began looking forward to June 1, the day set for my departure. I had represented *Svenska Dagbladet* in Berlin since February 1941, but for the first half year I had had a variety of duties, and my real work had begun late in the summer of 1941. Early in May, I let the German authorities understand that I wished to leave Berlin. It was very satisfactory to both sides of the Wilhelmstrasse. Many of those with whom I had had close personal contacts expressed their regrets, but they also stated flatly that my decision was wise. My family had already left for Sweden. On May 31, I was driven to the Tempelhof airfield and took a seat in the Stockholm plane. It was a definite farewell to the Third Reich, and with no regrets.

ЛЛЛЛЛЛЛЛЛ **II** ЛЛЛЛЛЛЛЛЛЛ

THE OUTBREAK OF
THE GERMAN-RUSSIAN WAR

THE FIRST HALF YEAR OF WAR

The Play Begins

THE Russo-German friendship pact of 1939 rested on shaky foundations. The aims of the two states were diametrically opposed and, even if the issues of conflict were being kept in the background, it was apparent that an open break must come sooner or later. That it would occur during 1941 was the general belief at the beginning of that year. In Berlin, one report after another described enormous German preparations in the East, troop concentrations in the Reich proper and in East Prussia, new flying fields and supply depots. Foreigners in Berlin became more and more convinced that the break must come soon.

Excitement began as early as May. Still, week after week went by and nothing happened. Rumors circulated wildly, each one more fantastic than the last. At seven p.m. on June 14, a Saturday, telephone connections with the outside world were suddenly broken off. Practically the whole colony of journalists in Berlin stayed awake that night in expectation of a call from the Foreign Minister summoning them to an extra special press conference at five o'clock Sunday morning. But no message came. During the following week it appeared that we might have to reckon with some alternative other than war. Well-informed circles—obviously "inspired"—were certain that Germany had presented an ultimatum to Soviet Russia and that Stalin had backed down and accepted German control over the Ukraine and the oil fields. In the general excitement and under the impact of the overwhelming might of the German war machine, an increasing number of people believed these rumors. Had not the Soviets only recently delivered something akin to an apology when Tass, their official telegraph agency, denied all reports of German-Russian tension?

For my part I did not know what to believe. The excitement was

25

unprecedented. One felt as though the whole world stood on the threshold of a crucial decision. Would the Russians yield? But there were other rumors which suggested that the question must be settled on the field of battle. It was said that linguists had been sitting for a long time in blocked-off rooms at well-known hotels working on translations of official documents, as had been the case prior to the 6th of April when the storm was loosed against Yugoslavia.

On the 18th of June came the pact with Turkey, a pact generally regarded as one step in the preparations for an attack on Russia.

By Saturday, June 21, it had become almost impossible to work since one could not write a single word of what was on everyone's mind. Some of us decided to suspend all work. Not only had the German-Russian situation become taboo; it had been made clear to the foreign journalists that any violation of this rule would be answered with expulsion.

That night the international colony of journalists in Berlin gathered at the Fasanenstrasse. Also present were a group of officials from the Wilhelmstrasse and several foreign press attachés. First-class Envoy Paul Schmidt, chief of the German Foreign Office press section, was there in person. As usual, he wandered about with a knowing grin, answering direct questions with his customary calm evasiveness.

I recall that the majority that night felt something would happen during the next 48 hours. But two days can be a long time. The hours passed—one o'clock, two, three. The company began to dwindle. Since my home lay close to the Wilhelmstrasse at the other end of the city, I decided that I might as well ride home. Before leaving I phoned a couple of colleagues, but still there was no news. At home I went to sleep with my head on the writing pad, to be awakened suddenly by the telephone at four o'clock. It was Dr. Gross at the press club in the Fasanenstrasse: "The press conference," he said, "starts at six o'clock in the Bundesratsaal." Then he hung up.

Since the subway was not running at that hour, I had to walk. On my way, near the Hotel Kaiserhof, a window opened suddenly. From within I heard, out of a hubbub of voices, the familiar radio harangue of Dr. Goebbels. A couple of night hawks gathered outside. By now dawn had broken. One of the watchmen at the Kaiserhof had already heard the news. "We expected it," he said. "Now it's Stalin's turn to get it on the chin!" In the Wilhelmsplatz my colleagues were already hurrying toward the Foreign Office. On arriving at Bismarck's old Bundesratsaal, I found the place packed with journalists, officials and photographers. Then, at exactly six o'clock, Ribbentrop arrived in uniform at the head of his staff, a row of functionaries from the Foreign Ministry and the Ministry of Propaganda. Into a breathless silence he dropped his bomb: that Germany had declared war on Soviet Russia; that three hours ago German troops and planes had begun the attack along the whole border. The immediate cheers were followed by a sudden quiet, whereupon Ribbentrop began reading the declaration of war, followed by its lengthy justification.

With everyone's eyes on him, many said to themselves: "What is the man thinking now, at this instant, while he himself is proclaiming the doom of the very principle of his own foreign policy?" That Ribbentrop had been a firm believer in the Russian alliance was generally known. On the desk in his inner sanctum there had stood for many months a large autographed portrait—of Stalin. Whatever his thoughts were now, he did not reveal them. Nevertheless, perspiration gathered on his brow.

Listening, one had a strong impression that this was not only an attempted justification of the German step, laying the whole guilt upon Russia, but also an apology for Ribbentrop's personal policy—that is, for the whole effort to find a modus vivendi between German big business and the Bolsheviks.

There is no doubt that the declaration of war against Russia was received with relief by the greater part of the German people. Real enthusiasm was lacking; and in fact there was an actual aversion to the war in some quarters, notably among the Communists and former Communists. But, on the whole, the Germans accepted the decision as inevitable.

Neither the German man-in-the-street nor his leaders realized then the significance of the attack on Russia. Most people expected a short campaign—anything from two to six months, after which the Russians would be out of the picture. Nor did the Germans only hold this view. To be honest, we must acknowledge the widespread impression in most countries (even more widespread after the Finnish-Russian war) that Soviet Russia could present effective opposition to the German war machine for only a short time. I must confess that I was one of those who believed this, not so much because I underestimated Russia as because I overestimated Germany's potentialities. It was particularly difficult to believe that the

German intelligence service had failed so completely in Russia in spite of the unlimited means at its disposal, especially when you remembered how well it had functioned in every other country.

It is easy enough, of course, to say this today. At that time, things were not so clear. The Germans were not the only ones to make a mistake. It seems odd, for instance, that the Russians should, to a certain degree, have been taken by surprise. Surely they should have known that an attack might be expected at almost any moment. They could have received first-hand information from the Bulgarians, since Professor Karl Boehmer of the Propaganda Ministry prattled openly at a reception where he had drunk too much for his own good. German reconnaissance flights along the frontier must have told an obvious story. Nevertheless, when the Germans attacked, they found one air base after another only partially manned. There is also a strong suggestion that Ambassador Dekanozoff never realized to what extent he was being made a fool of on his nightly visits to the Foreign Minister. It was later said that the Russians regarded the German troop concentrations merely as a means of applying pressure on behalf of the expected German demands on their country, and that the Soviet leaders did not believe war was imminent.

It now seems certain, in the light of what we have learned concerning relations among England, Russia and Germany before June 22, 1941, that it was hardly possible to avoid a Russian-German conflict. As soon as Hitler had come to this conclusion, as had Napoleon before the campaign of 1812, it was only natural that he himself wished to choose the date. Before the march toward the East began, the German leaders obviously sought security from attack in the rear. This is probably the explanation of Hess's trip to England. Possibly Hitler sought English co-operation in a crusade toward the East or at least an understanding with England before Germany took upon herself that great struggle. Another phase of this effort was the attempt to force Yugoslavia into the Axis alliance. A great mistake was made when, despite warnings from informed persons, the Yugoslav government was pressed too hard. But neither Ribbentrop nor the man who devoted himself entirely to the negotiation of a pact with the Yugoslavs, Dr. Schmidt, would listen to these warnings. As a consequence there came Simovitch's coup, the military campaign against Yugoslavia and a delay in the attack against the Soviet Union.

It is less well known that another circumstance also delayed the Russian campaign. Originally the attack had been set for June 12. Hitler at that time figured largely on employing the plan of attack which was launched ten days later, but with one exception. From the beginning he had counted on Hungary as an ally. But the Hungarian government flatly refused, adding that recently its relations with the Soviet Union had been improving. Despite every pressure the Hungarians persisted in their refusal, and there was nothing to do but change the plan of campaign. What, again, seems to have contributed to postponing the date of attack was the Japanese Foreign Minister Matsuoka's non-aggression pact with Stalin. This for a long time bewildered the Germans; and its import, so far as we can judge, first became clear to them only after the Japanese Foreign Minister returned to his country.

In seeking explanations for the relatively late date for the attack, one must not forget that military considerations would have made it late under any circumstances, delaying it until the end of May or the beginning of June. The German military command proposed to carry on a blitz campaign, which it hoped could be completed in a few months. This required the selection of a date which from the meteorological standpoint was most favorable for the mobile German armed forces.

It is always tempting to wonder what would have happened . . . . If, for instance, the attack had come in the beginning of June, the situation might have been different. It may well be added that if Hitler had not had dominant influence in planning the campaign, or had not persisted in the idea of three large attack wedges, there is the greatest likelihood that things would have developed in another fashion.

An expert has told me that another plan was proposed, but that Hitler turned it down. It was prepared by General Marcks, a staff officer of General von Schleicher who was murdered on June 30, 1934. Marcks proposed, à la Schlieffen, to strengthen the right wing, prepare a tremendous mass concentration in the South, then quietly permit a Russian advance to the offensive in the center and in the North, which would result in considerable losses for the Russians even if the German forces there were relatively small. All attempts to advance from North to South would be halted at the Carpathians, which were to be held from the South at all costs.

The main forces on the German side would be concentrated south of the Carpathians and in the Balkans, whence they would drive into the Ukraine, making a tremendous sweep toward the East.

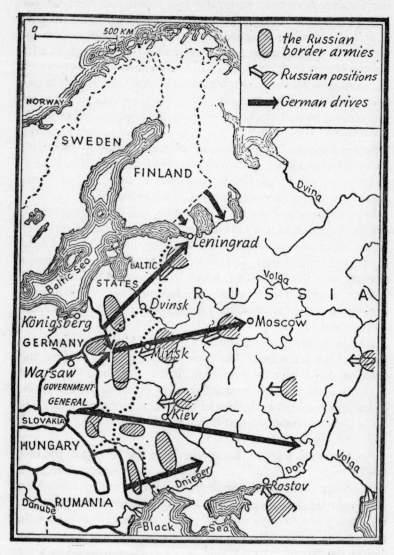

APPROXIMATE GERMAN AND FINNISH LINES OF ATTACK
ACCORDING TO HITLER'S PLAN OF CAMPAIGN.

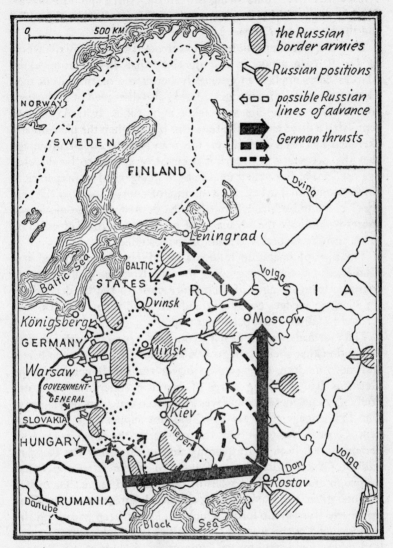

PRINCIPAL FEATURES OF GENERAL MARCKS' PLAN,
WHICH WAS REJECTED BY HITLER.

Afterwards they would swing toward the North and, in a powerful drive beyond Moscow, surround the Russian forces as Hannibal
did the Romans at Cannae.

Even if it were impossible thus to surround and destroy the whole
of the Russian army, it is quite clear that an operation along
Marcks' lines implied an essentially better use of the forces than
Hitler's three uniform wedges. Marcks also disagreed with the need
for reaching a decision as quickly as possible. Instead, he contemplated a drive against the Caucasus if and when the plan already
sketched had been carried out. His plan had the added advantage
that the preparations need not necessarily appear to be directed
against Russia, since they could also be construed as preparations
for an attack on Turkey. Its weakness, of course, was that the base
area's communications left much to be desired. But the motorized
forces would have the advantage of proximity to the Rumanian oil
fields and the favorable terrain of the Ukraine.

The plan of operation followed by Hitler likewise aimed at a
Cannae. But it took for granted that the Russians would concentrate the main strength of their army close to the border, where
the German wedges could split and surround them. The Russians
refused to fall into that particular trap.

The Germans went into battle on June 22, 1941, with the firm
conviction that their strategy was superior, their weapons better
and more modern, their soldiers better trained. Beyond this, the
Germans had a strong sense of intrinsic superiority and undoubtedly considered themselves as western crusaders driving east.
The first engagement, however, did not support the overconfi-
dent German strategy. On the contrary, the enemy matériel
demonstrated, both as to quantity and quality, that the Russians
understood exceptionally well how to profit from the Polish
campaign and from the lessons of the war in France. There was
just one great and important exception advantageous to the Germans: the Russian air force, which could not keep pace with developments. But this was the only positive entry which the German
leadership could register to support its judgment of Russian
strength. Moreover, doubt regarding plane statistics arose at an
early stage. Various quarters took it for granted that the Russians
were using "come-on" tactics. Articles from German soldier correspondents, for instance, described how the Russian planes were
lined up in rows on the flying fields, how the whole airdrome be-

came a flaming sea of burning planes. It was hard to believe that Russia, in the year 1941, could make such mistakes.

During the first week the German High Command was silent; not before June 29 were the first war communiqués issued. Meanwhile Berlin seethed with rumors: German parachute troops had taken Kiev, German troops were on the threshold of Moscow. Frequently these rumors were started by official German circles that knew—or should have known—just what was happening east of the Polish border.

Despite the lack of factual information, no one doubted that Germany had won a great victory along the frontier. On the German side everyone was filled with hope, believing that the battle was already won. In answer to the question as to when "the big journalists' trip" to Moscow would take place, a prominent German publicist replied that we "should know" by the middle or end of July. In Berlin, both the officials and the public were intoxicated with joy; in Party circles the goose was hanging high. Russia's many peoples became a popular subject of study, and when multicolored maps of the races of the Soviet Union were distributed, it was obvious that there were great "New Order possibilities" in that part of the world. Well into the fall many Germans believed that Russia was practically crushed. Time and again there were positive reports disproving this happy picture, but these were shunted aside with references to German superiority.

But even if none of the neutral journalists questioned the German successes, there were many circumstances that seemed difficult to explain. One of these was the high figure of prisoners taken. These had to be compared with constantly repeated announcements that the Russians would not surrender, but would continue to resist even when their situation was hopeless. There is now reason to discount the importance of the early fighting. That the Germans won battles and that the Russians suffered relatively great losses is certain. What those in journalistic circles in Berlin could not judge was whether or not the main Russian forces had actually been close to the frontier and had been defeated by the Germans.

The German view was that they had gotten the jump on the Russians when the latter sought to launch a general attack against Europe. There was much evidence to show that the main Russian forces had marched up relatively close to the border, prepared to move forward when the signal was given from Moscow. Reports from those who had been in the battle zone all testified to their having seen huge quantities of the most modern Russian matériel. In German circles, at any rate, it was believed that from the very start they had fought the main forces of Soviet Russia. A well-informed German journalist, Dr. Otto Kriegk, wrote in *Der Montag* on June 29 that the German Wehrmacht had opposed "the largest and strongest units of the Soviet Russian army and air fleet" and, from every point of view, had proved itself superior. Gradually, however, it became evident that the Germans had made a fundamental error when they reckoned on meeting the greater part of the Red Army at the frontier. And although there are many indications that the Russians had been planning to attack Germany sooner or later, they were still unprepared in June 1941.

From the outset one fact was clear to everybody—that the Germans were encountering soldiers of an entirely different mentality than they had hitherto met. "The Soviet Russian soldier," said an article in the *Völkischer Beobachter* as early as June 29, "surpasses our opponent in the West in his disdain for death. The tenacity and fatalism of the Russian soldier persist till he is blown sky high together with his bunker or falls in close fighting man to man." And the *Frankfurter Zeitung* on July 6 commented: "The enemy in the East reacts to the German tactics of wedges and extensions in a wholly different manner from the French. The spiritual paralysis which usually followed the lightning-like German break-through in the West did not occur in the East, or not to the same degree. In most cases the enemy did not lose his capacity for action, but instead tried in turn to encircle the German pincers." In conclusion the German newspaper declared that the Bolshevik leaders had attempted to create the most highly mechanized army in the whole world and that the German soldier had encountered for the first time an opponent who sought to meet him with the same technical weapons with which he himself was equipped. This should not have been surprising to the Germans. Nevertheless, it was a surprise; it was also a surprise for them to learn that the German command actually planned the campaign in the East on the model of the campaign in France.

In the greater privacy of political circles, no one concealed his disappointment that the Russians did not follow the rules of the game and surrender when they were encircled, but rather forced the Germans to continue the fight. The Russians, said the Germans, fight unfairly and against all the rules of international law. They

lack all chivalry and consider it their duty to kill the enemy, regardless of when, where or how. To cap all this, they calmly destroy their own land. Various German circles were quick to realize
what this Russian mentality really implied. The German soldier
had met an opponent who held fast to his political faith with
fanatical zeal and established *total defense* against the German blitz
attack.

During the first week, the three attacking wedges made large
territorial gains. The fastest progress was made by the German
armies heading toward the Baltic states. Within a few days, in fact,
the Germans had pushed to Lithuania.

One of the reasons for the rapid advance was the co-operation
of Lithuanian patriots. As early as the night of June 22-23, they
raided Russian arms depots and committed sabotage on a large
scale. On the following day real street fighting broke out both in
Vilna and Kaunas. The main force of the Soviet Russian army
abandoned these places on the night of June 23 and, after fierce
fighting with remaining Russian military units and especially Jewish
contingents in the two towns, the Lithuanians seized power the
following morning. They succeeded in occupying strategically important points such as the railway stations, the post office, telegraph,
telephone and radio buildings.

Although Lithuania was certainly a start, it was not more than
partially pacified when the Germans decided to send us journalists
to that country. In the great forests there were still some shattered
units of Russian troops making spasmodic attacks on the towns in
search of food. To prevent these attacks was difficult; the Germans
simply had too much on their hands. A systematic combing of the
huge forests was practically impossible. The Russians, moreover,
had considerable training in this kind of warfare. It was guerrilla
fighting and new to the Germans.

There were some Russians left even in the cities. In Vilna, for
instance, quite a number had escaped by underground passages to
the Jewish quarter, where they went into hiding. While we were in
the city there was constant shooting after dark. The Germans had
already started their executions on a large scale. Among the first
to die were 60 Jews who had fought as partisans. Even though large
groups of Jews had fled with the Bolsheviks, a considerable portion
of the population in Vilna, Kaunas and a number of other towns
was Jewish.

The advance northward continued at great speed. On June 30, the first troops entered Riga. The incidents of the warfare in Latvia differed from those in Lithuania in that no substantial national organizations could be formed. Small groups did succeed in hampering the Russians' defense, but the work done by these volunteers was not so important as that accomplished in Lithuania. German military officials, however, paid high tribute to their services.

It has been said that the battle for Smolensk upset Hitler's time-table. The blitzkrieg began to lose its blitz-like quality. Events made it clear that the Russian army was a wholly different opponent from what anyone had suspected. Winter warfare, which till then had not been seriously considered, grew into a haunting threat. Hitler certainly tried, in a gigantic race against the Russian winter, to reach a decision in the East during 1941. But as early as August a leading representative of the Propaganda Ministry told me that they had unquestionably to figure on a winter war. He explained further that the Russians had installed themselves with this in mind and that their great reserves of cavalry had so far not been under fire. My informant added that, to some degree, the Russians also had nature on their side.

Meanwhile, the German offensive in the South rolled on and, since things were calm in the center, several offensive units were shifted to the Ukraine. One of the most powerful operations of the whole campaign now began to unfold. While one army corps drove deep into the Ukraine and, in the beginning of September, crossed the Dnieper, a gigantic encircling movement developed around Kiev, ending on September 19 when that city and Poltava were reported captured. Eight days later came the High Command report of the victory: no fewer than 665,000 Russians, it said, had been captured. I remember that even those who had hitherto accepted the official German figures, now simply refused to believe this news. It was absurd to suppose that Budenny—even if the cavalry general with the large handle-bar mustache had been a complete fiasco—would permit five army corps to be trapped inside Kiev. Then it was explained that the High Command, in an attempt to take the public's breath away, had included all male inhabitants of the captured regions.

The Ukraine campaign, meanwhile, was one of the German Wehrmacht's greatest triumphs. It led gradually to the conquest of the Crimea, with the exception of Sevastopol. That this city, despite every effort, could not be taken was due primarily to the contribution made by the Russian Black Sea fleet. Though it was technically not in the same class as the Red Army, its value was demonstrated not only in the Crimean campaign but also during the evacuation of Odessa, which was carried out with its help.

German military officials began to hold the Russian fleet in much higher esteem, despite their confidence that the Russian warships would eventually be forced to take refuge in Turkey. In the German announcements regarding the Russian fleet, we began to notice significant inconsistencies which to this day haven't been cleared up. On November 15, for example, the High Command announced that one battleship, two cruisers, six destroyers, two submarines, and some smaller vessels had been sunk in the Black Sea. A large number of ships were described as damaged, including one heavy and six light cruisers. To my question as to whether the battleship which had been sunk was the *Pariskaya Kommuna*, built before the First World War and transferred from the Baltic Sea, there was no reply. Two weeks later the famous naval expert, Rear Admiral Lutzow, stated in *Das Reich* that the Russians probably had three battleships in the Black Sea in the spring of 1941; one had been found in drydock at the Nikolayev naval base, another was the *Pariskaya Kommuna*. But what about the third? This mystery was never solved.

While the campaign in the Ukraine was under way, the Germans made an all-out effort to take Leningrad. On September 14, all defense lines were reported pierced. Nevertheless, it was stated that the defense was astonishingly strong, the advance slow. A few days later Leningrad was not mentioned. The attempt had failed.

As the campaign developed from a blitzkrieg, in the areas with relatively good communications, to more "normal" warfare on the great plains, the customary eastern problem became all the more difficult for the German Command. To repair railways and change the tracks to the normal European gauge consumed an incredible amount of labor. The difficulties of delivering food and ammunition increased day by day. So did the activity of the partisans.

There now began that special brand of Russian warfare. With the exception of their limited experiences in Yugoslavia, the German war machine up to this time was utterly ignorant of this kind of war. The Russians, on the other hand, had spent years preparing for it, storing up ammunition, food supplies, building munitions depots, radio stations and systematically training soldiers in partisan warfare. When the regular army retreated, the partisans immediately went to work. They dynamited bridges and seized transport facilities. They laid mines and spied. But they waged not only this "little war" with every modern weapon and with specially tested tactics; the partisans also operated directly against the main lines. They concentrated on important centers, operating from their own bases in the peaceful areas. The partisans would let huge numbers of trucks pass by, then strike suddenly when a car with high-ranking officers appeared. They also shifted their activities from district to district, according to the changing war situation; they would lie low for weeks, then suddenly appear just before a German offensive or a Russian attack, and try to deal the German war effort the greatest possible indirect blow.

The Germans simply didn't know how to tackle them. The local German military commanders soon realized that they had to get on good terms with the population. But this, considering that they wanted at the same time to exploit the people as far as possible, was easier said than done. Since the Germans had been so long contemplating their expansion in the East, one would think they might have studied the basic psychological aspects of the problem.

In its time the pact with Russia had certainly brought about a number of changes in the German eastern policy. In 1939, Russian Whites and Ukrainian nationalists in Berlin had been forced to withdraw from public view. Germans from the Baltic states, who had always cried for revenge on the Soviets, now had to observe the greatest caution; in fact, everything that might have indicated a German desire for expansion at the cost of the Soviet Union had been pushed into the background. But this was only a surface change. The eastern question had been carefully studied even during the years of silence. Berlin had good connections with the Baltic states and was well oriented as to the situation there. The capital was even well informed as to conditions in the former Polish territory east of the German-Russian demarcation line. But the Germans had little knowledge of the Russian hinterland.

They could thank the Ukrainian émigrés in Berlin for the fact that they had some knowledge of the Ukraine. These people were successful in maintaining sporadic connections with their homeland. Highly trusted scientists from Lemberg University edited the information which came in. The Ukrainian colony in

Berlin had a wholly different character from that of the White
Russians; one reason for this was that ever since 1918 new blood
had been flowing into the Ukrainian colony from Poland.

The Ukrainian nationalists placed great hopes in Germany—in
the beginning with some reason, perhaps. After large tracts of the
Ukraine were conquered, however, the Party took over control
from the Wehrmacht and the Nazi bureaucrats were permitted to
swarm over the land like locusts. Before long, it was the same old
story: the people began to hate the Germans. In view of the fact
that the Germans had placed the greatest hopes on the additional
food and raw materials which should have been available from
the Ukraine, this shortsighted policy was very surprising.

Nor was it only in the Ukraine that the Germans blundered.
Even in the Baltic states it was apparent that the Party quickly
gambled away the sympathies which the German military had won;
it converted the populace, whose only desires were to work and
fight Bolshevism, into enemies who were forced to wonder what
difference there was between one oppressor and another. The pro-
visional Lithuanian government was disbanded and the Lithuanians
were robbed of control over their internal affairs. In Latvia the
formation of a responsible government was prohibited. In both
countries, and again in Estonia, citizens were not allowed to display
the national flag or play the national anthem. An arbitrary exchange
rate of one mark for ten rubles was established, making it possible
for German soldiers to buy at bankrupt prices. The three countries were hastily plundered of every essential commodity left
behind by the Bolsheviks. The Germans lived like the proverbial
Herrenvolk and let the Estonians, Letts and Lithuanians sense their
inferiority.

I have already stated that the German intelligence service,
despite its resources, was a complete fiasco in Russia. It had not
been possible for them to build up either an espionage organization
or a fifth column. This is no easy task when dealing with a totalitarian state. It is probable that the Russians had not succeeded any
better in Germany than had the Germans in Soviet Russia. The
Germans, however, suffered more from this situation, since they
were the aggressors. Even during the military campaign, the German intelligence service made little progress, and its only attempt
to organize a revolutionary group—in Leningrad during the
autumn—failed. The Russians, on the other hand, learned from
their partisans what was going on behind the German lines. They

also went to great lengths to make both espionage and reconnaissance more difficult for the Germans. They saw to it, for instance, that the Germans "discovered" detailed, carefully faked maps; on fallen Russians the German soldiers found papers which proved, later, to have been planted there for the purpose of misleading them.

Dr. Dietrich and the Great Offensive Against Moscow

At the end of September, the German Command once more concentrated all its available forces in the center with the intention of striking the decisive blow at Moscow and crushing the flower of the Russian army, which we heard was being commanded by Marshal Timoshenko himself. The operation was developing into a mighty encirclement of the Russian forces, carried out in feverish haste and with tremendous expenditure of men and matériel. It was one more race with winter.

The official world of Berlin was confident that the offensive would be successful. On October 2, Hitler issued to the armed forces an order of the day, to which everybody listened by radio. "Today," he said, "begins the decisive battle of the year. It will mean the annihilation of the enemy." This dramatic prophecy was announced in the Berlin Sportpalast, where Hitler had chosen to give his traditional Winter Relief speech, thus breaking the silence he had observed ever since the outbreak of the Russian war.

His appearance was a model of Nazi staging. Yet, despite the chorus of applause, one could not help noticing a radical change in the man since his last public appearance. Hitler gave the impression of being under pressure, like someone playing his most important card and at the same time trying to convince himself and others that it would take the final trick. It also struck both my colleagues and myself that there was something frenzied about the Nazi leader. With great fervor Hitler again voiced his unshakable will to victory. In the last 48 hours, he said, an operation of gigantic scope had begun, an operation that would contribute to the utter destruction of the foe in the East.

Not for a week did we hear another word concerning this "gigantic operation." Then, on the morning of October 9, the Propaganda Ministry called a special press conference for twelve o'clock, when Hitler's press chief, Dr. Otto Dietrich, was to make an announcement. Dietrich was brief. The war in the East, he said, was practically over. Only policing operations remained.

Could this, we all asked ourselves, be true? On the other hand, how could it be a bluff? If it were, the truth would immediately contradict not only Dietrich but also Hitler, on whose orders he spoke. Could Hitler risk such a colossal blunder?

We foreign journalists, especially the Scandinavians, viewed the pronouncement with skepticism. There were too many facts that could not be explained away. Yet, on coming to the conclusion that the whole thing could only be a gigantic fabrication, we were compelled to ask ourselves for what reason it could have been fabricated. So far, there has not been a satisfactory answer to this question. It is possible, of course, that Hitler believed he had surrounded Timoshenko, much as General Gallas, during the Thirty Years' War, believed that he had Banér and his Swedes in the bag. But this explanation did not, and does not, satisfy me.

When, later, it became evident that the Dietrich episode had been a crashing blunder on Hitler's part, two reasons for it were offered: first, that it was an attempt to bluff Japan into active participation by presenting Russia's annihilation as a fait accompli; secondly, that it was an attempt to bluff Russia. If the Russians found themselves in a serious situation in the center—which was actually a fact—and the Germans made it clear that they were putting into the battle everything they had in order to force a decision, might it not be possible to scare them into making a separate peace? The idea may seem naïve, but it should not be completely rejected. One thing we heard said in this connection, but which no one has ever been able to check, is that at the time of the Dietrich episode a high Bulgarian emissary visited Moscow in order to offer his country's good offices.

It soon became very clear that Dr. Dietrich was as far from the truth as can possibly be imagined when he proclaimed that the war was practically over. The German High Command's more cautious report issued the same day was significant enough. During the following days, as my American colleague, Howard Smith, has pointed out,[1] the headlines of the *Völkischer Beobachter* and other newspapers told a strange story to those whose eyes were open.

---

[1] *In* Last Train from Berlin, *where the whole episode is described in great detail.*—Tr.

But it was interesting for a neutral observer to witness how this announcement of victory—the contents of which, after all, were soon known all over in Berlin—left the Berliners completely unmoved. Here my experience differs radically from that of my good colleague, Howard Smith. True, the weather was none too good that day, yet neither then nor the day after did I observe any reaction whatever. There were no gatherings at street corners, no sign of rejoicing; on the street cars and in the subways the chief topic of conversation appeared to be no different from that of any other day. I traveled all over the city, finding the same thing everywhere. The simple fact was that the German people were clearly beginning to get sick and tired of the whole war. Deep down inside themselves they no longer believed in the slogans of victory.

On October 13, it was announced that operations were proceeding according to plan. Then, three days later, the German communiqué gave statistics of Russian prisoners that were only slightly smaller than those issued after the fall of Kiev: 648,000 men. The whole of Timoshenko's group of eight armies was supposed to have been crushed and the majority of the men taken prisoner.

Even though this was gross exaggeration, it was beyond doubt—and should still be kept clearly in mind—that the Germans had made significant advances toward Moscow in the first days of their offensive. The Russians themselves considered the city's position critical, and on October 21 it was announced that the Russian government was leaving Moscow to establish itself in Kuibyshev. At this time, there was a pause in operations. Military quarters in Berlin claimed that this was the calm before the final collapse. The Russians, declared Captain Sommerfeldt, had only 40 divisions left out of 300; and he added that even if they still had 100, the result would be the same. It was some time before the German leadership realized to what extent they had misjudged the magnitude of the Russian reserves.

The Germans were still misjudging even the weather. Having stated earlier that the weather would not influence the fighting seriously before about November 10, two days before that date the claim was made that, though the weather had recently been bad on the central front, the Russian climate had shown a tendency in the past three years to approach that of Central Europe, thus making the temperature in Moscow approximately the same as that in Berlin. Consequently the "Russian Winter" was not to be expected before January. On November 12, there appeared some statements concerning winter warfare upon which we eagerly jumped. The basic idea behind these remarks was that it was by no means certain that the winter would prove advantageous to the Russians. Moreover, a great many details about German plans for a winter campaign were disclosed with intent to show that Germany was in reality well prepared for what might come. A few days previously it had been stated that almost the entire German textile industry had been working for the war machine since October 1940.

On November 23, Captain Sommerfeldt explained that the outcome of the operations against Moscow was regarded most optimistically. A few days later he was wondering how long the Russians were going to postpone their acknowledgment of the loss of Rostov, which had been taken by SS troops. On the 28th Captain Sommerfeldt explained that German troops had reached the Greater Moscow region, in other words, that they were between 25 and 30 miles from the city.

And then came the first unequivocal reverse. After the Russians reported on the evening of the 30th that Marshal Timoshenko had succeeded in recapturing Rostov, the Germans acknowledged, on December 1, that the city had been lost. There followed long explanations which did, of course, contain at least a grain of truth. The military spokesman declared, for instance, that the Soviet leadership, after great efforts, had succeeded in acquiring tremendous superiority at a single point, that the population had joined in the battle as snipers, that the German troops in the city had been greatly hindered by mines, and finally that the Russians had attacked regardless of losses.

In spite of these words of consolation, and in spite of the fact that it was quite well understood in political circles that Rostov had only limited military significance, on December 1 great gloom prevailed in both the Propaganda Ministry and the Foreign Office. For the first time the Russians had succeeded in retaking a great city. That the German troops were suffering tremendous casualties soon became plain. Officers of the regular army recognized with a certain satisfaction that what had happened was a complete fiasco for the SS, but that was all. Incidentally, losses sustained by the SS "Viking" division, composed of volunteers from various Germanic countries, were especially heavy.

But the fall of Rostov was soon to pale before events on the central front. On December 3, Berliners were still being told that the semicircular belt around Moscow was being drawn tighter and tighter. Then, on the 6th, the Russian cold suddenly became intense. All at once, in a single night, the temperature sank to 40 degrees below, and lower. The offensive against Moscow had to be called off. We were told that the German war machine had been paralyzed by the climate—the same climate that had earlier been hailed as an ally.

Effects of the War in the East, Inside and Outside Europe

The outbreak of war on June 22, 1941, had, from the German point of view, both favorable and unfavorable repercussions among Hitler's vassals, but an overwhelmingly unfavorable effect upon the German policy in the occupied countries.

On the positive side, Germany acquired Finland as an ally. But the joy over this was qualified by the fact that Finland from the beginning assumed an independent attitude; the Finns even ignored Hitler's attempt to force a quick decision by his declaration of war, in which the Finns were hailed as valiant brothers in arms even before their own declaration of war on Russia.

Another advantage for Germany was the attitude of the Baltic states. The overwhelming majority of Lithuanians, Letts and Estonians—more than 95 per cent of them, the Germans claimed—regarded the Germans as liberators. No doubt there had never been such an expression of real sympathy toward Germany since Hitler's rise to power. Many correspondents who visited the Baltic states were impressed by this spontaneous enthusiasm. In those days the Lithuanians, Letts and Estonians had seen no German officials or policemen; they had seen only the Reichswehr, which behaved with its customary discipline and was trying, so it seemed, to treat the population decently.

The Baltic patriots, of course, expected to see the independence of their countries re-established. Lithuanians felt they had good reason to expect that a Lithuanian army would be formed from the volunteers who had fought bravely and helped the Germans in their campaign. "To the last man—not less than 200,000 in all—we are ready," had been a popular cry.

Anyone who had had personal experiences in Nazi Germany received the impression, however, that there was a great deal of political naïveté in these activist Lithuanian circles. For the time being the German army was still in power in Lithuania. But what was going to happen when the Party management and the Gestapo made their entry into the country? On a trip I took to the Baltic front in July 1941, I had the good luck to be admitted to an inner circle of Lithuanian activists. After much hesitation, I decided to give them a warning. Should any one of them still be alive, he will no doubt recall the surprise and indignation with which they received my fears that they were counting not on the Third Reich, but on a Germany that did not exist. I warned them against placing their hopes in the policy of Nazi Germany, advising them to prepare for a new battle for liberty.

A third advantage for Germany was naturally the latent, or rather instinctive, anti-Bolshevist sentiment still existing in most nations. This could very well have been utilized to further German interests if the Nazi regime had not piled up such a huge debit balance with the peoples of Europe. Goebbels did what he could. But his only achievement was to make Germany look a little more sympathetic in the eyes of certain countries. With extreme care everything possible that could be interpreted in her favor was recorded. Every feeble sign of generosity toward other nations was called "a contribution to Europe's battle for freedom."

After the outbreak of the Russian war, the German authorities deemed it wise to avoid discussing the New Order; there was little doubt that almost everywhere enthusiasm for the New Europe had dropped to a low ebb. But once in a while a blunder showed the smaller nations only too clearly what Nazi Germany had in mind. The most notorious instance probably was Dr. Arthur Seyss-Inquart's speech at Cologne in November 1941. In it he announced that no country in Europe, the New Europe, of course, was to have complete independence, because a Germanic Lebensraum implied a united front, including a common defense and a single economic system. It was the will of the German leader, he continued, to incorporate the Netherlands in the German Lebensraum and to make them equal partners inside this area. In a brief commentary on the address it was said at the Wilhelmstrasse that Germany would never retreat from the North Sea coast. This could be interpreted to mean that the Nazis certainly planned to incorporate the Netherlands with Germany at once.

Reports of Seyss-Inquart's speech reached all the smaller countries of Europe, causing even Italians in Berlin to make inquiries as to the meaning of the term "Germanic." The same speech helped greatly to dampen whatever little enthusiasm there may have been for a battle against Communism under German leadership.

But from the newspaper quotations which the German press cited from all European countries, the German people, as such, could easily have received the impression that all Europe stood on Germany's side. On one occasion Dr. Schmidt in the Foreign Office even went so far as to say that Germany had won "the good-will battle for Europe." The German public, nevertheless, gradually began to understand that the "great daily papers" in the neutral countries were in reality insignificant sheets, financed either directly or indirectly by Germany.

Even the enthusiasm of the Axis partners for the eastern campaign was comparatively cool. Tokyo fell into a profound silence, showing not the slightest sign of wishing to intervene. Nor was a campaign against Russia included in what Italy had planned when she entered the war on June 10, 1940. But since Italy was, after all, forced to participate, she naturally did not hesitate to make the best possible use of the situation. In Berlin she issued claims in advance on certain Caucasian areas, not to mention demands for decisive influence over territories as far away as Turkestan.

As for Hungary, she had not entered the war until after the Russians had bombed Budapest; and when the Hungarian Government did declare war on Soviet Russia it was stated in Budapest that Hungary had no territorial ambitions beyond the Carpathians. In Rumania, on the other hand, there was more enthusiasm for participation in the war in the East. The disgrace suffered by the Rumanian army, which had been compelled to give up Bessarabia and half of Bukovina without firing a shot, would then be wiped out. Moreover, on the eastern horizon loomed possibilities of acquiring further territories and of getting the best of Hungary—a country which might perhaps be forced by Germany to surrender its newly reacquired share of Transylvania. At the beginning of November the already existing tension between Hungary and Rumania began to increase. At Arad a portrait of Admiral Horthy was solemnly burnt, an act all the more challenging as this city, even according to Rumanian statistics, still has an overwhelmingly Hungarian population. In the Rumanian press violent language was used, and from Budapest, in return, threatening rumbles were heard. But at that time Germany was still powerful enough to keep her two allies apart without much trouble.

The clash between Germany and the great Slavic power had far-reaching consequences on the Slavic areas within the Reich itself—the Bohemian-Moravian Protectorate—and on Germany's Slavic allies. In the fall of 1941 the ferment in the Protectorate came to a head. On September 28, the Germans took action, dismissing the former German Minister for Foreign Affairs, Baron von Neurath, who was then Protector, and appointing in his place the most brutal of Germany's police officials, Reinhard Heydrich, as Deputy Reichsprotector. For some reason the Germans wanted to preserve outward appearances, so they allowed von Neurath to retire for "reasons of health."

The most sensational move, however, was the arrest of the Czechoslovakian Premier, Alois Elias. The moment this arrest was announced, a wave of executions broke out. (Elias was spared at the time.) By October 1 no fewer than 123 Czechs, including two generals and several well-known businessmen, had been put to death. Some of the 123 victims were hanged. Among these were four from a little village which, by a quirk of fate, happened to have the name Höllengrund (Hell's foundation). Later, a considerable number of former high-ranking officers in the Czechoslovakian army were shot, as was Dr. Klapka, the former Mayor of Prague. There were the usual charges—sabotage, membership in secret national organizations and contacts with Czech refugees in England.

The situation in Croatia became particularly strained. There the new state, which had been set up under not too unfavorable auspices, had not had time to get organized before partisan riots upset public order. To this was added the pressure the Italians exerted upon the Croatian government, a pressure which during the spring had the peculiar result of compelling the Croats to accept a king from their hereditary enemies. The situation was further complicated by German-Italian rivalry in regard to Croatia. The German efforts to gain influence in the country were due chiefly, perhaps, to the fact that the Nazis wanted to be able to make "concessions" to Italy if and when it was necessary.

Originally Pavelitch had stood some chance of having his government accepted by his countrymen, since he expressed the old Croatian desire for a separate national existence. But he came back to his country suffering from two handicaps that eventually proved too much for him. The first was that he had been forced to tie himself to Italy, which had supported him during his long exile and which in return demanded large sections of Croatian territory; the second was that he had brought with him from other countries 800 faithful followers, the so-called "Ustachis," who to a great extent were simply cutthroats. Furthermore, he failed to come to terms with Dr. Matchek, the man who had the greater part of the Croatian nation behind him. Within the first six months, therefore, it was clear that the Pavelitch regime had been stillborn. Because it lacked troops, it could not take part in the war against Russia; it did, however, send volunteers—the so-called Croatian Legion—to the eastern front.

In Slovakia conflicting emotions, to put it mildly, prevailed at the outbreak of the war. As in the German war against Poland, the German-supported Tiso regime took part in the Russo-German war, with the result that Slovakian troops were sent to fight against Russia. When they reached the front, however, they sometimes acted as though they weren't sure which side they were fighting on.

As far as Bulgaria was concerned, the Germans encountered a long-established pro-Russian feeling. This, combined with Communist sentiment which had been prevalent in Bulgaria ever since the First World War, was utilized to the full by the Soviet Union. On the German side there were complaints that the mass of Bulgarians had failed to distinguish between "the earlier Russia which had liberated Bulgaria, and the Soviet Union whose aim was pure Bolshevism, with the consequent destruction of the Bulgarian state and the final proletarianization of the Bulgarian people." In any case, Bulgaria took no part in the war against Russia.

In the occupied countries the most unfavorable reaction came from Serbia, Montenegro and other parts of Yugoslavia. Unrest was kept alive by Pan-Slavic agitation from Moscow. "Hold on," urged a leaflet found by the Germans, "until the great Russian brother arrives to liberate all Slavs." As a matter of fact, the Serbs did rebel in masses and, as time went on, became increasingly bold. Mikhailovitch, then a Colonel, became a legendary figure whose troops made havoc of the highways and railroads. Whenever the Germans captured some of his Chetniks or some of the Communists, who had formed their own Partisan Army, they gave them short shrift. Likewise, whenever a German soldier was murdered, they applied reprisals at the rate of a hundred for one.

In the non-Slavic areas, the situation grew even more tense. To some extent this was due to the fact that the Germans found it necessary to continue draining these regions of their food and other supplies. In addition, the Communists, who in France, Belgium and Holland had at times worked to a double purpose, fighting their own governments as well as the invaders, now turned against the Germans. Another contributing factor was the feeling among the occupied nations that at last their overwhelmingly powerful oppressor had taken on an enemy who obviously could not easily be destroyed.

The first six months of the war with Russia saw a whole series of radical changes in Germany's political situation. It was natural that the new campaign would absorb many forces that previously had been used on other fronts, and that this would result in a considerably reduced freedom of action. As early as the summer of 1941 it became increasingly obvious, as many Germans had feared, that the expedition against Russia had involved a tremendous relaxation of the pressure against Britain. The sinkings of ships had decreased, and the air offensive against the British Isles was almost nonexistent. With growing apprehension, it was observed in Berlin that the British were beginning to lay in stores, and that American aid was increasing from day to day. Nor was it possible to close one's eyes to the fact that active American participation in the war was only a question of time. In some ways the official state of peace was more favorable to both England and the United States than it was to Germany. President Roosevelt's order to fire on Axis warships caused German submarines to abandon a considerable portion of their area of operations. Inch by inch the President moved forward his positions, until the feeling grew in Germany that it was once more a game of cat and mouse, in which the Germans, who so far had been accustomed to playing the cat, now had to be satisfied with the role of the mouse. Both Mr. Roosevelt and Hitler knew that it was as yet impossible for the Nazis to declare war on the United States. And both of them also knew that the American President might resort to any extreme, but that he would not do the German Führer the service of declaring war.

In German political circles there was helpless rage at repeated acts of defiance which could not be answered as they would have been if the United States were a helpless little country. The Germans were taking care not to exceed the limits of technical neutrality, and their feelings were revealed chiefly in the language they applied to President Roosevelt personally rather than to the country as a whole. This language now became so coarse that foreign journalists many times had to chalk up new records. As tension grew, however, it became impossible to preserve any distinction between the President and his country. Thereupon the Germans—or rather the Nazis—began offering their new picture of the United States as a country ruled by Jews and gangsters, where Negroes were lynched every morning before breakfast.

On September 12, after one of Mr. Roosevelt's most forceful speeches, the situation became critical. Neither the German press nor the German radio mentioned the speech, but the Foreign Office spokesman did not mince his words. Ever since Munich, he said, the American President's policy had been a continuous series of acts leading to war. In several countries he was looked upon as a warmonger. The chief responsibility for the outbreak of the war in 1939 fell on Mr. Roosevelt. His order to fire on German warships had been justified by "lies, forgeries, hypocrisy and pure inventions." Next day, in the *Hamburger Fremdenblatt*, Dr. Adolf Halfeld wrote that "Roosevelt had just fired the opening shot in an undeclared naval war."

Thereafter, the Germans followed developments in Japan closer than ever. With obvious emphasis the German press repeated that Japan was threatened by the Allies. They claimed, however, that a resolute and skillful policy was possible.

By the end of October, after the sinking of the American destroyer *Reuben James*, a new crisis in German-American relations had arisen. Mr. Roosevelt's speech in this connection was characterized as "vulgar, ridiculous and shameless," and the President of the United States was described as "insane, a criminal, a fool."

A circumstance favorable to Great Britain was the fact that she had the time, slowly, to build up her position in the Middle East, which has since played such an important role. The Germans were powerless to prevent the occupation of Iraq by the British; likewise they were compelled to sit back and watch them conquer Syria. That accomplished, the British were masters of the entire region from Egypt to Turkey. For the time being, Iran was left untouched, but it was thought to be only a matter of time before the need for a southern link with Russia would lead to British action against that country as well.

Aid to Iran was possible only through Turkey: that much was immediately clear to Berlin. But despite every reminder of the Sadabaad pact, which should have obliged the Turks to aid the Shah of Iran, despite all hints that Turkey was threatened by the new developments, the Turks showed no sign of readiness to intervene. And this being the case, the Germans had no choice but to observe passively how Iran, too, was forced to become a part of the British sphere in the Near East.

Berlin's only consolation was that Soviet Russia was also allowed to occupy its share of Iran—a fact duly utilized by German propaganda. At one moment it looked as though Germany had decided to put a stop to the British victory march through the Near East by taking up matters with Turkey. In September there were rumors of German-Bulgarian troop movements along the Thracian border and Russo-British concentrations at the eastern frontier of Turkey, but for once the storm clouds passed without a lightning war.

The War and Germany's Internal Problem

I have already mentioned that the declaration of war against Russia was received in Germany with a feeling of relief. To many Germans, both Nazis and opponents of the regime, the strained relations with their eastern neighbor had become an infernal nuisance. The fact that Hitler's recent ally was now Churchill's was something that pleased many Germans. Now, they said, it will be Churchill's turn to dance with the Russian bear. On the other hand, Germans couldn't suppress a guffaw when Dr. Goebbels, with self-righteous indignation, started talking about the treasonable act England had committed against Europe by allying herself with Russia. This interpretation was accepted only by those capable of forgetting that England's new ally was formerly Germany's or of accepting Goebbels' thesis that a fundamental difference existed between the Anglo-Russian and the German-Russian pacts.

Many Germans gave much thought to this enigma. While discussing the subject with three well-informed and unprejudiced Germans, I asked: "Supposing the Soviet Union had gone to war against the Allies. Would you have refused to accept Russia as your ally?" To this they were honest enough to answer no, quoting the old maxim about my enemy's enemy being my friend.

When the campaign against Russia got under way, the German people began to feel the real impact of war. Until then the lives of people on the home front had been comparatively undisturbed; nor had they suffered much from air raids. But soon after June 22 it was realized that the territory conquered in Russia couldn't be compared with the rich and apparently unlimited resources of France, and that it was impossible to supply German troops in the East to the same extent that they had been supplied in the West.

The initial successes in Russia were received with satisfaction. People were inclined to believe that the war might not last so very long. The German Wehrmacht, penetrating deeper and deeper into the colossal Russian country, achieved an unbroken series of victories. But when was the Victory to be expected? This was what the Germans wanted to know. When soldiers came home on leave from the eastern front and began talking about this enemy which refused to surrender, which possessed, apparently, unlimited material resources and reserves in man power, Germans on the home front could not help feeling uneasy. They could not help observing the increasing casualty lists, nor remain ignorant of the hospital trains which, under cover of darkness, came rolling in one after another. Gradually more and more rolling stock, construction matériel and supplies were shipped to the newly acquired territories—to be replaced by long columns of poorly clad prisoners of war.

As winter approached, and the fighting did not appear to abate, the public began to show increasing signs of anxiety. The pessimists recalled Napoleon's war in Russia, with the result that there was an immediate rush for every book dealing with the Grand Army's campaign. The fortune tellers' prophecies stressed Napoleon's fate, and astrologers realized a boom. Finally, the press had to be mobilized to offset the winter psychosis. The papers ran long and detailed articles on why this campaign could not possibly be compared with that of 1812. The first ten weeks of the war, said the *Frankfurter Zeitung* on September 14, demonstrated that the Russian armies were now defending their territory, instead of making voluntary retreats, as they had done in Napoleon's day. At that time the Russian generals could have withdrawn their troops to the Urals without losing the war, but that was impossible in 1941 for reasons of supply. Moreover, the German leaders, the article continued, had no intention of marching endlessly on, of garrisoning every village in the Soviet Union. On the contrary, Germany's military goal was "to bring about such a decisive weakening of the Russians that Bolshevism would cease to be a danger to Europe." This, by the way, was one of the first signs that the campaign now had a more limited goal.

The Nazi propaganda machine also began to stir itself into bolstering the flagging morale. Realistic stories were published about miserable conditions in occupied territories; newspapers displayed horror photographs; German workers were shown a model of so-called workers' quarters in Soviet Russia; day after day the German public was reminded of what Hitler's decision had saved them from.

"Look at the quantities of Russian war matériel captured along the Polish border," the German propaganda machine was saying in effect. "Any fool can see that Hitler waited until the very last minute before striking." And the Germans apparently swallowed this story, too. Hitler was still immune from criticism, but not the Party. It was the relations with America that caused the greatest anxiety. German propaganda against the United States and disparaging remarks about American production figures were in themselves disturbing evidence that there was danger of another 1917. Not even the most ardent Nazis wanted war with America. Every German felt a profound respect for America's strength. No one had forgotten how American intervention had decided the outcome of the last war. Despite every declaration to the contrary, many Germans were aware that something of a similar nature might occur again. For this reason, also, the attitude toward the regime became more critical. But the Nazi Party was by no means ignorant of these changes in the public's attitude, and with due discretion precautionary steps were taken.

The foreign correspondents immediately noticed the change. Press regulations tightened. The attitude toward the Americans—who, until then, had often been favored, even admired—altered completely. The change became noticeable even to the neutrals, if this formal term may be used to cover all the newspapermen in Berlin hailing from non-Axis states. Suspicion increased, and we were under strict and constant supervision. Foreign businessmen, too, were subjected to closer scrutiny. New campaigns were started to prevent people from listening to foreign broadcasts. These were supported by police raids and a spreading of rumors that the police had at its disposal a device with which they were able to ascertain not only whether a radio was tuned to a foreign station, but also the very name of that station.

But listening to foreign broadcasts was not the only danger. During the autumn Moscow suddenly began to inject remarks into Germany's own broadcasts. It was said in Berlin that a German Jew in Russia acted as an extracurricular announcer. He wasn't at all bad, and for several weeks he forced the German announcers to read in a very loud voice and so fast that it was a wonder their lungs didn't burst. But the Germans had prepared their comeback, with the result that one day in the middle of October a derisive voice injected itself into a British broadcast. I happened to be listening to a London station broadcasting to Canada, when a clear voice suddenly asked: "How much are the Jews paying you?" And later: "Why don't you tell the truth?" When the British announcer declared that the RAF had shot down some German planes, the voice cried: "And lost nine of their own." Sometimes this voice attempted some real Bronx cheers, and sometimes both voices spoke at the same time. A similar voice was heard over the Rome radio, denouncing Fascism to Italian listeners. But after a week or so all was quiet again on the radio front. Possibly the two antagonists found this kind of warfare too much of a bore.

In spite of the sharp police control, consisting of the establishment of SS posts all over Berlin, it was soon clear that war weariness was on the increase. The war spirit had fallen to a low ebb. All manner of bartering flourished, especially during the fall when the tobacco supply ran low and long lines of people queued up outside every tobacco shop. There was no end to the barter trade. Luxury goods were especially in demand. With more and more articles completely disappearing from the market, the businessmen's standing slogan became: "*Alles für die Wehrmacht*"—everything has gone to the army—whether it was a question of candy, women's stockings or liquor.

Another sign that things were not going too well at home was the renewal of the anti-Semitic campaign. In September the Star of David was made compulsory for all Jews, and Goebbels again began turning out one anti-Semitic editorial after another. The purpose of this was partly to prepare the German people for war against America, a country, according to the Nazis, dominated by Jews. The Nazis went so far as to publish a purported Roosevelt genealogy showing that he, too, was a Jew. Fundamentally, however, the campaign served purely practical aims. Nobody could seriously believe that those Jews still remaining in the country, mostly old people who kept themselves alive only with the greatest difficulty, constituted a danger to the German people. But the Jews did have something that was highly desirable, and that was a roof over their heads. It was said quite openly, in fact, that the mounting shortage of housing facilities was sufficient justification for the transfer of the Jewish population to territories in the East. What happened to them there, or en route, is known all too well.

Doubtless Goebbels also thought that he would obtain the same results on this occasion as he did by his previous anti-Semitic campaigns, and that morale would soon show signs of improving. This time, however, he was mistaken. The people of Berlin reacted against the Star of David in a manner that must have given Goebbels and his crowd many anxious hours. Time and again there were demonstrations in favor of the Jews, and the stoic calm with which these miserable people endured their fate did not fail to impress even the most fanatical Nazis.

It would be incorrect, on the other hand, to state that the situation was critical in Germany in the fall of 1941. It is certainly true that the Russian war began to get on the Germans' nerves. But even if they did feel dejected when the large-scale operations in the East failed to produce the desired results, they nevertheless did not believe that the Russians—whose defensive strength was pretty generally admitted—would be able to take the offensive against the German army. The Wehrmacht was still considered invincible.

What did impress foreign observers was the rapid depletion of all reserve supplies. Civilian life was naturally first to suffer, but it was clear enough that military supplies were also limited. With this in mind it was permissible to suspect that the dynamic type of war Germany had so far been waging might move into a static phase. Meanwhile England, the chief enemy, would be slowly rising to her feet.

THE WINTER OF 1941-1942

Pearl Harbor and Germany's Declaration of War Against America

THE secret of the attack planned on Pearl Harbor was closely guarded. It was of course known in international circles in Berlin that for several weeks the situation in the Far East had been extraordinarily tense, and that the Germans for many months had pinned high hopes on Japan. When my German informants had spoken about this matter during the autumn, they had taken it for granted that Japan would act as they always hoped she would—in other words, that she would help to crush the Russians by attacking them from the rear, or possibly open hostilities against England. That the Japanese were to direct their main attack against their most dangerous enemy, the United States, had not entered the minds of the Germans. On the whole, they desired to keep America out of the war and had every reason to believe that this would be possible.

With the news of the attack on Pearl Harbor, everything seemed to indicate that even if Japan's action was to the temporary advantage of the Germans, still the island empire had acted in its own interests, and that Germany would have to pay for Japanese aid by waging war against the United States. During the first days we gained the impression that the Japanese had failed to inform their German allies about their plans for attack until the very last moment. We also noted that enthusiasm in Germany for this new war was very lukewarm indeed. When later on it became evident that the Japanese had succeeded in making much bigger gains than anybody had anticipated, the mood of the Wilhelmstrasse changed entirely.

The Japanese in Berlin—with the probable exception of their ambassador, General Oshima, and his closest advisers—were doubtless never told that the war was to start at this time and with an attack on Hawaii. But the Japanese journalists in the German capital knew that the situation was serious, and possibly some of

56

them suspected that the outcome would be a sudden attack like that on Port Arthur. On the night of December 6, one of the Japanese newpapermen became gloriously drunk and began offering toasts to the Japanese-American war. "It will start tomorrow," he shouted. But nobody paid any attention to him, as he was known to be an alcoholic and sometimes made rather wild remarks.

The day after Pearl Harbor was strange indeed. The Americans were dejected, but they still did not suspect the whole extent of the catastrophe. One of my close friends among them said, "We needed something like this to make the people back home understand that this is a serious business."

Americans, Germans and neutrals—all of them thought that war between the United States and Germany was unavoidable. But even on December 7 it was quite evident that the Germans wished to wait a few days, hoping that Roosevelt would spare Hitler the necessity of declaring war. Two days passed and Roosevelt took no action against the Germans. At the beginning of his press conference on December 10, Dr. Schmidt asked all the Americans to leave the room and urged the representatives of the foreign press not to regard them any longer as colleagues. They rose quietly and left. Dr. Schmidt stood at the door to shake hands with each of them, beginning with Louis P. Lochner, who for many years had been head of the Berlin bureau of the Associated Press.

The press conference then proceeded in a heavily charged atmosphere, but it did not produce any more sensations. After it closed, the discussion became very lively, everybody wondering what was going to happen now. People with special connections said that the Reichstag had been called into session at three o'clock that afternoon, and that Hitler, acting on pressure from Japan, would declare war. However, it was not until the next day that we were told we could get our cards for this event at the Propaganda Ministry, and when we did get them we noticed that the date had been changed from December 10 to 11.

There were fewer cars than usual outside the Kroll Opera House, for the cut in gas rations for official cars had made itself felt; and there was not a specially big crowd inside, either. A long time had passed since meetings of the Reichstag had attracted great masses of people.

The ceremonial was the same as always and the audience was also the same. Some prominent foreign guests had been placed in the boxes—among others the Grand Mufti of Jerusalem in his colorful costume and Anton Mussert, the Dutch Nazi leader. Quisling was there in person and had been given a place of honor. He looked very pleased with himself, like an errand boy who for the first time in his life had been invited to travel first class.

Hitler entered, and the Reichstag greeted him with the usual well-drilled ovations. After a few words from Goering, the Führer started to speak. He began by giving some incredibly low figures of German losses in Russia, where the fighting had tapered off for the moment but was soon to start up again. The main point of his speech, however, was the business of settling accounts. It was typical of Hitler that he should devote about half an hour to President Roosevelt and his wife, berating them personally, and in such mean and vulgar words that those present applauded only with hesitation. In the long row of field marshals, generals and admirals, I saw not a single hand move. I glanced around at the officials of the Foreign Office and the Propaganda Ministry, who were seated close by, in order to see if they too found the performance revolting. Most of them applauded his "sallies" with enthusiasm, but some appeared to be uneasy, and they looked surreptitiously at one another and at the neutrals when Hitler screamed out his hatred for the American President—the "cripple" —and his wife. Had they the same thoughts as we? It is possible that even eight years of the Nazi regime had not rubbed out all sense of generosity and good manners.

When the paroxysm of hate was finally over, the information came at last—during one of Hitler's "quiet" periods, which always come after the shouting and exert a tremendous influence on his audience—that the German Foreign Minister had presented the American chargé d'affaires with his passport. Then the entire audience applauded, and this time even the military had to clap their hands.

When Hitler, in the rest of his speech, loudly thundered against those who dared to disturb the inner front, he seemingly spoke to persons not present in the Kroll Opera House. Nevertheless, a peculiar silence fell over the hall. The eyes of the spectators rested on the generals, especially when Hitler with great emphasis exclaimed: "Back of me stands the Party, of that I am certain—the Party, which has grown great through me and through which I have become great." What attracted attention was not the emphatic tone but—why did only the *Party* stand back of him? Didn't the armed forces support their commander-in-chief and the people support their Führer? The words contained an unmistakable warning, but to whom? A few weeks later part of the secret was to become publicly known.

I had been present at quite a few sessions of the German Reichstag, but this one had a more depressing effect on me than any of the others. The gigantic duel with the United States was announced to the German people in words which were unworthy of a barroom brawl.

The Scandinavians were particularly interested in the fate of their American colleagues. In response to inquiries, we were told that they were to be treated as members of the diplomatic corps, provided the United States accorded the same privileges to the German journalists in America. On the previous day the Americans had been confined to their homes. They were now transferred to a hotel before being interned temporarily at Bad Nauheim. An exception was made for Guido Enderis of the *New York Times*, because his health was failing. The courtesy was only natural, since Enderis had been dean of the foreign correspondents and had been interned once before during the First World War.

The German people received this new declaration of war with resigned calm and without the least trace of enthusiasm. Many persons had dire forebodings and began talking about the First World War. Above all, the Germans now became fully convinced that this new conflict would be a long one. Even the greatest optimists among them were forced to realize that the final outcome was doubtful—and this in spite of the early Japanese victories, which had been considerably greater than the German in the street had dared to expect.

Ever since the end of November a terrific battle had been raging in North Africa between the British and Rommel. The latter seemed to have the situation in hand, although there were some signs of worry in Berlin because of what was said to be the superior strength of the enemy. The situation in Russia, on the other hand, caused real anxiety.

The Threatened Catastrophe in the East

On December 7 news of such a sensational nature arrived from the Russian front that it could easily compete with the bulletins from Pearl Harbor. The temperature had fallen to 40 degrees below zero, and the German offensive against Moscow, which had been making further progress since the end of November, had suddenly been paralyzed. This news was confirmed by the High Command, which announced on December 8 that, because of the cold, the war in Russia had come practically to a standstill, and that "on large sectors of the eastern front, only local skirmishes now take place."

At the press conferences, Captain Sommerfeldt admitted that the winter had arrived earlier than had been expected, and that the cold made it impossible to use any of the German armored vehicles; even the motor oil had frozen. The fall of Moscow, therefore, could not be expected in 1941. From other sources we learned the same day that the situation was critical. Tanks were immobilized and had to be dynamited, quantities of trucks had been lost, and in view of the Russian counteroffensive all the way from Leningrad to the Black Sea, the Germans were now in full retreat, leaving behind them large quantities of war matériel.

These violent attacks by the Red Army were a real surprise to the Germans. They had failed to consider the possibility that the Soviet leaders might be able to organize counterattacks on a large scale—above all, not when the weather was so cold that, according to the German view, it made practically all fighting impossible. To top it all, the Russian offensive was obviously going ahead in accordance with a carefully worked-out plan—a fact that the Germans hesitated to admit, although they were later forced to do so.

The situation became so dangerous that well-informed people in Berlin began to admit the possibility that the central German front might crack. In the German capital and especially in the government offices, the atmosphere was dismal. The neutrals, too, began to envisage a Russian victory, although they had believed until then that the Germans were certain to win. For two or three exciting days the fate of the whole eastern front hung precariously in the balance. That the crisis was surmounted and the Russian advance gradually brought to a standstill was due above all to the fighting qualities of the German soldier. Even though he was confronted by an entirely new method of warfare and a climate that ninety-nine out of a hundred Germans had heard about but had never experienced, and despite the total lack of suitable winter equipment and weapons, the private soldier did his utmost time and again.

A large part of the credit for stabilizing the front must also be given to the stubbornness of Hitler himself. Yet in this case there are qualifications to be made. His military advisers recommended retreat, and whether they were right is hard to determine. Even if it was Hitler who then took a correct view of the situation, he must nevertheless be held responsible for the mad tempo during the fall which had exhausted the German war machine. And even though the front became stabilized, Germany suffered a real defeat in the winter battle.

As soon as the real heat of the battle was over, the German soldiers began to express their whole-souled bitterness over their miserable equipment. Until that time it had been said that the German forces were better equipped than any other army in the world. But that December the Russian troops appeared in sheepskin coats, felt boots and white parkas, whereas the winter equipment of the German soldier often was limited to a white cloth around his helmet. Even worse was the fact that the German army completely lacked training in winter warfare and knew nothing about fighting in the darkness and in wooded terrain. The Alpine regiments had some knowledge of how to meet these conditions, but even they were trained for a special kind of warfare, far different from what they had to practice in the East. It is obvious that the lack of training for winter warfare was an unforgivable blunder of the German High Command—just as serious as the failure to understand the role of tanks in modern warfare which helped to cause the defeat of the French.

The announcement by the High Command that in order to avoid unnecessary losses the German troops had "voluntarily" withdrawn from all salients, had retreated to a winter line, and had undertaken "correcting" movements, seemed like a piece of bloodstained mockery to the men at the front. Something had to be done, and it was Dr. Goebbels who had to do it. On the evening of December 20, he delivered an address over all the German radio stations and many of those in the occupied countries. He announced that a gigantic collection of winter equipment for the armed forces would take place between December 27, 1941, and January 4, 1942. The speech was made in a tone quite different from the one that Goebbels generally used, and it told all Germans quite plainly that the situation was critical. Hitler's short appeal, which was read by the Propaganda Minister, was also significant. Goebbels himself touched only briefly on the reason why the collection had to be made. The Wehrmacht, he said, had made great efforts to supply the soldiers with winter equipment, but winter had arrived earlier than expected, and in spite of everything that could be done, the German soldiers still needed warm clothing. He concluded with an exceedingly urgent appeal to the solidarity of all Germans.

The speech hit the people like a bomb. Many asked themselves where Dr. Dietrich was, with his famous announcement that the war was over. They wondered whether it wouldn't have been more reasonable to prepare for winter before the middle of December, considering that even in Berlin it was usually icy cold by that time. But the dominant feeling was that fate had touched the German nation in a way that it had heretofore escaped during this war, and that a catastrophe was to be feared. With the possibility in mind that the Russian masses might roll westward through Europe, even the most violent anti-Nazis became willing to sacrifice something. The collection campaign led to a tightening up of German morale.

But the people at home were to have still another shock. On December 19, I received a telegram sent through Stockholm by a colleague in London, who informed me of reports that Hitler had dismissed Marshal von Brauchitsch and had in person assumed command over the army. This fitted in perfectly with something we had sensed for a long time, especially after the meeting of the Reichstag: that a conflict had arisen between Hitler and the higher officers. For two days I could get no confirmation of the report; none of my friends in Berlin knew anything. But on the evening of December 21, when most of the Swedes were assembled at the home of a colleague, there was a telephone message announcing that Hitler had decided to take command of the army himself, and that he had issued a proclamation to the soldiers. We scattered as quickly as possible in order to get in touch with our papers. On reaching home, I decided to call Sommerfeldt in spite of the late hour. At first he told me to go to the devil—I was the tenth person who had called—but he calmed down after a little persuasion. What he could tell me was very little. "Don't get into trouble," he said, "by going beyond the official announcement."

During the next few days, we received nothing more than a few evasive comments. It was by no means the symptom of a crisis, Sommerfeldt said, after he had found out what it was safe to say. The measure had been planned a long time ago, and what we heard now was merely the formal announcement of something that was already a fact, namely, that Hitler was personally in command of all the armed forces and, consequently, of the army as well.

Sommerfeldt went on to explain that Hitler had personally worked out the plans for the invasion of Norway, for the war against France and for the operations against Russia. In the explanation sent out by DNB—the German News Bureau—it was said that the German Chancellor had had a determining voice in the equipment and operations of the army, that in exercising his leadership he had followed his intuition, and that he had reserved for himself the right to make all important decisions. The only answer to further questions was that the subject was closed.

Berlin, of course, was filled with rumors about the Brauchitsch story. It was by now quite clear what had been the cause of the conflict. In 1941 Hitler regarded himself as "the greatest general of all times," to use an epithet that many Germans, two years later, would apply to him ironically. Without a doubt the autumn campaign of 1941 showed traces of his interference. Dr. Dietrich's pronouncement to the foreign correspondents, the desperate offensive against Moscow and the resulting strain on the whole German army—all this could only be Hitler's work. His point of view was quite natural to one whose guiding star had been the motto, *"aus dem Unmöglichen ein Mögliches zu machen"*—to make the impossible possible. At Moscow the Germans came close to achieving the impossible once more. Theoretically they might well have entered the city before they were overtaken by winter; in practice what stopped them was the presence of Russian reserves. When they failed to allow for these reserves, the High Command and Hitler himself were acting like amateurs in the art of war.

Field Marshal Walther von Brauchitsch is surely no such military genius as was his predecessor, General von Fritsch, but he is a good Prussian officer. He comes from an old Silesian noble family with military traditions and was brought up in a soldier's home, his father being a cavalry general. Brauchitsch made a good record in the First World War. Afterwards, as a major, he entered the newly formed Reichswehr, and in 1931 he became a major general. Under Hitler, he played a rather important part in organizing the new German army, especially its motorized units. As commander-in-chief of the army, from February 4, 1938, he was not an outstanding personality and politically he was of no decisive importance. But he was a generally respected, capable officer, greatly trusted by the armed forces and of quite a different type from his colleague Keitel, who was regarded as being too compliant.

Marshal von Brauchitsch had been opposed to Hitler's tactics during the fall of 1941 and, according to rumors that now have been verified, several serious clashes occurred between him and the Führer. Brauchitsch was by no means alone; in addition to a number of army commanders who resigned when he did, Reichsmarshal Goering had strongly opposed the offensive against Moscow. Developments proved Brauchitsch to be right, but that only increased Hitler's anger. It is surprising that the decisive conflict was delayed until December. When the Germans retreated, Hitler made a scapegoat out of the man who had committed the crime of judging the situation more clearly than his Führer.

The Party tried to spread the rumor that it was the generals, after all, who had insisted on taking Moscow in 1941, whereas Hitler had warned against it and had only reluctantly agreed to their plans. The joke was that Hitler's own words effectively squelched this rumor, as did the remarks of the official commentators when they pointed out that Hitler himself had decided all basic questions about the equipment of the army—including its winter equipment—as well as questions of strategy. They had left no doubt concerning the responsibility for the German defeat.

The crisis among the generals was not ended by the resignation of Marshal von Brauchitsch. Several of the high commanders declared themselves on his side: for example, Field Marshals von Rundstedt, Ritter von Leeb, von Bock and List, as well as Generals Guderian and von Kleist. All of these resigned.

The Christmas of 1941 was gloomy. The many death announcements now reaching German families were felt especially keenly during the holidays. The scarcity in commodities was so great that it was hard to celebrate Christmas with even a trace of the old traditions. Nevertheless, the holiday was deeply appreciated, especially because it gave most Germans a chance to rest for a few days. By the end of 1941, the effects of poor nourishment and extra work had begun to show themselves in the form of physical fatigue. For days on end, everyone talked about the extra chance to sleep, just sleep.

All through January, the battles in the East continued, and so did the difficulties of the High Command. The "winter line" that had been mentioned in December was only a geographical term. In reality it was simply the line where German units had been able to stop the Russians. The German troops suffered keenly, quarters were bad, and when a human habitation was found, it was infested with millions of lice. The situation is best described in a soldier correspondent's article, written in this case by the man who was formerly chief editor of the *Lokal Anzeiger:* "During the summer, no German soldier ever entered one of the stinking houses. Today we are grateful for any hole that has a more or less solid roof, under which we can squeeze in like sardines. But the straw doesn't keep you warm in these huts, which would be complimented if you called them stables, according to German standards. The floor is icy cold and crawls with lice, fleas and bedbugs. How is it possible for people to exist year after year in this awful filth?" [1]

Along the whole front, the Russian attacks were ferocious. It was not only in the central sector that they were beginning to assume a rather dangerous character. The Russian General Staff utilized its control of the Black Sea to make landings in the Crimea. Kerch and Theodosia were recaptured in rather short order by surprise attacks, although the Russians failed in their repeated attempts to land troops west of Sevastopol, especially at Eupatoria. The German position in the Crimea, however, was not easy to hold, considering that all supplies had to cross the narrow Perekop Isthmus, and considering also that the powerful fortress and naval base of Sevastopol still belonged to the Russians.

In the North, the Red Army made a shrewd move by bringing up fresh Siberian troops who could stand the extreme cold better than Europeans. Nevertheless, a rather stationary battle zone developed. This we could tell by reading the German press, which heretofore had carefully avoided mentioning any Russian place names. In the middle of January, however, it specified a number of towns in such a manner that it was possible to visualize a front extending from Taganrog, in the South, along a line that ran east of Kharkov, Belgorod, Kursk and Orel to the Kaluga section; then east of Mozhaisk across Lake Seliger, Valdai and Lake Ilmen up to Schlüsselburg, cutting all Russian land connections with Leningrad. The Russians, however, had been able to hold strong positions at several points behind this line. Especially between Kholm and Toropets the Russian command had succeeded in driving in a deep salient that was fifty miles wide at the base. But it was evident that the Germans had succeeded in holding the large towns, which not only served as breakwaters against the Russian tidal

---

[1] *The Russians, on the other hand, were amazed by the filthy habits of the German troops. See especially Maurice Hindus' account of a visit to the liberated regions, in* Mother Russia.—*Tr.*

wave, but also provided quarters for the German troops. This was all the more important because German resources in this respect were of poor quality and wholly inadequate.

Though the main crisis had passed for the Germans by the middle of January, the situation was far from stabilized. Captain Sommerfeldt had a hard time making his statements correspond to what he had said some weeks before. But what he did say made a rather curious impression on those of us who had good memories or kept accurate notes. He admitted, for instance, on January 21 that the Russian winter was Stalin's best ally and that the climate would favor Russian operations until March.

Meanwhile the Germans showed that they were still superior on the North African front. The British offensive of November and early December had resulted only in small advances and by no means justified the cheers that were at first heard from London. Berlin was greatly amused at Churchill, who had shouted a little too early and had expressed himself in a manner quite contrary to his usual attitude of careful realism.

At the end of January, General Rommel made another of the quick counterthrusts of which he had proved himself a master; he forced the British to retreat with heavy losses. On January 25, military quarters in Berlin declared that the British were in full flight, and that panic was sweeping eastward like waves after an earthquake. It was only by dint of the greatest efforts that Rommel was stopped a short distance from Tobruk.

Dr. Goebbels' New Propaganda Technique

When it became evident that the German situation in Russia was critical, little Dr. Goebbels decided to meet the situation with a new kind of propaganda. Instead of maintaining the previously adopted sanguine attitude, the aim of which had been to minimize first the British and then the Russian strength, the Propaganda Ministry began to paint everything in somber colors. It spoke only in general terms, but these were plain enough to scare the German people to increased efforts. Stories began to circulate about what would happen to Germany if the British and the Russians were victorious. The transition was a little too fast for many Germans, but the propaganda was carried on so cleverly that the only con-clusion to be drawn from Goebbels' presentation by the man-in-the-street was that he had to do his utmost. "If the Russians should reach East Prussia, I'm going to take my rifle down from the wall," said one of my friends who was a confirmed opponent of the Nazi system. Obviously, the Propaganda Minister had spent quite a little time on phrasing his explanation so as to make the situation look as black as possible without causing people to despair of victory.

The winter collection of clothes for the front was utilized to the utmost for propaganda purposes. Every day the newspapers published pictures of prominent persons, especially film stars and athletes, who were donating all sorts of clothing, and more than once the announcement was made that famous or even historic fur coats had been sacrificed for victory. The collection, which was supposed to end on January 4, was extended to January 11— "to give all who had not had time to get their gifts ready a chance to contribute." On the last day the result was published, and it showed that some 56,000,000 separate garments had been collected. Of equally great importance was the fact that the collection brought about a definite improvement in morale.

Propaganda also had to be adjusted to fit the mental state of soldiers at the front. Promi reasoned that when they came home on furlough, their language would have to sound not too different from the statements being issued by the regime. Many of them had been deeply shocked by the lack of winter equipment and by the faulty tactics their officers had employed, and it was deemed necessary to turn the expected criticism "in the right direction."

The first line was to stress the fact that Hitler himself had once been a common soldier at the front. It was repeated over and over that his heart bled for the soldiers and that he lived as simply as they did. It was also said—and in all probability it was true—that Hitler was exceedingly severe with those who had never served in the front lines. Somewhat cautiously at first, the newspapers emphasized the eternal contrast between the home front and the battle front. In order to forestall criticism by the soldiers, the civilians themselves were criticized. One publication was given this specific task—the SS weekly, *Das Schwarze Korps*.

This paper, published every Wednesday, had always tried to assume an attitude that was regarded as suitable for the soldiers at the front. Now its language became even coarser and slangier, and one could almost smell the sulphur after Goebbels changed his propaganda line. Often articles in *Das Schwarze Korps* sounded phony, and you couldn't help feeling that the writers themselves had never smelled powder. On the other hand, soldiers who had served at the front were asked to write about various problems pertaining to morale, and then the words rang true.

Thanks to the bitterness with which it criticized conditions at home in the name of the front-line soldiers, *Das Schwarze Korps* became an excellent medium for dispelling the soldiers' discontent. It minced no words in attacking merchants, officials charged with civilian supply, war profiteers, the black market, the bureaucrats and everything else that soldiers in Russia detested. It was widely read and, for correspondents, it was the most revealing of the German periodicals.

Other clear signs of the new propaganda line were evident in Hitler's New Year's message, which Goebbels read over the radio. They were also evident in the New Year editorials of the German press, many of which were written on the theme, "The war has become harder." Even in propaganda released for foreign consumption, changes could be noticed. The new situation seemed to have brought about a different attitude toward the smaller countries. Previously these had been treated with a certain haughtiness and told in no uncertain words what the New Europe demanded of them. But in the New Year's article he wrote for the *Berliner Börsenzeitung* Karl Megerle said, "Germany does not want a Europe held under duress but a Europe of good will."

The German people were tensely awaiting the first public appearance of the Führer after the defeats in Russia. It had been expected that he would speak at the memorial service for the late Marshal von Reichenau on January 23, but instead it was Goering who delivered the address. Rumors had been circulating about Reichenau's death. We heard from usually well-informed people that four high SS officers had paid him a visit—"and then he died," our informants would add significantly. Others claimed that the scene of his death was a hospital in Leipzig. A police officer claimed that he had been murdered by the Monarchists. I should judge that some of these rumors had a basis of fact. The official cause of death was heart failure, but Reichenau was known throughout Germany for his remarkable physique.

On January 30—the ninth anniversary of his taking of power—Hitler made a speech in the Sportpalast. The audience consisted of the usual picked élite of faithful Party members. In contrast to earlier occasions, however, some 40 high army officers were present, obviously to make the ceremony more official in character than any of the earlier commemorative celebrations. It was a new Hitler who appeared before the audience and the members of the foreign press. Colleagues who had been able to observe him for years before I came to Germany immediately said, "You can see that he has his first serious defeat behind him." His face now seemed ravaged and his manner uncertain.

But Hitler always seems unsure of himself at the beginning of his speeches and takes at least half an hour to get really under way—a fact that was now more obvious than ever. He began by stating that he thought he should return to the place from which he had sprung—to the people. Then followed the usual review of events since 1918. Eventually he mentioned his adversaries with even more than his usual lack of taste. Churchill was "a chatterbox and a drunkard"; Roosevelt was a "pitiful lunatic" (*armseliger Irrer*). It was easy to see the same reaction among the listeners as at the Reichstag meeting in December; many stirred uneasily in their seats.

At last Hitler approached the heart of the matter. It was not, he declared, the military power of the Soviets, but a temperature of 50 below zero that had forced the German armies to halt and occupy a defensive position (the word "retreat" was not mentioned in his speech). The difficult operation had now succeeded and "when spring comes," the German army would launch a general attack. "The greatest of our difficulties lie behind us," he said. But the home front would have to work as never before. Extraordinary means would be taken to increase production. Finally Hitler directed an impassioned appeal to all persons in industry, transportation and other fields to do their utmost.

As early as January, a gigantic mobilization of all available resources of man power had begun. The barracks were filled once more, and a vast training program was launched on the double-quick. Great numbers of German workers had been called up; their places would be taken by prisoners and foreign labor. Small business-men had to close their shops and join the army. Masses of university students, who so far had been exempt, were also drafted. The Government departments, too, were forced to yield many men—for example, the Foreign Office and the Propaganda Ministry each supplied a war-strength battalion. The men to go were selected by the chiefs of personnel, who had to see to it that the prescribed number was produced. The Ministries lost some of their best people, and this was particularly the case at the Foreign Office and Promi. Those who remained were the physically unfit, and the ones who, often by petty intrigue, had gained the favor of the personnel directors.

As one step in the progressive mobilization, a proclamation was made to all former officers of "German or closely allied blood" who were now German citizens. Included were those who had once belonged to the Austro-Hungarian army, the Austrian Republican army, and the Italian, Czechoslovakian, Polish, Belgian and Yugoslavian armies. All these were ordered to report to the police stations in their home districts.

To augment the reserves of man power, action was taken even before Hitler's speech to employ all available technical and economic resources in order to compensate for lost war matériel and bring production to its highest peak. On January 27, Ministerial Director Mansfeld was ordered to import new hordes of workers to Germany (it was estimated that 2,200,000 foreigners were already at work there). Simultaneously it was announced that recruiting bureaus would be opened in the Ukraine and that forced labor was to be introduced in the occupied countries. From the Baltic states came trainload after trainload of men and women workers. Some of them had been recruited by means of veiled threats, while others had been lured by the promise of high wages and good working conditions. During the first days of February, the first Russian civilian workers arrived, among them a consignment of miners from Krivoi Rog.

Women workers were employed to an increasing extent, especially to take the places of men drafted from government or municipal bureaus. It was said in February that a forced labor law was being prepared that would mobilize practically all the German women.

From the beginning, the two catchwords of this new drive were "efficiency" and "concentration." These, however, were not the only aims behind it. The German leaders were also thinking in terms of propaganda, and were hoping to compensate the German people for their hardships by making them feel that their strength was becoming concentrated and was being used more effectively.

Military and Political Problems of the Late Winter

From a military point of view, the situation did not change materially in February. The Germans were still forced to repulse strong Russian attacks made while the mercury was far below zero. Spokesmen in Berlin, however, were beginning to be more hopeful. They pointed to the heavy Russian losses and said that the Red Army would bleed to death in its winter offensive. It was, indeed, attacking with fanatical courage and without any regard for the losses it sustained. The Wehrmacht found it hard to meet the tactics that the Russians were using; they not only made frontal assaults but filtered through the German lines, or rather, through the zone that was under German observation. At certain vital points, strategically placed, the Germans built so-called "hedgehogs," which were defended by units as large as a full division and were stocked with large stores of supplies. These hedgehogs were a continual threat to the flanks of the Russian advance. On the other hand, their store of supplies had to be replenished mainly from the air, since the Russians controlled the highways. This method succeeded in 1942, but not in 1943, when the hedgehog tactics were tried once more.

On February 22, the German High Command made public a tabular summary of the fighting since January 1. This was done to forestall an expected Russian communiqué on the jubilee day of the Russian Army, February 23. The number of Russian prisoners was given as 56,800, a figure which, for once, seemed fairly reasonable.

Naturally, there were no figures given for the German losses, since Hitler was supposed to deal with these on one of his more important appearances. There was no doubt, however, that German casualties were extraordinarily high, in spite of the fact that the Reichswehr was on the defensive. Cases of frostbite had reached a record high. If a soldier sustained even a minor wound at a temperature of 40 below zero, he had slight chance of surviving. Lieutenant Colonel Soldan in a radio address set the Russian losses during the two and a half months at 800,000 to 1,000,000 men killed. Well-informed Germans gave an estimate of at least 350,000 for their own dead during the winter. Undoubtedly, the figure is much too low.

The winter war had shown that the Russians were capable of large-scale offensives despite their losses. It also showed that the wastage of German man power and matériel in the East was considerably greater than anything that Germany had so far experienced. On both sides the lines began to stiffen, and the terror-spreading blitz tactics were followed by what all German experts had warned against—the war of attrition.

At the beginning of 1942, Germany expected great things from submarine warfare, principally because the Americans lacked experience in combating the U-boats. By now these had an increased radius of action, effected in various ways, which also contributed to the sharp rise in Allied losses, especially in American waters. An increase at the beginning of 1942 was to be expected in any case, since during the latter part of 1941 the Germans had been hoping to avoid a war with the United States and had recalled their submarines from wide stretches of the Atlantic. The increase was, however, more rapid than had been anticipated, and for a few months it actually looked as if the U-boats might paralyze Allied power to wage war. The tabulation of losses, followed in Berlin with the keenest attention, was compared with information about new tonnage, which reached Germany in various ways. Toward the end of spring, it began to appear that the U-boat blockade had been partly broken.

Meanwhile the news from Russia was being scanned with strained attention. The Germans were vastly encouraged when they saw that the Japanese, with their swift conquests, were shaking the British Empire to its very foundations. They said that with Singapore as a base, Japan now dominated the Indian Ocean. Leading Party circles counted on the possibility of making contact, in some way or another, with the apparently unconquerable Japanese. At that time Germany was pinning hopes chiefly on Rommel.

The fact that the German battleships *Scharnhorst* and *Gneisenau* managed by a bold stroke to steam through the English Channel did not, of course, increase Germany's respect for her arch enemy. "Where is the British Navy?" Berliners asked. Sober observers, however, set no great military importance on the escape.

When the British report on the dash of the German battleships reached Berlin—the German communiqué had not yet been issued—one of the most respected foreign journalists asked whether it wouldn't be possible for the authorities to arrange a trip by plane to one of the battleships so that the journalists might interview the officers while they still had vivid impressions of the battle. The answer was a point-blank refusal, much as everybody had expected. Several of my colleagues, however, couldn't refrain from pointing out to the gentlemen in the Propaganda Ministry that the British

THE WINTER WAR IN THE EAST, 1941-42.

surely wouldn't have neglected such a chance to glorify the Royal Navy.

From a political standpoint, February was rather uninteresting. It began with the elevation of Quisling to the post of Norwegian Minister President, as an appreciation of the faithful services he had rendered the country that had attacked his own. Various Berliners expressed their deep contempt for the man and his mission, while admitting cynically that they intended to use him to the utmost, the situation being what it was. According to report, the contempt for Quisling's person was not shared by Hitler, who revealed the same fondness for him as for all the other foreign gangsters who have served the Third Reich.

A small incident occurred one day at the Propaganda Ministry, when Grundvig Gundersen, the foremost representative of the "Q-men," as we called journalists of his type, protested in a loud voice because somebody had asked about "the Quislings" instead of "the members of the National Union." Before any of the Germans had time to answer, a mild-mannered colleague inquired, "Are you ashamed of your lord and master?" Shortly afterwards there was another amusing incident. An older Swiss newspaperman asked how large a percentage of the Norwegian people supported Quisling. A murmur rose. After a painful pause the chairman of the conference, Dr. Brauweiler, changed the subject. Herr Grundvig Gundersen kept silent that time.

As early as in 1941 it became evident that Hungary was taking an increasingly independent attitude. The Hungarians had certainly never been popular in Berlin, where for many years there had been complaints about their cantankerousness and obstinacy. One sign after another revealed that they were more and more concerned with their own interests, and less and less concerned with those of Germany. When the question rose of a deputy for Admiral Horthy, the Germans were not a little interested. Neither of the two leading candidates—the Regent's son, Stephen Horthy, and Archduke Albrecht of Hapsburg—seemed specially desirable. Against the former it was charged that his political opinions were far from friendly to Germany, that he possessed a will to act independently, and also that he had good personal contacts in England and the United States, where he had worked as a common laborer. The only charge against the Archduke was that he was a genuine Hapsburg. On the other hand, he might be played against Archduke Otto, the head of the family, whom Hitler had always regarded as his number-one enemy. The Hungarians, however, made some minor political concessions, and in return the Germans voiced no objections to Stephen Horthy's election, on February 19, as his father's deputy.

There had been growing difficulties in the Balkans. The partisan troops ravaged the countryside, and from time to time succeeded in disrupting communications. Famine reigned in Greece, to such an extent that it seemed the whole population would starve to death. Owing to the lack of coal, the street cars stopped running in Athens, and evening newspapers were no longer published in the capital because of the paper shortage. The Allies had promised to help, but shipments were delayed because they feared that the Germans would seize precious vessels and their cargoes as well—or at the very least would use the relief shipments as an excuse to seize any Greek food stocks they had so far left untouched.

Meanwhile the Greeks were the spectators and innocent victims of a war of nerves. The Germans would not or could not transport foodstuffs to Greece. They stated on several occasions that such and such quantities of food had been placed at the disposal of the civilian population, but the quantities were small even as announced, and in practice they were probably even smaller. Claiming formal right on their side, the Germans were determined to force the Allies to feed a German-occupied country. This time no mention was made of the "New Europe," which was supposed to be self-supporting in food supplies, and therefore should have been able to take care of its own starving. The Allies, on the other hand, were determined to force the Germans to use *their* supplies for the purpose. At last, however, the international relief action got under way and the situation improved, though slowly. The Greeks expressed deep gratitude for what Sweden had done, along with other nations.

The domestic situation in Germany underwent some improvement in February. The gnawing worry over the situation in Russia that had been felt in December and January—Germany's time of "moral winter crisis," as it was known in certain quarters—abated slowly and gave way to a more hopeful attitude. Air raids during the winter had not been severe. The bitter cold was beginning to lessen, and the coming of spring also stimulated some improvement in the general mood.

Wild rumors continued to circulate, however, and the usual

measures were not sufficient to combat them. One incident that occupied the minds of the German people was the airplane accident early in February, when one of Germany's foremost men, Reichsminister Todt, was killed. This time the correspondents were ready to believe that it really was an accident. The Germans, however, were more doubtful. They had fallen into the habit of taking for granted that official stories about the deaths of prominent persons were always untrue and were always intended to conceal a murder or a suicide.

ѦѦѦѦѦѦѦѦѦ **IV** ѦѦѦѦѦѦѦѦѦ

THE SPRING OF 1942

The Political and Military Lull

SPRING was unusually late in 1942, but early in March the Russian winter offensive seemed to be over. It was the beginning of a lull that would last for two long months, while every day people were expecting to see the battle resumed. Everything seemed to indicate that Hitler intended to keep his promise by launching a general offensive as early as possible, so as to have more time at his disposal before autumn and winter once more balanced the scale in favor of the Russians. It seemed very doubtful that he would accomplish any decisive results. On the other hand, we correspondents took it for granted that the Germans would inflict great losses on the Russian armies and gain much territory. The Germans themselves counted on being able to reach the oil fields on the Caspian Sea.

Early in March we could see that the German preparations for an offensive were being carried out on a large scale. A new system of roads was built by Todt Organization according to a plan drawn up by Dr. Werlin, who had been given dictatorial powers over the use of motor vehicles. In April an expert told me that, in order to make the roads firm enough for heavy transport, cement or some other binder was mixed with the mud, after which the steam rollers were run over it. Thousands of trains with brand-new matériel were also sent to the East, and stores of food and fuel were heaped up behind the front.

In the beginning of April, there were signs that the Germans were trying to straighten out the front. But neither of the two belligerents had as yet launched any greater offensive, since the snow was not completely melted until the middle of April. The airfields were in a hopeless state, the roads were bottomless, and the entire countryside was transformed into a quagmire. This enforced lull was a piece of luck for the Germans, who had time to reorganize their exhausted and depleted troops.

There was no great military activity during the spring in the Mediterranean or on the continent of Europe, excepting the war in the air. The British attack against Lübeck toward the end of March came as a shock to the German people, because it was one of the cities in which the architecture of the Middle Ages had been admirably preserved. The RAF continued its hard blows against the Baltic ports, including an attack on Kiel. The damage to industry at Lübeck and Rostock was probably not large, even though the Heinkel factory received some direct hits and was forced to transfer some of its activities to other regions. The damage to dwellings and warehouses was more severe. The German authorities were forced to evacuate almost the whole population of both cities. This, of course, created a new organization problem to add to all the others that demanded solution. For the moment these British air raids had very little effect on German morale. That would come later, when it became evident that the Luftwaffe was not allowed or was unable to retaliate with more impressive attacks on England; people could see that the so-called "Baedeker raids" on historic English towns were only pinpricks. Plainly Goering's boasted weapon could no longer be used simultaneously and in full force against both the British and the Russians, and although the aerial activity on the eastern front had slackened off because of inclement weather, this did not result in heavier raids against Great Britain. The only thing that did rise in pitch and tempo was the press cannonade and the threats of vengeance. Even the extremely severe regulations for the foreign press in reporting the British air attacks were somewhat relaxed, so that we might be able to express our indignation.

The Germans observed the enemy's preparations with the keenest attention. Since Berlin decided that the Russians themselves could replace only a small part of the destroyed or captured war matériel, the shipments from the Allies to Russia were regarded as being of the greatest importance. The northern route was regarded as the strategic one, and the logical consequence was increased submarine warfare in the Arctic Ocean. From their bases in northern Norway the Germans watched all transports in arctic waters. Although the Allies tried to keep as close to the ice fringe as possible, the German command in northern Norway had great success in its attacks on convoys, both when the vessels were en route to Murmansk fully loaded, and when they returned from there empty. The loss of ships in the North must have been a heavy blow to the Allies.

A period of calm on the battle fronts usually implies that the diplomats are busier than ever. To superficial observers, this rule appeared to hold good in Germany during the spring of 1942. The truth was, however, that a truce existed on the diplomatic front as well. The Germans made no serious attempts to win new allies. It is possible that King Boris of Bulgaria, during his visit to German headquarters on March 24, was asked to take an active part in the war against Russia, but in that case his answer must definitely have been *no*.

Germany, on the other hand, was having the greatest difficulty in maintaining peace between two of her "most eager" confederates, Hungary and Rumania. The origin of the conflict between these two, which flared up in March, was the speech delivered in Bucharest on the 19th of that month by the Rumanian Prime Minister, Michael Antonescu. In this address he stated that the Rumanians were the guardians of civilization at the mouth of the Danube, and that their consciousness of this mission had led them to march on Budapest in 1919, so as to "destroy the Communist crop planted by the Hungarian government then in power, which threatened to engulf the whole of Southeastern Europe." In addition, Antonescu accused Hungary of having broken the "press peace," i.e., the agreement not to print attacks on Rumania in the Hungarian newspapers, besides insulting the Rumanian army, making "attacks and challenges" during the past year, harassing and persecuting the population of Northern Transylvania. "It is our duty," Antonescu said, "to declare that this cannot continue."

It is easy to imagine what a storm this attack aroused in Hungary. The words about the march into Hungary in 1919 could not be construed as anything but an intended insult. On government orders, the press kept silent in the matter, but Hungary let Germany understand that if the Germans could not keep the Rumanians in their place, Hungary would not be responsible for the consequences. The tension grew when not less than 64 border incidents occurred within two or three days, and matters became still worse when the Rumanian press comments on Antonescu's speech had been made public. They were remarkably outspoken. "We have," said *Timpul*, "long kept silent with clenched fists and gnashing teeth, but we will forget nothing." *Unirea* said, "In our army's trumpet blares there is heard the signal that cannot now be mentioned. Some day it will be the sign of vengeance for humiliations." Troops were drawn up on both sides of the border. The Hungarians greatly outnumbered their opponents, one reason being that they, unlike the Rumanians, had no strong armies tied up on the Russian front. By dint of great efforts, Germany succeeded in averting an open conflict which, if it had occurred, might have smashed the whole German system of alliances, since the Germans themselves probably would have sided with the favorite, Rumania, and Italy with Hungary. There were also many who suspected Antonescu of playing a double game. He wanted to extricate himself from the present situation, and above all from the sanguinary war in the East, by provoking a war with Hungary. Perhaps he had an idea of thereby gaining the gratitude of the Allies at a future peace table. If that was his game, Germany was still sufficiently powerful to outplay him and to prevent an open conflict between Rumania and Hungary.

It had often been hinted during the spring that there would be a new meeting between Hitler and Mussolini. The meeting took place after the German Reichstag had been convened in April. The joint communiqué issued by the two dictators on May 1 had the usual contents. Reading between the lines, Berlin guessed that action in the Mediterranean had been the principal topic of discussion. The official communiqués laid much stress on the fact that the situation of the British in the Mediterranean theater must be regarded as precarious. What this threat meant was shown a few weeks later, when Rommel made his attack on the British lines.

Meanwhile the main topic of conversation at the Foreign Office during March and April was—India! Seldom has so much eloquence been wasted on us journalists as when First-class Envoy Schmidt and Baron Braun von Stumm delivered long lectures, nay, sermons, on the shoddy treatment by the British of the poor Indian people, whom Japan—and Germany—wanted to liberate. Time and again an argument was used that baffled the neutral correspondents: If what was said were applied to Germany's neighbors, it would mean that she would have to evacuate the occupied countries, liquidate the Quislings, and retire to her own borders.

But the Japanese and the Germans have their special Quisling where India is concerned. The former mayor of Calcutta, Subhas Chandra Bose, is certainly no unimportant person in himself. It is difficult for him, however, to play an independent role as a tool of the Japanese and the Germans. When he paid an extended visit to Germany, he spoke over "an unknown radio station"—as it was mysteriously described—and German officialdom rejoiced over the effect that this was supposed to have. In Berlin a handsome newspaper was devoted to the interests of India, and a journalist from Delhi, Habibur Rahman, who had landed in Germany, conducted violent propaganda for the liberation of his country.

On April 14, it was said that the failure of the Cripps mission meant "the dissolution of the British Empire" and that "England's historic role is finished." But in spite of all these eloquent prognostications, the British showed a remarkable unwillingness to do what Berlin expected of them. Of course, the British Empire had been dissolved many times in the Wilhelmstrasse. Meanwhile the month-long rapid-fire gave many people the idea that Germany and Japan were preparing a common move to make contact with each other, and that Berlin at all costs wanted to popularize the Indian question. This question achieved great importance later on when Rommel threatened Alexandria. In April, however, one hardly looked for such a development, and almost all the journalists including the Scandinavians yawned when some Quisling did his duty by asking whether there was "anything new on the Indian problem," a question that unloosed another flood of eloquence.

Soon the Vichy problem was back into the news. In the middle of April, Pétain had yielded to German pressure and had named Pierre Laval as chief of Government. When the English suddenly attacked Madagascar early in May, the German government tried to force Vichy to declare war against England. Laval seemed to be willing; at least he made some vehement speeches, but he suddenly fell silent when Roosevelt expressed solidarity with the English and made it quite clear that war against England also meant war against the United States. Neither Pétain nor 99 per cent of the French people wanted that to happen.

Growing War Weariness

A consequence of the waiting period was that the problems of the home front attracted more attention. Even a cursory view of the situation proved that morale had perceptibly deteriorated from what it had been six months earlier. The general tendency, to be sure, was not unbroken, and quick changes might occur, but usually these were merely eddies on the surface. The trend was downward.

The German government clearly saw the need for keeping the public occupied in order to make it forget its war weariness. Conference after conference was held at the Ministry of Propaganda and, according to report, opinions were sharply divided. Apparently the decision finally reached was to continue the new Goebbels line. In general this meant that the war picture was painted in dark colors, with emphasis on the fact that all official statements were "realistic." There was much talk about the Russian menace, but at the same time the propagandists tried to instill the feeling that this menace could be averted if the Germans made great enough efforts. The first and foremost of these efforts was to be the spring offensive. Without specifying the objective of this drive, the propagandists were to indicate that its aim was not necessarily to crush Bolshevism, but to force it so far back that "it will not be a menace to Europe." They would thereby leave open the possibility of halting at some "quarantine border."

Nothing was said about how long the war would last beyond the fact that it would be long, but alert observers could draw their own conclusions from the warning about the need for increased endurance and the talk of how victory would come to him who could keep alive "a quarter of an hour longer than the enemy." German propaganda was beginning to use purely defensive concepts, including the term "Fortress Europe." People were told that this fortress would be able to sustain itself from its own resources and would, in other words, be "blockade-proof."

The Goebbels policy in its expanded form included a recipe for dealing with purely internal difficulties. These had previously been dismissed as trivial or simply ignored, but now they were discussed openly. Reading Goebbels' articles in the spring of 1942, I frequently felt that the new "open" and "realistic" policy regarding domestic affairs was among his greatest achievements. Essentially it consisted in discussing the general atmosphere and the varying public reactions, point by point, and assuming that everything was rather natural and of no great significance.

As early as February, Goebbels struck the keynote in an article he wrote for *Das Reich*, in which he recapitulated the reasons for the 1918 collapse. It is no trick to have faith in victory, he said, when the radio gives you news of fresh triumphs every hour, but it is another matter when the news is bad. The German people, however, have a confidence in their destiny that is not affected by the fact that everyone from time to time feels the need of getting mad about something. One man complains about the lack of heat, another about the shortage of potatoes and coal, a third about the overcrowded trains, a fourth about events on the eastern front and a fifth about the war in Africa. This is nothing alarming, "for we are all under a strain and hence somewhat irritable," Goebbels concluded.

Variations on this theme were played in almost every number of *Das Reich,* and to some extent they were doubtless effective. Gradually, however, Goebbels had to shift over from calm analysis to admonition. "We have the deepest appreciation of the fact that many of us are exhausted and hence more irritable than usual. Nevertheless this doesn't give anybody the right to vent his ill humor from morning till night. A pleasant, friendly and encouraging word in the right place works wonders, even in the case of an angry person. People at home should follow the example set by the soldiers."

That the soldiers were quite different was an observation that anyone could make. "Why is Civilian Mueller always so cantankerous as compared with Private Mueller?" asked the well-known journalist Schwarz van Berk. He maintained that "anybody who is impolite throws sand into the war machine." Berliners never had a reputation for being polite and agreeable, but their conduct in the spring of 1942 came close to being intolerable. Many individuals felt they couldn't keep in good physical condition unless they relaxed by having at least one good quarrel per day. Wherever you turned, you were likely to meet with scowls or imprecations. The causes of this ill temper were perhaps various but in the end they all went back to the war.

It became necessary, therefore, for the propaganda authorities to take measures beyond those that were strictly part of the new policy. Dr. Goebbels chose to bear down on impoliteness as such without raising the issue of what caused it. The newspapers in the German capital began insisting to their readers that politeness was needed in wartime, and soon came the announcement that May was to be a special "month of politeness." Politeness is oil on the everyday seas, said one paper. People collect stamps or keep canaries, said another paper, but it occurs to no one that politeness is an ideal cure for nerves. "The worst thing is when the polite use impoliteness as a medium for teaching politeness to the impolite."

On May 5, Dr. Goebbels announced a contest in politeness for the population of Berlin, in a proclamation which maintained that politeness and a co-operative spirit are fundamental conditions for peaceful community life. Then came long harangues to the effect that the Berliners were, of course, polite, spoken in the flattering voice that the Nazi authorities always adopt when speaking to the people of their capital city. Nevertheless, in order to provide an incentive for even more politeness, Dr. Goebbels established forty prizes for polite Berliners in various occupations.

The politeness campaign was only partially effective, and many people took pride in sabotaging it in every conceivable fashion. But at least it had one result that pleased the authorities: it diverted attention from what was really deep-seated—the German people's doubt of victory and their lack of faith in the government.

Anyone could see that the growing war weariness in Germany, and particularly in Berlin, had caused a decline of moral standards in business and industry. The fortunate persons who possessed anything that could be eaten or drunk, any extra clothes, furniture or other desirable goods, could ask any price for them. In the shops, customers were short of funds and had to beg humbly for credit, which after investigation was bestowed with an air of lordly condescension. The restaurants were perhaps the worst places. There the waiters, who reigned supreme, had in many places developed their own system of favoritism.

Black markets and bootlegging grew to enormous proportions. Bartering became brisk. People pretended to observe the price-control regulations, but among acquaintances these were not taken too seriously. Everyone mobilized his own resources, using various things of actual value—food stores, clothing, household equipment and commodities in general. Currency came to have less meaning, and anybody who lacked goods for exchange had to pay out comparatively large sums for anything he needed.

Das Schwarze Korps was the paper that had to deal with the deterioration of civilian morale, particularly morale in the field of consumption goods. It began at once to criticize institutions and individuals openly, making public the names and addresses of erring businessmen, both those who were liable to penalties under the laws and those who in form, though not in fact, kept on the right side of the line. The paper did not content itself with pillorying these people in its columns. It argued incessantly that it was not enough to observe the letter of the laws, but that their meaning should be determined in harmony with Hitler's pronouncement: "Anybody who tries to profit from the war must perish."

Of course, there were certain disadvantages in bringing the question to public notice. For one thing, *Das Schwarze Korps* was read by all foreign correspondents—by this writer perhaps more carefully than by most of the others—and we were now able to mention in our dispatches a whole group of domestic problems that had formerly been taboo. Indeed, the editor of the SS organ was several times warned to use phrasing that would make it more difficult for us to utilize the material. Naturally warnings were not confined to the publisher, Herr Gunther d'Alquen; correspondents were informed again and again that the authorities most certainly disliked to see us "butcher" *Das Schwarze Korps*, as we had lately been doing. But the effect of such a reminder usually lasted only a few days, at least so far as the Swedes were concerned, and then we were back on the subject again. The German authorities didn't dare at the time to forbid us from using the paper. The only other course was to make *Das Schwarze Korps* "tamer," and this was done.

It was often entertaining to read about all the smart people who wanted to procure something *ohne*—"without"—this being the technical term for everything that did not require ration points. *Das Schwarze Korps* had a staff of assistants which in numbers, at least, was respectable. Anyone who had anything on his mind that would contribute to winning the war was invited to write to the editor. As a rule, though not always, the editorial staff was careful to check up on the information given. But even if they were careless and allowed some poor innocent to be pilloried as a black-market operator, they weren't running much risk—for, after all, who would dare to take action against *Das Schwarze Korps*?

There were cases where the authorities amended a law after letters to the editor had pointed out that it left too many loopholes for profiteers. Often, however, the only means of getting at the culprits was to print their names.

The gentlemen on the editorial staff of *Das Schwarze Korps* cast an affectionate eye on trade journals. If a big dealer in photographic supplies advertised in a grocery trade journal that he had a large stock, the editors asked why this particular journal was chosen. If a tobacco manufacturer or a liquor dealer bought space anywhere, the case was clear—no such firm needed to advertise in order to dispose of its products, unless it was selling them at black-market prices. And that is exactly how they were being sold, under cover of these seemingly innocent advertisements. Many dealers went even further and informed their customers that, while they couldn't deliver anything, they might be willing to talk things over. In other words, "We have an illegal stock of tobacco or liquor that we'd be willing to trade for other illegal merchandise. Let's get together." Sometimes people specified what they wanted in exchange, but they were careful to mention only unrationed supplies—for example, rabbits.

Whenever the authorities were able to catch the jobbers they put the clamps on, and death sentences were common. Butchers especially suffered punishment. At the end of March two nurses in Königsberg were condemned to death because they had in an extraordinarily unscrupulous fashion sold the food supplies provided for their institution and let their patients starve. Death sentences also were imposed on several Germans who tried to print their own food-ration cards, which, being very simple, were not hard to copy. But the campaign of the authorities was, of course, not directed at the numerous and big thieves inside the Party. That spring many stories were being circulated regarding the exploits of politically powerful racketeers.

Concentrating Power Against the Opposition

Even if the war spirit in general showed a tendency to sink, the National Socialists in the spring of 1942 were not yet forced to cope with any extensive opposition, although there were many signs that the authority of the government was weakening.

The Nazis decided upon comprehensive measures to prevent the growth of any opposition groups. They organized roundups of Communist agitators, and a number of arrests were made among intellectuals of the middle classes. The judges, however, irritated the Nazis by sometimes refusing to impose sentences when the accused were brought before them without legal warrants. Demands for a purge of the bench had early been raised within Party circles.

Although there had been a general expectation that action would be taken against the courts, there was great surprise when Hitler made this the principal subject of his Reichstag speech on April 26.

The news that a meeting of the Reichstag was to be held late in April brought one of the richest crops of rumors I had ever seen in the German capital. It was pretty clear that there would be a review of the winter campaign now ended, but besides that came all sorts of predictions—a new crisis for the generals, an attack on Turkey or perhaps Sweden and the announcement of the spring campaign against Russia.

The Reichschancellor seemed to be in better spirits than in January. Contrary to custom, he wasted little time getting down to business, or at least the review of events since Adam and Eve was briefer than usual. Then he launched into what the audience expected to be his main theme, namely, the winter campaign. He reported that there had been danger of a catastrophe but that it had been averted, and that he himself had been compelled to take a hand on several occasions in order to make the machinery function. He made an indirect admission that the government was planning a new winter campaign when he reported that the German railroads would be quite differently equipped the following winter, in order to prevent a repetition of what happened in Russia during the phenomenal winter of 1941-42.

Then came the surprise of the day. The measures he had taken were authorized under "the sovereign power which I have received from the German people." But for the future Hitler requested the Reichstag to give him formal authority to hold everyone to his duty and, regardless of the laws involved, to imprison all who fail to perform it, regardless of their rank, office or position. Everyone must be enlisted for victory, and no one has a legal right to a vacation. Those who had earned one first of all were the frontline soldiers. "Since 1933," he said, "I myself haven't had three free days in a row."

How Hitler was to use this enormous power, unique in European history, became partly apparent in his vigorous attack on the German courts. The courts exist for the nation, he said, and not the nation for the courts. Then he repeated a number of similar axioms, all of them enthusiastically applauded by the audience, which seemed relieved to find that only the judges were being singled out for attack.

After the Führer came Goering. Usually Hitler's most faithful paladin makes only a short speech of tribute to his master. This time, however, he talked at greater length, and in his sketch of the campaign in the East, he surprised everyone by using more somber colors than the Führer himself. If the front can now be held, he said, thanks are due not only to the bravery of the soldiers but also in large part to Chancellor Hitler, who had restored order even during the days "when it seemed that everything was hopeless."

As the foreign journalists walked out of the Kroll Opera House past the elegant cars of the Party bosses and the ranks of troops on parade, a lively discussion arose as to the nature and aim of this new authority which Hitler had demanded. We hardly knew what to believe. Even many well-informed Germans completely lost their bearings during the next few days. Several feared a new June 30; others held that the whole thing was an eruption of political dynamism, which continually demanded new measures of force, and which had to create an artificial need for such measures if none arose naturally out of a given situation.

The new authority was not favorably looked upon by the people. During the days that followed, you could hear ironic comments from all sorts of persons, who sometimes added that they feared the consequences of this further concentration of power. As a matter of fact, the new measures probably didn't change the situation greatly, but there is no doubt that Hitler's speech made the public nervous.

Well-informed circles pointed out one factor that might explain his action—the new concentration of power increased his control over the Reichswehr. Until that time it had been hard for the Gestapo to get at the army, for the officers tried to maintain their solidarity. Now they were also exposed in fair or foul weather. Later developments proved that these analysts were to a large extent correct, even though they did not give the whole explanation. It is evident that the general power of the Gestapo was increased. Hitler's warm praises for the SS units were also revealing; Himmler's star was rising steadily.

Still another purpose of the new measures was to increase Hitler's personal authority, and it wasn't hard to see that other steps were being taken in the same direction. One of these steps was an article in the May 10 issue of the *Völkischer Beobachter* proving that Hitler was among the great captains of history. Colonel Walther Scherff, the author of the article, is a military historian who has been summoned time and again to demonstrate the warlike genius of the Führer. This time he surpassed himself. His article began with a quotation from Schlieffen to the effect that no military leader at the outset of his career, not even Frederick the Great or Napoleon, escaped criticism. As evidence of his surpassing genius, Scherff reviewed the situation at the beginning of December 1941, when German troops were caught unprepared by the severe cold. At that time many people wondered whether it wouldn't be better to retreat at once on a broad line and thus shorten the front; they had even begun citing the situation in 1812 as a warning, and this was a blow to the morale of officers and men. Then Hitler took hold, with his battle cry of war to the utmost; the line was held and the situation stabilized. The article closed with a quotation from Clausewitz: "It is a striking peculiarity of the great captains that in times of hardship and misfortune they depend as confidently as ever on themselves and Fate to bring better times without heavy losses."

We hadn't long to wait before we discovered that the government had begun imposing tighter restrictions. There were more arrests than before, and it was clear that they were leading to many executions. Severe measures were taken against rumormongers. During the spring, gossip had enjoyed a genuine boom; much of it dealt with the many prominent persons who had died, but there were also stories about those still living, and Hitler himself was not spared. I heard persistent rumors from widely different sources than an attempt had been made on his life and that he had been wounded in his left arm. It was said that two young officers had been involved, and that both had been executed. A typical story dealt with Colonel Moelders, the most famous of the German pursuit pilots. It was to the effect that he broke with the Party before his death because his sister, a nun, had been thrown out on the street by SS men who were cleaning out a nunnery. There were in circulation copies of a letter that Moelders was said to have written to a priest, confessing himself a devout Catholic. This was, of course, a big scandal, and Das Schwarze Korps was ordered to print a refutation.

During the spring a series of measures was directed against the churches, now regarded as the most dangerous enemies of the National Socialist state. Wherever possible the restrictions were justified on the ground of war needs. Most of the religious journals received no further allotments of paper and hence had to cease publication, religious literature could not be printed, and even Bibles and hymnals were hit by the decree.

The Catholic Church, because of its organization and international connections, was considered more dangerous, but it was easier to get at the Protestants, and they had to endure almost everything. Few of their protests ever reached the public, although a letter to Goebbels from Dr. Wurm, bishop of the Württemberg Evangelical Lutheran Church, was circulated in thousands of copies. The Württemberg bishop did not mince words. He referred to Goebbels' own article, "Free Expression," published in *Das Reich*, and explained that he intended to speak openly with the minister. What he first pleaded for was a just distribution of the burdens that everybody had to bear. To suppress religious periodicals was not just, considering that anti-Christian literature in great quantities had been thrown on the market or sent to the front. The restraint imposed upon the Christian population was nothing less than a continual abuse of their meekness. One measure of force follows another, said the Bishop, and the laws are disregarded. No government official listens to the cry of the oppressed.

The Russian people, continued the Bishop, are told that Adolf Hitler and the German Army have restored the freedom of Christian worship. The Germans, on the other hand, are persistently admonished not to take part in religious ceremonies. Is such a contradiction justifiable? Is victory for an anti-Christian world philosophy more important than victory for the Germans? Does the present state insist on forcing a uniform faith upon its subjects?

Finally, the Bishop recommended a thoroughgoing change in the political attitude toward religion and an end to the "meaningless heresy against the Christian faith," the hobbling of the Church, and the persecution of conscience carried on against many Christians, especially those who think they can combine Church membership with Party membership. "I pray earnestly that the Christian portion of the people, constituting the overwhelming majority in Germany, may have the privilege of seeing something of the harmony between the Government and the people which you have so emphatically declared is a fact." Of course, Bishop Wurm's plea had no effect.

Police measures were not the only ones employed to prevent a rise of opposition. Continual innovations in propaganda were also made by the National Socialist Government in order to meet the altered situation. Particularly effective were the special honors for war-production workers. The first of these awards was made with great ceremony by Goering at the Chancellery on May 21. The ceremony itself seemed to make a deep impression on the war workers and countryfolk present, especially the awarding of the highest distinction, the Knight of the War Service Cross, described as a symbol of gratitude from the battle front to the home front. It was presented to a certain foreman named Hahne, by a corporal who had been made a Knight of the Iron Cross for courage in action.

Another propaganda device was the exhibition called "The Soviet Paradise," which was opened in the Lustgarten. It was a "warranted genuine" collection of Russian dwelling places—horribly squalid outhouses filled with rags—brought from Minsk, it was declared. Thousands of visitors poured in every day. The stench was loathsome, and many visitors came out as fast as they had gone in. Doubtless some people were susceptible to this form of direct propaganda, but there were also many who saw through the trick.

On May 27 there was an attempt to destroy the Soviet Paradise. The culprit was not caught, but the authorities shot some 200 Jews and Communists, claiming that they were among "the spiritual originators" of the crime. News of this affair spread widely, and there was much grumbling. After the close of the exhibition a joke went the rounds in Berlin:

"Why did they close the Soviet Paradise?"——"Because the people in North Berlin wanted their things back."

THE EARLY SUMMER OF 1942

Armament and Supplies

THE military lull in the East lasted longer than had originally been expected, but it was possible to put most of the blame for this delay on the unusually long winter. In German propaganda, the much-talked-of spring offensive gradually became the summer offensive, and while the people were waiting for that event they were treated to repeated descriptions of the enormous preparations made by the German armies. It was clear that the resources of the nation were being drawn upon to an extent that would be exceeded only by the total mobilization of the following spring. In May 1942, a special production board was appointed which was to correlate all war orders and to promote further consolidation and simplification in German industry. The council included a row of high-ranking officers and several prominent industrialists. A few weeks later the War Production Office was formed. This was headed by General Thomas, and since the office belonged in the government department headed by Minister Speer, the latter became in fact the dictator of German industry.

Ever since the beginning of 1942 industry had become more and more aware of government control. In February, the newspapers carried the story of two managers who had been sent to concentration camps because they hadn't been getting enough work out of their employees. It was a story that was read with great attention. Further troubles for the industrial leaders were created by new decrees providing that all products for military purposes should be sharply reduced in price.

The spring of 1942 marked the beginning on a large scale of the eastward migration of industry, which had been planned much earlier. Certain easily damaged factories had already been moved to Poland, but now came the development of Upper Silesia into an East European Ruhr. The production of iron and steel was to be doubled and coal mining was to be speeded up from 100 to 150 million tons a year. There were ambitious plans for transporting iron ore from Krivoi Rog in the Ukraine and bauxite from Hungary, while power was to be provided by new hydroelectric stations in Germany, the Protectorate of Bohemia and Moravia and the Government General of Poland. Workmen by the tens of thousands were to be brought from various countries to Upper Silesia. Since then the work has progressed and, in the spring of 1943, it was greatly intensified. The principal reason for this gigantic project was the destruction of vital industries in the West by the Allied air raids.

Accelerated German war production in the spring and early summer of 1942 meant that all reserves of raw materials had to be mobilized. In May, all factory stocks of iron and steel were seized, with certain exceptions. The same kind of blow descended on the skilled trades. At the end of the month came a new campaign to collect clothing for war workers, and it was announced that even the smallest contributions were needed—if only a rag were given, it would be utilized in a textile factory. "Make a general inventory of your wardrobe," was the slogan. At the same time the collection of waste paper in the schools was speeded up, and strict orders were given to office managers not to waste anything that could be used. This collection of all waste proved to be an expensive means of providing raw materials, requiring the co-operation of tens of thousands of persons. But the various shortages had become so serious that the campaign was indispensable.

The man-power problem was partly solved by importing foreign workmen, who were being recruited in many European countries. By an order of Gauleiter Sauckel, at the end of June, German workmen were virtually made serfs, since no change of position could be made without the approval of the Labor Office. At the same time an effort was made to conserve labor by eliminating unnecessary administrative work, by standardization and by simplification. The civilian consumption of goods was further cut by a series of drastic regulations. Thus, at the end of May the manufacture of machines not necessary for war was prohibited, and printing presses were classed as such machines. The newspapers, furthermore, were hard hit by a rigorous rationing of paper and from June 1 onward they were as a rule limited to four pages.

Drastic cuts were made in transportation. Diners were taken off the trains, and there were new limitations on the right to reserve a berth. Freight and express service for civilian purposes was further reduced, and at the same time efforts were made to speed up loading and unloading. A clear result of this intensified work was that a respectable volume of matériel of various kinds was made available to the army. New models of various weapons began to appear, and in certain cases entirely new weapons were developed.

Meanwhile it seemed to many foreign observers that, despite the gain in war production, the food problem had reached a crisis that might bring about the downfall of Germany. It is possible that many of us overestimated Germany's difficulties in supplying food during the early summer of 1942. But the winter had been unusually severe, and a substantial part of the winter grain had been destroyed by freezing—more than six million acres, according to a report of Undersecretary Backe at the end of June. The damaged fields were either reseeded to grain or were planted with potatoes; but this meant that food stocks had to be drawn upon for seed. Rye was severely damaged, and wheat suffered from the sharp cold spell in January—which came before any snowfall had given protection to the ground—as well as from the frosts in March and April and the drought later in the spring. The worst damage had been done in the central region of Germany, between the Weser and the Oder.

Spring work was delayed four weeks, and no greater supply of labor was available. Consequently a crisis loomed in the food supply before the end of the year, and certainly not later than the following spring. Every German household had been clearly warned by the sharp deterioration in the quality of bread during the winter. Many critics felt that it would have been better to cut the bread ration deliberately, rather than to eke it out with all kinds of indigestible matter. The black bread procured with ration cards was not good for weak stomachs. To make sure that it wouldn't be injurious it had to be toasted, and then it became unpalatable.

In other ways, too, the German people had been reminded, during the winter and spring, that food was getting scarce. The milk was blue and watery, green vegetables sometimes disappeared from the stands for days, and there was even a bad shortage of potatoes. Unrationed food, with which people tried to eke out the scientifically determined minimum they could buy with their ration cards, gradually disappeared from the market. There was an old Berlin joke about people who tried the impossible, that is, to subsist on rationed food. That spring it turned into dead earnest.

Even more serious was the fact that a scratch of the pen reduced the scientific minimum of the rations to something below the minimum. It became more and more obvious that a big cut would be necessary; the winter damages to the crops had made it inevitable. But the authorities waited until April, when, with the coming of joyous spring, they felt that an unpopular measure could at last be taken. The weekly bread ration was cut from 2,250 to 2,000 grams (about 4½ pounds); beef from 400 to 300 grams (10½ ounces); and fats from 269 to 206 grams (7½ ounces) per week.

Actually it looked as if the problem of food supply was a most serious one. But Germany was to be partly delivered from the dilemma by the good crops which, in spite of all forebodings, were harvested in the autumn of 1942. In the spring of that year, not even the seasoned agricultural specialists had ventured to predict such a stroke of luck.

Spring Operations in the East

During the early summer the chief aim of the German military propagandists was to advertise the new weapons which the High Command declared to be available. The claim was based on Hitler's statement about "new and better weapons," and through hundreds of "indiscretions" fantastic stories were spread about them.

The neutrals in Berlin thought it quite probable that Germany would introduce previously unheard-of weapons. Yet everyone recalled that "new weapons" were always talked about when there was a lull at the front, and hence we remained a little skeptical. There was, however, one story we had some reason to credit, and later it proved to be true—the story about the so-called "atom gun." Very well-informed people reported that this weapon hurled grenades that were charged with liquid air under enormously high pressure and a new explosive which could kill a great many persons within a limited area, leaving no visible trace. But there were reports, also, before the weapon had been put to use, that its operation was extremely hazardous for the crew, made up only of volunteer officers, and that the effectiveness of the piece was limited. It was further reported that the cost of manufacturing the gun was fantastically high, and that its use would be senseless extravagance except when it was fired into a dense concentration of enemy troops.

The new weapon was utilized in the attack on Kerch, which the

Germans started on May 8. Here large forces were concentrated within a small area. The operation was preceded by an artillery bombardment, unusually intense even for this war, and was started with a German air raid in the old style, in which 2,000 bombs were dropped on a single sector in one day.

Hence it is hard to judge how great a role the "atom gun" played in the Kerch operation. The Germans would undoubtedly have gained their objectives in any case, thanks to their enormous artillery and powerful bomber forces. But evidently the "atom gun"—to use this convenient but incorrect term—had no small effect upon the tightly packed masses on the Kerch Peninsula, and a couple of days later there was a charge from Russian and Allied quarters that the Germans were using gas in the East.

Just what is meant by gas is debatable. Everything considered, the Germans were in the right when they stoutly maintained that the stipulations in the Geneva Convention regarding poison gas could not be applied to the new weapon. But when Churchill threatened in a speech that the Allies would retaliate with gas warfare, the matter no longer depended on an interpretation of the Geneva Convention. Faced with this direct threat, Hitler beat a retreat. On May 12 a spokesman for the War Office explained that Germany intended to respect the agreement not to use gas, as long as her opponents did the same.

It was his impression, he said, that Churchill had based his statement on Russian reports regarding the new weapon, and that the effect of the new guns upon the Russians had led to "the erroneous notion that gas had been used."

Captain Sommerfeldt told us that the new weapons were a guarantee of victory in the East. But in spite of his boasts and those of other officers, Kerch was the only place in the East where, so far as can be ascertained, the "atom gun" was used to any great extent.

Kerch was a typical preparation for a greater offensive on the eastern front. Before these operations in the Crimea were completed, however, the Russians on May 12 took the initiative, to everybody's surprise. Timoshenko made an elaborate attempt to crash through the German positions south of Kharkov, and in fact succeeded in making a deep penetration of the German lines. But the base of his drive was too narrow, and the Germans, after a week of fighting, were able to develop great counterattacks from the North and the South, which encircled Timoshenko's army in an oblong pocket south and southwest of Kharkov. By the end of May, the German High Command was able to report a great victory. Was it as great as the Germans officially claimed? Neutral observers in Berlin were impressed by the private comments of military men, who told us that, although the Russians had suffered heavy losses, they had nevertheless gained one of their objectives, which was to delay the German major offensive.

No particulars on the direction of the projected thrusts were available, but it was apparent that the weight of attack would be on the southern front. The oil problem had, during the past year, become more and more pressing for the Germans, who had to apply one restriction after another. Therefore an offensive ought to safeguard the war effort through a conquest of the oil fields in the Caucasus.

There were other burning problems of supply that made a southward movement probable. On the road to the Caucasian oil fields lay one of the richest agricultural regions of the Soviet Union, the Kuban district. The Ukraine, because of extensive industrialization during recent years, had not had its former surplus of food supplies, but had easily met its needs by imports from the Kuban. It was considered very important to get this rich district into German hands.

Even on purely military grounds the southern sector was indicated as the intended theater of action. Kerch had been captured as early as May. On June 2 an intensive drum-fire had been started against Sevastopol, as the prelude to a systematic attack. In the middle of the month there was a large-scale preparatory operation in the Kharkov sector. Furthermore, the southern area had been pretty well cleared of partisans, supplies were coming up, and lines of communication were being rapidly extended.

Sevastopol proved to be an extremely hard nut to crack. In spite of a murderous fire from the heaviest mortars the Germans possessed, besides continued dive-bombing and various new technical developments, the fortress held out week after week. Not until July 1 could the High Command report the capture of the city; actually the last defenders held out for two or three days more.

The delay was largely caused by the activity of the Soviet Black Sea fleet. Despite the vigilance of the Luftwaffe, the Russians succeeded, almost without interruption, in bringing convoys to the fort and in sailing the vessels back empty under protection of strong naval escorts.

Sevastopol was a clear example of how important a fleet may be, even in narrow waters dominated by the enemy's air force. To keep watch over the entrance to Sevastopol harbor was in itself a comparatively simple task; and besides, the Russian war vessels were technically of no great power. Nevertheless, it was frankly admitted by the Germans that connections with Sevastopol were maintained by sea, at the cost of only moderate losses.

The Russians announced that the city had been evacuated in about the same way as Odessa. This was categorically denied by the Germans, who gave picturesque descriptions of the "graveyard of ships" in the harbor and talked about enormous masses of prisoners.

On July 5 a number of foreign journalists were sent by special plane to the newly conquered city to certify, as it were, to the accuracy of the German claim. I wasn't one of those chosen to make the trip. Back in Berlin, there was no evidence to make me doubt the official German reports. Yet if the garrison had consisted of 100,000 men, as we had been told, the figure of 97,000 for prisoners taken seemed too high. Some Russians must have escaped and others must have fallen. But when Captain Sommerfeldt replied to a cautious question by saying that the garrison undoubtedly consisted of nearly 120,000 men, I let the matter rest.

A few days later my colleagues came back sick and miserable; they were victims of the so-called Crimean fever, the symptoms of which were annoying abdominal pains and weakness. But the trip had evidently provided all the sensations a journalist could reasonably ask for. To begin with, they all declared that the "graveyard of ships" was nowhere to be found: there was only one small vessel in the harbor. If many others had been sunk, they would have expected to see their masts, at least, sticking out of the water; but the harbor was as smooth as a mirror. They also said that the prison trains they had seen had been of a pretty modest length. Their most interesting report was that some of the younger officers had evidently talked too much, and had admitted that the Russian navy had succeeded in evacuating a large part of the garrison. They said that the Russians had transferred several thousand men every night and that, among other means, they had even utilized rafts camouflaged as little houses. As they lay along the piers, which the Germans did not wish to destroy completely, these rafts, seen from the air, could hardly be distinguished from harbor sheds. These stories and others showed that the Germans had exaggerated the number of prisoners taken and made us feel skeptical about the German account as a whole. I do not mean to say that the Russian version was entirely correct, but in this case it was clearly nearer the truth than the report of the German High Command.

Most people had the notion that the great German offensive would be launched on June 22 at the latest, and an earlier date was widely expected, both in Germany and abroad, since the 1941 campaigns had shown the need of beginning as soon as possible in order to overcome the vast Russian distances. But when the first anniversary of the war in Russia passed uneventfully, many observers began to wonder whether there would be a great offensive after all. The majority opinion was that Hitler was so bound by his statements that he would have to go into action. On June 24, Moscow reported that the Germans were attacking, but Captain Sommerfeldt explained to us in his stiff Prussian fashion that they were merely improving their positions. But the attacks were pressed home in greater force at the end of the month. On July 1 the German High Command used language which showed that the battle in the Ukraine had begun on a large scale.

The March Against Egypt

During May and June, when the situation in Russia was comparatively quiet, General Rommel had struck a heavy blow in Africa. He had been receiving reinforcements for several months and, according to what was understood in Berlin, the transport losses had been notably small. This, they said, had been due chiefly to the fact that Germany and Italy had succeeded in keeping Malta out of action by intensive air operations during the spring of 1942. The forces had not been sufficient to conquer the island, but they had been able to minimize the British threat to the German supply lines. On May 26 the battle in Libya blazed up again with a German-Italian assault on the British positions. For the moment, however, neutral circles in Berlin looked for no great shifting of the front, and everything indicated that the Germans themselves held the same view, although they justly pinned great hopes on Rommel's capacity for taking full advantage of a situation. Partly because of his great reputation, the battle was intently followed in Germany, although no official announcement was made until June 7, when the struggle had already continued for thirteen days. But as if to compensate for the delay, the Germans began speaking as if victory were certain. We were given to understand that the new Axis advance—the first assault had been thrown back, and was followed by a British counterattack, which had been similarly fruitless—had developed with extraordinary success, and that this time one might expect something extra special from Rommel. The journalists said to themselves, "Wait and see." None of them yet believed that anything more was involved than forcing the English back to Tobruk, and then everything would continue as before. The capture of Bir Hacheim and the encirclement of a considerable English force on the coast made it pretty clear that Rommel had succeeded in winning the first round. But subsequently, we felt, he would be halted by the Tobruk garrison.

Tobruk had become an idea, a legend. Nobody believed that this fort, which had so long defied Rommel, could be stormed. Well-informed Germans were of the opinion that a long siege was inevitable, and they also thought that the growing heat would soon prevent all further operations.

But Rommel apparently paid no attention to the climate, and made no allowance for the theory that the fort was well-nigh impregnable. He was at the head of his troops when they stormed Bir Hacheim; he drove them ceaselessly onward, and his rapid advance was supported by large air forces. Beginning on June 17, his troops were called the Africa Panzer Army (instead of merely the Africa Corps) and Berlin announced that it had received strong reinforcements, especially of planes. On the 19th Tobruk was encircled, and, after concentric assaults had been made, the incredible happened—on June 21 the High Command was able to announce in a special communiqué that Tobruk had been stormed and captured and the entire garrison were prisoners.

The fall of Tobruk made a tremendous impression in Berlin and all over Germany. Instantly the general feeling throughout the country rose to a pitch that had not been reached since the end of the Battle of France in 1940. Rommel was the man of the hour, the general for whom nothing seemed impossible. Perhaps we can win the war after all, everybody said, and the Germans joyfully congratulated themselves over something they felt was a real victory, not so far away or so hard to judge as the successes in Russia.

Those inclined to criticize were silenced for a moment, and near-panic broke out among those in direct opposition. In Vienna and throughout Austria there was great excitement; the Austrians al-

ready had the vision of a hard peace that would leave National
Socialism in unmolested possession of their country. The fall of
Tobruk, furthermore, had a catastrophic effect on Britain's pres-
tige inside Germany, which up to then had been rising. Even
Hitler's bitterest enemies began saying to themselves that they could
place no hopes in the British.

We gathered from foreign reports that the surrender of the
Tobruk garrison had led to a moral crisis, not only in England, but
even more among the troops that were now making an orderly
retreat toward Egypt, pursued by a fast and ruthless foe. Egypt
was at stake, one of the jewels in the crown of the British Empire.
The pace quickened. On June 26 it was openly declared in Berlin
that the Eighth Army was completely shattered and that its fragments were in full flight eastward. At the Libyan-Egyptian frontier,
Indian troops had been overpowered, and Marshal Rommel—the
new rank had been conferred on him after he took Tobruk—already
stood at Sidi Barrani.

The German journalist, Lutz Koch, in a lecture before the foreign
correspondents on June 22, explained that Rommel had aimed at
Tobruk from the start. But there was much evidence that the scope
of the victory was as much of a surprise to Berlin and the German
government as it was to the British. Rommel achieved a result which
Hitler with his bold flights of fancy had probably not counted on.
But when it looked as if nothing could stop the onrushing Axis
forces and Egypt hung in the balance, people in Berlin were not
slow to take advantage of the opportunity for spinning dreams.
Didn't this victory mean that the much-desired junction with the
Japanese was already in sight?

As early as the beginning of June, there had been a notably strong
interest in Egyptian political problems, and Premier Nahas
Pasha had been the object of insane attacks for his "betrayal of the
country's real interests," and his subservience to England. There
was more faith in other Egyptian nationalists, and there was confidence that a significant faction among the Arabs was in principle
friendly to the Axis. However, the Quisling problem was complicated by the fact that there were two European Axis powers, and
that Italy, the second, was intensely unpopular in Egypt. There, to
be sure, people were eager to get rid of British rule, but they by no
means desired to exchange it for Italian rule.

After Tobruk had fallen, Berlin speculated on still another source
of strength for the Germans in their advance into Egypt. The

insiders kept repeating reports from Cairo which indicated that Rommel's successes had made a great impression on the country, that its youth had caught the Rommel fever, and that the Arabs awaited emancipation by the great general. When I asked a good friend if the Egyptians really imagined that Rommel would have anything to say after the conquest, or that he could keep the Party bosses from pouncing down like vultures on the rich land, he replied with an embarrassed smile that in any case there were influential persons who thought the Egyptians "had a different view of the matter." In this connection he declared that the Grand Mufti and former Prime Minister of Iraq, Rashid Ali el Gailani, who was friendly to Germany, would play a certain role when Rommel had plunged farther ahead toward Alexandria.

The airtight blockade of Egypt that was established by the British when they realized the seriousness of the situation, clearly handicapped the Axis powers in getting reliable reports from Cairo. Of course, the Axis agents there had a great number of radio transmitters, through which they were in communication with their superiors, but there was also the story that the English police had confiscated many of them and had calmly continued the conversation with Italy and Germany.

The pace of Rommel's advance hardly slackened, and apparently the field marshal was trying with a single thrust to force his way into the Valley of the Nile. Would the English be able to achieve something parallel to the miracle of the Marne? All Berlin was tense until tidings of victory came again. The Matruh position had been stormed, and enormous stores had fallen into the hands of the victors. The attack was kept up incessantly without giving the English any rest. The temperature was said to have risen to 105 in the shade, and fighting theoretically should have stopped because of the weather. But Rommel seemed to have beaten the weather— with the help of his air-conditioned tanks, said military spokesmen —and it was expected that Alexandria's turn would come after that of Matruh. Of course, there were cautious soothsayers who pointed out the risks of the long-extended supply lines; but they were soon howled down by others who pointed out that Rommel could, of course, live on the immeasurable resources of the conquered land. The average German, like his government, believed that Egypt would fall within a few days. All official Berlin was completely intoxicated, and particularly so because the offensive in Russia was launched in earnest just at that moment. "We shall squeeze the Middle East between the jaws of the pincers," said a well-informed person in the Wilhelmstrasse, "and after a month or so the two jaws will meet in the Gulf of Persia. At the same time, we shall push down to the Caucasus, and then you shall see a new campaign against India, like that of Alexander, combined with a gigantic Japanese attack from Burma and the appearance of a strong Japanese fleet on the seas between India and Arabia." Another reliable source stated, at about the same time, that parachute landings in Afghanistan would be part of the vast operation.

The idea might seem fantastic, but the problem of joining forces with the Japanese continually absorbed all Germans. In this they speculated rather heavily on Japan, which then seemed to be almost invincible. But my first-mentioned spokesman also had something to say about Turkey.

"Well, what do you think she can do? Maybe she can remain neutral, like your country, which also has German troops to the North, South, East, and West. But we shall see. Ankara offers no problem for us." It would seem that the projected attempt against India did not necessarily presuppose an invasion of Turkey. But at the beginning of July, I definitely learned from one of my best sources—he was a man with excellent military connections—that the German government was planning before long to undertake an attack on Turkey. The whole scheme for the thrust into the Middle East depended on whether Rommel would succeed in conquering Egypt.

During those days when the fate of Egypt appeared decided, and when we expected every day to hear that Rommel had advanced to the outskirts of Alexandria, we could see how much reason there was for the cautious policy that had been followed by at least the majority of the Swedes in Berlin. There had been various Germans, even in rather high positions, who had not concealed their conviction that Nazism was a poison, who maintained that Germany ought to make peace, and that her chances of winning the war were equal to zero. But, in spite of this, something had deterred us from abandoning the role of attentive listeners, and talking things over frankly with these men. Now many of these same persons revealed themselves as triumphant members of the master race. They told us and others what was in store for truculent little Sweden after Germany had broken through to the Indian Ocean and had thus created a position that would be invincible. Meanwhile the real opponents of Nazism were in a somber mood.

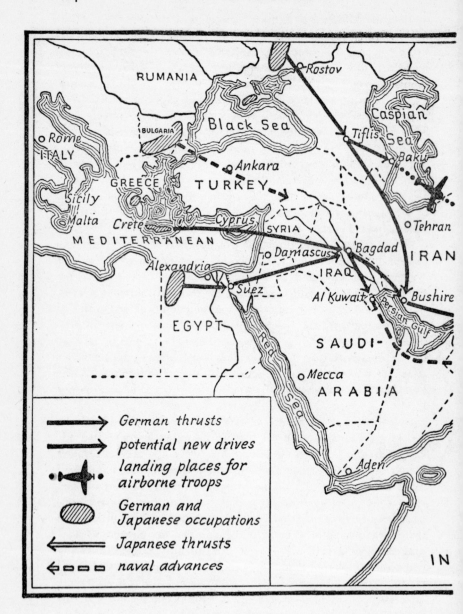

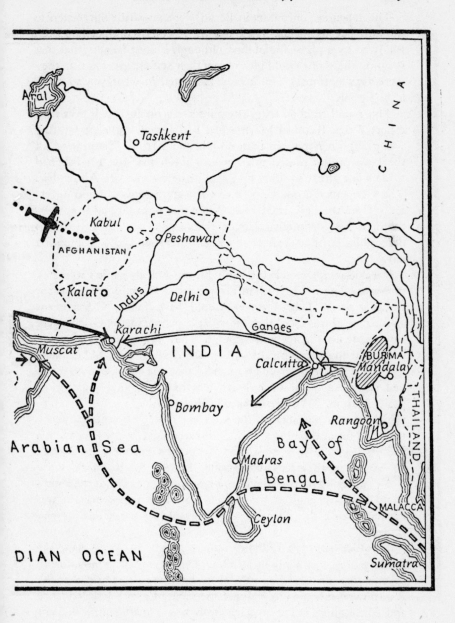

The Japanese journalists in Berlin were unusually interested in the new developments. Their usually reserved conduct had been followed by a pleased affability, although it must be admitted that the only thing one could glean from their statements was that they were very optimistic and keenly interested in what was to come after Egypt.

This mood reached its greatest intensity on July 1. It was then reported that Rommel had reached El Alamein and that fighting was going on not more than 60-odd miles from Alexandria. All the insiders interpreted this news to mean that the English had made a last effort to draw up a line of defense before Alexandria. The Germans did not suppose that the attempt would end differently from the fight at Matruh. After that position had been captured, it was definitely claimed that, so far as was known, no defensible position existed between there and the Alexandria naval base.

It was also indicated in the Wilhelmstrasse that a panic had struck or was striking the English in Egypt; and it was added that except for this panic Tobruk never would have fallen. Government spokesmen also insisted that the volatile people of the Orient were susceptible to the Rommel legend. They said that the German marshal who swept onward swift as the desert wind had become a legendary figure even in Egypt, and that the English themselves had contributed substantially to this by their loudly expressed praise of him. "We Germans would certainly be careful not to praise an enemy general to the skies like that," a German military man told me at the time. "Why," said an official in the Propaganda Ministry with a smug look, "the Egyptian youngsters are already showing how they feel by shouting, 'Hurray for Rommel.' "

A couple of days passed without any announcement of the anticipated break-through at El Alamein. On July 3, however, it was explained that the fighting was favorable to the Germans and Italians.

The Germans felt that the time was ripe to supplement the military blows with a political blow. On July 3, Dr. Schmidt with solemn formality read an official declaration which said that the Axis powers intended to "respect and secure Egypt's independence and sovereignty." The proclamation was a masterpiece of Axis bombast. The Axis troops, it explained, were not treading on Egyptian soil as enemies; their aim was to drive the Englishmen out of Egyptian territory and free the Near East of British domination. The policy of both the Axis powers was an application of the principle, "Egypt for the Egyptians." In conclusion, the Egyptians were harangued as an independent and sovereign nation —that is, after they were released from British chains. Dr. Schmidt in his commentary described the declaration as a historical event signifying that the Egyptian people had been invited to take their place within "the European folk family." The Mediterranean lands were declared to be an integral part of Europe.

Schmidt said that the Egyptian answer could be left to negotiation, but the days went by without our hearing any more about it. Little by little there was so much irritation over the correspondents' questions that the matter was relegated to the limbo of unpleasant subjects not to be mentioned at press conferences.

In the meantime, military developments had taken a turn that nobody had foreseen. On the 3rd, the communiqué declared that operations were developing favorably and that several important positions had been seized. On the 4th, it was announced that the English counteroffensive had been repulsed, and likewise on the 5th. One of the afternoon newspapers said that gaps in the English defensive positions had been enlarged, but that the enemy offered stubborn resistance and that the temperature had risen to 115 and 120 degrees. The whole El Alamein position was favored by nature, the paper added, but nevertheless the break-through had been successful. "This last attempt to block the way to Egypt with troops hurried from the Near and Middle East will fail."

To anybody who understood German military terminology, it was obvious from this account that Rommel's lightning thrust had been repulsed. What we still did not know was whether the British would be able to withstand the new attacks that would come after reinforcements had been rushed over from Italy. Meanwhile the latest developments showed that the British had greater supplies in the Nile Valley than the Germans or the Italians could get from their bases. Captain Sommerfeldt told us on July 7 that the British could utilize bases in the immediate vicinity of the battle zone, while Rommel had to depend on a 300-mile supply line that ran all the way back to Tobruk. We were beginning to realize that the miracle of the Marne had been repeated at El Alamein. But the fate of Egypt was still not finally decided.

By bringing all his strength to bear Rommel had made a grandiose attempt to destroy the British position. After it failed, his troops were left in a position that offered great disadvantages for defense.

The natural thing for him to do was to make a new attack—or to retreat. The British Empire was saved for the time being. The southern jaw of the pincers around the Middle East had failed to close. Both the British and other peoples—for example, the Turks, who had been extremely nervous—began to recover from the military and psychological shock that Field Marshal Rommel had given them.

When it gradually became clear to anyone in Berlin who was at all intelligent that Egypt was being wrenched out of German hands, a quiet discussion was heard behind the scenes. Why was it that Rommel had been victorious but had not won the Victory? Most often you heard that it was the fault of the Italians who, it was said, had committed one act of treason after another. The truth is that the Germans had good reason for being violently irritated with their allies. In Italy the fall of Tobruk had been greeted with disappointment. Two Germans who began to shout "Heil!" when the radio announced that Tobruk had fallen were thrown out of a big Italian restaurant by other patrons. But even if the repulse at El Alamein could be blamed partly on Italian sabotage, it appears that the principal reasons for it were the utter exhaustion of both the German and Italian troops, the furious exertions of the British, the breaks in the Axis supply lines and finally the fact that the German command was surprised by the extent of Rommel's victory and unprepared to take quick advantage of it.

The Death of Heydrich; Troubles in the Occupied Countries

From the political point of view, the early summer of 1942 was dominated by an increasing spirit of rebellion in the occupied countries. It was becoming more and more difficult to solve the problems that confronted the occupying forces. But the only true crisis occurred in a country that was not formally considered as occupied, namely, the Protectorate of Bohemia-Moravia.

The feeling there had been relatively peaceful during the spring. On May 27, however, two unidentified men fired some shots at the automobile of Reinhard Heydrich, the Deputy Reichsprotector, who was on his way to Prague. Seriously wounded in the back, Heydrich was taken to a hospital in Prague.

The attempted assassination created a sensation in Berlin. At first, we were given to believe that Heydrich could be saved, but after some days it was hinted that the wounds would prove fatal.

In the Protectorate, there was a whole series of rigorous measures —a state of emergency was declared, houses were searched, the border was closed. All those who had guests in their homes were given until Friday midnight, May 30, to notify the police. After the stroke of twelve, all those who had failed to report their guests, as well as the guests themselves, would be executed. By June 1, the list of people sentenced to death had already risen to 111, including many accused, in what was by now a stereotyped phrase, of having "approved of Heydrich's assassination." Among the first victims were officers in the former Czechoslovakian army, professors and members of the former Czech ministries.

When Heydrich died, on June 4, high-ranking Nazis made open threats, without bothering to be temperate in their choice of words. Germany's patience is at an end, they said, and it would not be surprising if the Führer answered by sending the whole Czech people to the Ukraine. There is no doubt that the Nazis were planning this wholesale banishment. When Heydrich's funeral was conducted in the Chancellery on June 9, poor little President Hacha was among those present. We heard it firmly asserted that Hitler had threatened him with the Ukraine during a terrible outburst of rage.

But this forced migration was impossible for a purely technical reason—the Protectorate was a most important source of armaments, and its production could not for a moment be disturbed. The Propaganda Ministry announced that the Czechs would be given another chance. Blame for the assassination was placed on the English and the émigrés.

One reason why more severe measures were not taken against the Czechs may have been that, so far as could be judged, they had nothing whatever to do with the assassination. This fact must have become clear even to Hitler after a most thorough examination had been completed. Even before that time, strange rumors had begun to circulate. One of them was that the Reichswehr had plotted Heydrich's assassination. Another rumor, more widely believed, was that the secret anti-Nazi opposition in the Gestapo itself had put Heydrich out of the way. Even more than Himmler, he stood forth as the representative of ruthless violence, and his colleagues had come to regard him as chief bloodhound in the pack.

It can now be stated with relative certainty that Heydrich was murdered by his own associates, although the crime had nothing to do with political opposition to Hitler. It was plotted by three high police officials who had made a fortune in conquered Poland through graft and peculation. On their return to Germany, Heydrich had seized most of their profits for himself, using his secret information for blackmail. When it was revealed that they had revenged themselves by murdering the Deputy Protector, two of the officials were executed and the third committed suicide.

The official story was that the actual assassins were found on June 18 in a church and were shot there while resisting arrest. It was afterwards learned, the official story continued, that the two men who fired the shots were former noncommissioned officers in the Czechoslovakian army. After having been trained in England, they had been carried by a long-range British bomber to the appointed place in December 1941, and had there been dropped by parachute. Their explicit task was to murder Heydrich. They had obtained shelter and help from various Czech families and had made contact with other parachutists.

The Czech press at an early stage had set the tone for public discussion of the case by laying the blame for everything that had happened on the émigrés. The "rescue program" for the Czechs, which was then outlined, was based on "loyal behavior toward the German Reich, the ruthless elimination of elements inimical to the Reich and increased production in the special war industries." The originator of this program was the Propaganda Minister, former Colonel Emanuel Moravec. How far this creature was willing to go is shown by some of his words in the *Action*, shortly after Heydrich's death: "The government of the Protectorate and I myself are faced with the problem of educating the Czechs to become good National Socialists."

Gradually the executions decreased in number. Among the later victims were a number of generals and other high officers of the former Czechoslovakian army, professors, school teachers and officials of various ranks, including mayors. The total number of executions officially announced rose during the weeks after the assassination to about 1,600, counting the total male population of two towns, Lidice and Levzsaky, all whose people were considered to be "directly or indirectly guilty" of an assassination with which they had absolutely nothing to do.

In the occupied countries, disturbances increased markedly during the early summer of 1942. This was, for example, the case in

Holland, where 72 members of a secret national organization were executed early in May; for the most part they were officers and noncommissioned officers of the Dutch army. The German newspapers printed sharp warnings to the Dutch people, and the German-controlled press announced that further acts of resistance would lead to court-martials. "Every person must know," the Dutch newspapers said, "that he is playing with his head as a stake. That the men sentenced to death were acting from patriotic motives cannot be taken into account. Germany could not excuse their crime on this ground without putting her own existence in jeopardy." Some days later, the military commander ordered all former officers of the Dutch army to report for control to the German authorities. On May 14, it was announced at The Hague that 24 more persons had been executed. At the same time 460 others were taken as hostages, to answer with their lives if there were any additional deeds of sabotage.

The battle between the occupation authorities and the Dutch Quislings on one side and the overwhelming majority of the population on the other became still more bitter. The fact that Dutch Jews were now required to wear the Star of David offered an opportunity for new demonstrations. Some Dutch youths wore the star, others went arm-in-arm with Jews, while still others lifted their hats to the star in the same way a Catholic lifts his hat when passing a church. The occupation authorities became increasingly embittered over these small insults, and soon announced that Hollanders who insisted on mingling with Jews or continued to "irritate the occupation forces through provocative conduct" would be treated as Jews.

In Belgium, too, restlessness increased markedly during May and June. There were several assassinations and acts of sabotage, and the German authorities answered them with executions and deportations. Some months earlier, a number of lawsuits had been brought in which the question at stake was the legality of the edicts issued by the General Secretary. Originally this official had limited powers, like those of a permanent under-secretary in Great Britain, but since the cabinet ministers had left the country, a special law had been passed authorizing him to act for the whole cabinet. Various loopholes in this law were used by the opposition as an excuse for questioning the legality of the decrees which the General Secretary had issued. Since the Belgian courts welcomed this opportunity to demonstrate against the occupation authorities, it looked as though the whole rationing system might break down. The Military Commander was forced to take a hand. On May 14, he issued a decree proclaiming that the conclusions of the General Secretary were endowed with absolute validity, regardless of anything the courts might decide. This decree led to great demonstrations and the resignation of several judges. Still the situation was not so serious as that in Holland.

Restlessness also increased in other occupied countries. In the Baltic states, strong measures had been taken during the spring, but not many of them came to public attention, although several of the foreign correspondents in Berlin had a pretty clear picture of what was taking place. The real trouble was the ruthless demands for grain and potatoes which the Germans inflicted on the Estonian, Latvian and Lithuanian peasants. Since these had no wish to starve, they withheld as much of their crops as possible; sometimes these were buried and sometimes sold on the black market. On July 15, a decree was issued in Lithuania providing that refractory peasants would be punished by confiscation of all livestock as well as by the eventual loss of their land and the shipment of the peasants themselves to work camps. The Germans got no more grain than before.

SUMMER WAR 1942

The Military and Political Offensive Against Russia

THE combat that began in the Kharkov salient at the end of June rose to so great a scale after a few days that it was evident the great offensive had begun. The German troops and their allies were attacking on a 185-mile front. At first the usual reticence was observed, but on July 4 a heavy break-through was reported in the direction of the Don. On the following day the attacking troops were stated to have reached the river on a wide front after crashing through between Kharkov and Kursk. Progress was unusually fast, and 24 hours later a bridgehead on the farther bank of the Don was claimed. On July 7, the commanding general announced the capture of Voronezh, though in due course it proved that the Russians still held parts of the city.

Berlin asserted on July 11, after the first phase of the offensive was over, that the great gains in territory were the result of new tactics as well as of the enormous concentration of various weapons. The new tactics, so far as could be judged, included an extensive camouflaging of points of attack through the constant transfer of units, as well as accelerated motorization which permitted supplies to move virtually in step with the advance. Added to this was the contribution of the tireless air force, which swept a path for the troops, all but cleared the air of Russian planes and confused the Russian retreat by bombarding important traffic junctions. The Germans were clearly superior in numbers on the southern front, and must have had available about 225 divisions in the East, besides which there were 22 Rumanian divisions, 9 Italian, 8 Hungarian, 3 Slovakian and 1 Croat—a total of some 270 divisions. The Russians certainly had 300 or more divisions, but the Germans, with their concentration in the South, outnumbered them there.

The quick advance became feasible, too, because of Marshal Timoshenko's rapid withdrawal and refusal to engage in heavy combat. The Russians' elastic defense prevented the Germans from taking large numbers of prisoners. It was only a question of whether or not the retreating forces could hold themselves intact.

Despite the great advances, the German command was remarkably conservative in its decisions. On July 9, *Das Schwarze Korps* warned against underestimating the Russians with their advantage of "an infinity of space." And by way of further caution: "Even an operation on a very large scale here becomes only a sectional action. The enemy still has a base territory; he still has reserves of men. War can grind him under, deprive him of his matériel, destroy his production centers, close his sources of raw supplies and choke the arteries of his existence only if pursued relentlessly, step by step."

With the extension of combat, the matter of Allied help to the Soviet Union became especially significant; hence the note of triumph in the German special communiqué of July 7, which announced that U-boats and aircraft had sunk the greater part of a giant Allied convoy on its way to Murmansk with war matériel for several armies. British battleships were said to have been in the convoy escort.

At first the Russians found it difficult to retreat in good order because the Germans harassed their communications from the air and drove tank wedges deep into the retiring troops.

Toward the end of July the German forces were divided, strong units proceeding in an easterly direction and other important forces moving toward the South. The whole Russian front wavered. Rostov was captured, and on a wide front the Germans crossed the Don. Russian communiqués took on a serious tone and the Russian radio revealed a growing nervousness. Oliver Lyttelton, the British Minister of Supply, held that the coming 80 days would prove the most significant period thus far. In Russia there was a growing demand for a second front.

The German troops rapidly spread themselves out over the plains of the North Caucasus, reaching Voroshilovsk on August 4; three days afterwards the High Command declared that German troops had reached the first ranges of the Caucasus along a front of more than 250 miles. Sommerfeldt's deputy (our usual commentator, promoted to major, was now on leave) stated plainly that the objective was Baku.

In the bend of the Don the Germans made a similar quick advance. Stalingrad was not regarded as a particularly difficult nut to crack; as early as the end of July a press attaché expressed the opinion that the city would be in German hands by August 3.

Berlin followed developments in the East with eager interest;

spirits rose upon news of successes and high hopes prevailed. Because of this mood the foreign journalists were the more astonished at a Dietrich story that a military spokesman in Tokyo had declared that the Soviet Union would have to make a separate peace with Germany, since Britain and America could not give Russia effective help.

Our curiosity was stimulated. This suggestion of a separate peace, with Japan as mediator, was no new thing. We speculated on the pronouncement of our oracle, noting that he seemed always to key himself to an imaginary listener in the Kremlin, whom he sought to convince that his allies were not only false but useless to him. When we saw Dr. Schmidt, the little envoy twiddled his thumbs as always, and said that the word "separate peace" in the Japanese announcement, about which he seemed informed, meant nothing other than unconditional surrender by the Russians. "This, gentlemen, is the German viewpoint," he said. "Victory first—peace afterwards."

We left the press conference in a whirl of conjecture. The confusion grew when, next day, a rare guest, Colonel von Wedel, chief of the High Command's press department, informed the newspapermen that German soldiers had discovered "somewhere during the offensive against the Caucasus" a Soviet order of the day, dated July 28, of really sensational content. Colonel von Wedel guaranteed its authenticity.

This order of the day started out by saying that certain troops on the southern front, seized by panic because of cunning propaganda, had abandoned Rostov and Novocherkassk "without the justification of serious opposition and without orders from Moscow, and had thus disgraced their banner." The order continued: "The people of our land have always regarded the Red Army with love and respect, but are now disappointed and distrustful. Many curse the Red Army for abandoning the people to the Germans and withdrawing to the East."

There followed a lengthy admonition against a continued retreat: "Not a step to the rear!" The only noteworthy point in this passage was a statement that Russia was no longer superior to Germany in the matter of reserve man power and grain supplies. "The Germans are not so strong as the panic-mongers would have us believe," the order of the day continued. They are straining their final resources. Russian victory is assured if we resist their pressure now in the months to come. But order and discipline are imperative. Commissars and commanders who desert their units will no longer be tolerated. Troublemakers and cowards must be liquidated on the spot. Commanders and commissars who leave their posts without being expressly ordered to do so shall be considered traitors and treated accordingly. Any commander who condones the withdrawal of troops without permission shall be court-martialed. There shall be a special punishment battalion of 800 men and punishment companies of 150 to 200 men, all of which shall be assigned to especially dangerous positions. . . . The order was signed by Stalin himself.

This order of the day had in part the air of being authentic, but other parts of it seemed naïve. If it were genuine, it was plainly a godsend to the Germans. But close scrutiny made it seem to most of us that here was another order "planted" by the Russians to mislead their enemies. The question of authenticity is less important than the fact that the announcement broke at the same time as the rumors of a separate peace.

August 8 brought still another surprise. That night a colleague telephoned to ask whether *Dienst aus Deutschland* had offered me a new fairy story. They had telephoned him a fantastic yarn about how Stalin was to be replaced, and more of the same kind. Inquiry among the correspondents revealed that the story had not been given to all. Here is the sensational thesis that *Dienst aus Deutschland* presented to selected subscribers: The Soviet Union faces political and military collapse. "According to information received in Berlin," the British and the Americans desire to substitute for the Bolshevik regime a military government, which in turn may be replaced by a constitutional monarchy. The 28-year-old Grand Duke Vsevolod, son of the Grand Duke Ivan Konstantinovich and the Serbian Princess Helena, who is married to an Englishwoman, is the favored candidate for the throne. The new regime will continue the war, putting aside any thought of a separate peace. The regime plans to gain popularity by promising an election for a national assembly after the war.

The journalists who got this stuff were reluctant to spread it. The Germans would sometimes use the unofficial *Dienst aus Deutschland* for rumors which they did not wish to sponsor and this seemed to be a typical case. How had the Americans, whom the Wilhelmstrasse called weak, and the English, whom the Wilhelmstrasse called impotent, suddenly acquired enough power to overthrow Stalin? For me, timeliness was the solution—if peace feelers were being put out, this report was a symptom. But I was nevertheless happy when I saw that the foreign editor of my paper captioned my telegram: "Rumor in Berlin."

Nobody ever explained what lay behind it all. The next day all questions were categorically waved aside, and after a few days the talk petered out. Nor have I since obtained any light on the episode; the only fairly plausible explanation came from a person with good Japanese connections. He stated that the Japanese were in fact urging Russia to accept a separate peace, and that the Germans, by claiming ulterior designs on the part of the Allies toward Stalin, hoped to induce Moscow to accept Japan's suggestions. The whole thing can be interpreted only as a political offensive against Russia.

In the middle of August the tempo of action in the Caucasus slowed down. Rain began to fall in torrents, and the German and Italian Alpine troops made no noteworthy progress. On the coast, the Russian Black Sea naval forces constituted a perpetual flanking threat. The Russians offered bitter opposition before Grozny and drew reinforcements both from Iran and the Turkish-Russian border, which became almost stripped of troops. The Germans, for their part, did not neglect to point out to the Turks the happy opportunity of disposing of their hereditary enemy, and in Germany there was talk of the oppressed Turkish minority in the Caucasus. They got no satisfaction, and it was plain that the Russians believed that their Allies could control Turkey, for they left only very weak forces, women's battalions among them, on their southern border.

On the other hand, the Germans made significant advances in the Stalingrad area. On August 12, their High Command announced the annihilation of Soviet forces around Kalatch, and late in the month a German tank corps crossed the Don northwest of Stalingrad, thus cutting off the city from the main Russian forces to the North. We were told on September 1 that these German troops were at the Volga, and on the 4th that Russian opposition had cracked and the whole Soviet position was doomed. Certain German troops had reached the suburbs. The Russians were being forced back, but only inch by inch. A military expert reported, as an illustration of Russian tenacity, that they kept right on operating their war plants in the city and turned out 20 brand-new tanks every day. On September 13, we had it unofficially that the business of storming of the city had begun. But as day followed day the German newspapers were increasingly hard put to it to describe the violent crescendo of the combat. The whole area is a single fortress, it was said, although meanwhile an officer straight from Stalingrad had averred that no really strong fortifications existed there. Gradually, the press began to let out, apologetically, that German regiments were no longer intact, and that soldiers had gone for days and weeks without sleep. The strategical objective had actually already been attained, it was said finally, and this pronouncement late in September was interpreted by the foreigners in the German capital as the forerunner of a retreat, at least on the propaganda front.

The campaign seems to have been planned by Hitler, Halder and Jodl. Its manifest aim was to create favorable conditions for an attempt on the Caucasus by first striking at Stalingrad. But the two enterprises were undertaken simultaneously, and with fatal results. The offensive took so long and made such heavy demands on the German soldiers that the Axis forces became exhausted. That is probably the main reason why the plan failed, despite the great advances. I was told, too, that a reason for the later inaction in the Caucasus was shortage of motor fuel. Oil transport had to be directed to Stalingrad. The offensive toward Baku was then halted by a shortage of oil. It takes oil to get oil.

The German Soldier Facing the Winter War

The whole enterprise had by this time proved to be much more difficult than was at first expected. Stubborn resistance at the bend of the Don had delayed the advance by two months. Already there were voices raised asking whether the capture of Stalingrad was worth the price. True, traffic on the Volga could be cut off, but the winter's ice would achieve that even more effectively. Some anxiety was in evidence, too, concerning the slow progress in the Caucasus. The Maikop oil wells fell into German hands early in September. The Russians, however, had done a lot of damage there, and besides, the area's total annual yield was only about 2,300,000 tons. Immediately upon the capture of Maikop a German commission of 40 experts arrived there. A few days later a military patrol thought that the house in which the members were quartered seemed deserted and entered to investigate. The guard was found dead and a room-to-room search revealed that the whole commission had been killed by partisans.

Even if the taking of Stalingrad was merely a matter of time, the long wait had its perils. The winter war would soon be a reality. At home the prospect was viewed with the greatest optimism, but there was much to testify that the German at the front did not share this view. Even if current preparations were much more extensive than in 1941-42, the prospect was not a cheerful one for him. As early as the middle of September he began to feel the cold nights, which were soon followed by autumn rains and storms. The offensive had been carried out with an intensity which necessarily exhausted the men, and it quickly became apparent that the resources in fully rested troops were limited. Even though the soldiers' knowledge of winter warfare had been much improved (they were self-taught under the pressure of necessity), there were many signs that they feared the Russian winter.

Nor did the soldiers at the front evaluate their Russian adversaries as did those at home. Many recognized the Russians' superiority in winter warfare. There were military experts who also had a healthy respect for the Russians, and some of this got into print. A well-known commentator wrote in August in a professional magazine that the Bolshevik soldier's greatest advantages over the German are "his highly developed animal instincts and his insensitiveness to weather and terrain." Further, that whoever plans to defeat the Russian must be at home in woods and marshes, must be able to orient himself at night and in fog as well as by day (the Russians almost always attack in fog or at night and time and again have surprised the Germans) and must be able to advance over the terrain like a hunter. The Russians, too, are masters of improvisation. They launch artillery projectiles from gliders, promptly utilize captured weapons and quickly form units of hastily assembled farmers, who supply their own weapons. Moreover, the Russians are ceaselessly active and hardly permit a day to pass without attempting an advance. The German soldier tends to become negligent if combat is long sustained, the writer continued. It must be impressed upon him that the Russians fight with craft and cunning. Destruction threatens the Germans in a thousand ways from Russian civilians and war prisoners, especially from those of the younger generation, "who are capable of all possible deceit" with mines, camouflage and ambush. Scouting is the be-all and end-all in Russia.

The German expert said further that service of supplies had to be maintained even at the cost of broken axles and dead horses. He emphasized the imperative necessity of personal hygiene:

"Whoever fails in that will be lost in Russia." There is no excuse for not washing oneself every day, the writer declared. There is always time and always water. This laxity must be conquered. Fighting at 40 below or 100 above in mud or thick slime to the knees demands real men. "Only such as retain self-mastery in the very face of death are fitted to fight against the Bolsheviks. Weaklings should know that their leaders are steeled to punish cowardice with death. In the present conflict between two world ideologies it must be clear to all that the life of an individual is virtually insignificant."

There were other experts to give respectful rating to Russia's resources in matériel. And in discussing the Soviet Union's Achilles heel, her air weapon, the facts showed that her production was important. The figures mentioned were 1,500 planes a month from 70 factories.

By 1942 the attrition of German human resources was palpably greater than in 1941. Echoes of many desertions were heard back home, and soldiers on leave commonly declared that the spirit at the front was unusually low, lower than at any time during the winter of 1941-42. Families in Germany would receive the terrifying announcement that "unfortunately we have found it necessary to shoot your son because of his cowardice in the face of the enemy"—*wegen Feigheit vor dem Feinde*. A young officer confided to me that a not inconsiderable number of deserters had joined the Russians and were fighting against the Germans. Even indirect desertion was ominously large. A new technical term had been created, *Verkümmelung*. This meant the soldier's losing his unit "by mistake." My informant assured me—and the fact was subsequently confirmed by other eyewitnesses—that thousands of men behind the front were busily engaged in "looking for their units." The German military authorities were impotent in the situation, he said, being reluctant to solve the problem by putting the "lost" men in the nearest unit at hand. At the front they were exasperated at the service of supply and the bureaucracy at home. An army doctor told me that even the SS troops had begun to curse *die Bonzokratie*, the Party hierarchy, and vowed to fire *Erinnerungskugeln* (souvenir bullets) at them on their return home.

I was credibly informed that religion was gaining strength at the front, particularly among the officers. Anthroposophy was particularly pervasive, and a book or pamphlet written by Rudolf

Steiner, founder of that cult, shortly before his death, was circulating covertly. Reports have it that the work is a telling prediction of dire developments in Germany, that it fixes the autumn of 1942 as Hitler's fatal period and promises a Hohenzollern as his eventual successor.

An ominous portent of disintegration was the increasing administration of drugs, as attested by all front soldiers. For the most part pervitine was used; it had long been given to troop units assigned to a particularly dangerous task. The habitual use of pervitine produces harmful effects. An influence of a positive nature, however, was the progressively increasing fear of the consequences of a German military collapse in the East. Not only the officers but the men had visions of the knife at their throats, and each one knew that an individual's chance of ever getting home, unless in regular troops units, was infinitesimal.

The War Against England on Land, at Sea and in the Air

During the summer it became increasingly evident that the war in the East absorbed so much of Germany's strength that only a fraction could be used against the British. Though a few spasmodic attempts were made to keep alive the idea that Britain could be invaded, the real problem was just the opposite.

German propaganda did its best to prove that a British invasion was impossible. They contrasted the strong Atlantic wall with the meager British tonnage. They even pretended that the Germans would welcome the British, so that they might "at least engage them in combat under equal conditions." That, however, was not merely propaganda. German officers advanced the same view privately. We hope, they said, that the British will yield to pressure from Stalin and start something before they are sufficiently prepared. If they act now, they will necessarily be soundly beaten, and nothing could be better from our point of view. In that case it is doubtful that they could come back better prepared next year. The effect of such failures is often permanent, and what we hope above all else is that the British will become convinced that it is futile to fight us and that a compromise is in order. That's our chance.

If this was the opinion of the German leaders, their propaganda should have been presented differently. I think it more likely that it was the private view of the more clear-sighted younger officers. At any rate, the British were stubborn enough to withstand the pressure from the East and to choose their own time and place of attack.

On the 19th of August they made a commando raid on Dieppe. Major Sommerfeldt cautioned us not to regard it as an attempt to create a second front, but by the next day he had received instructions, and he declared—obviously embarrassed—that it had really been an attempt to set up a second front, an attempt at invasion which from a military point of view was madness. In accordance with practice, the tone from across the street was even more emphatic. Dr. Schmidt declared that the operation had been nothing more nor less than an "enormous catastrophe," "a new Dunkirk." The attack had been undertaken by command of Stalin—thus suddenly again the dominant factor in the hostile coalition against Germany—who had "ordered" the British Prime Minister, then on a visit to Moscow, to open a second front immediately. That American soldiers on the occasion had been buried in European soil was the fault of President Roosevelt, "and will bring the American people to a turbulent awakening. The American soldiers who died yesterday at Dieppe are received by the Germans and their friends with a clear conscience as a contribution to the New Europe."

In justice it must be stated that not even Dr. Schmidt was in the habit of insulting the enemy so grossly. On that occasion it was evident, despite the well-trained expressions of admiration always visible on the countenances of the officials present, that everybody in the room who had not lost his feeling for chivalry and dignity felt stung by Schmidt's bad manners.

By the irony of fate, however, it was the Germans themselves who smashed the already punctured theory about the attempt to open a second front. The national edition of the *Deutsche Allgemeine Zeitung* on September 1 published a few pages of the captured British order of attack. This presumed five phases of the operation. The last ones were demolition, retreat, re-embarking and—debarkation in England and "dispersal of troops."

When somebody called the Propaganda Ministry's attention to the fact that an expedition planned for demolitions and quick re-embarking could scarcely have been an action for a second front, there was great commotion in the beehive. But it was too late then to change the official story.

The Dieppe expedition was, however, a German victory, even considering its limited range. Among other things it had proved that the German mobile forces could appear on the scene of action with extraordinary speed and also that the coastal defense was of considerable strength.

Somewhat later the Germans attempted to defeat the British on the only land front then existing, which was in North Africa, and failed. On the night before August 31, Rommel staged an attack according to established rules and customs, but was met by a different enemy than the one he had defeated in the spring, and he was forced to give up the offensive after heavy losses. The Germans and Italians tried to make light of what happened, and claimed that Rommel's attack was only a reconnaissance push.

Submarine warfare, in which the Germans placed great hope, continued with undiminished fury. Sinkings in June, July and August amounted to approximately 800,000 tons and in September the German High Command reported the record-breaking figure of 1,012,000 tons. Admiral Doenitz, in an interview, told the German soldier-correspondent Gerhart Weise that the battle between the North-South and the East-West supply lines in the Mediterranean had been decided to the advantage of the Germans and that although the Allied air force could doubtless destroy single U-boats, it could never eliminate them all—"just as a crow can never defeat a mole, inasmuch as God has given them both different spheres of life." The German expert added that the anti-aircraft batteries on U-boats were more perilous to planes than bombs were to U-boats when submerged.

The actual effect of U-boat attacks on Allied shipping was extremely difficult for foreign observers in Berlin to estimate. As a rule we took a rather skeptical attitude towards German optimism —and rightly so, as events proved.

Air warfare, like submarine warfare, continued almost without intermission. Sometimes the weather diminished the intensity of the attacks, but generally one could count on continued English raids on western Germany. And the Germans could not retaliate by counter-raids on Great Britain.

In the beginning the Germans tried to minimize the importance of the British air raids. The great raid on Cologne (May 31-June 1) was described as having been made with only 70 planes instead of 1,000, the British figure. Only a few days later it was admitted by well-informed Germans that the attacking planes had numbered between 300 and 400. We concluded, however, that the British statement was also incorrect, and that somewhere between 400 and 500 planes must have appeared over Cologne proper.

Gradually German propaganda changed its policy. The importance of the British raids was no longer minimized. The Germans could not retain this attitude in the face of the severely afflicted population of western Germany—but it was pointed out that the military damage was exceedingly small, and that the attacks were aimed chiefly at the morale of the German people.

Official spokesmen emphasized that these attacks must be repelled—and they cautiously cited the endurance of London to prove that it was possible. Retribution would come in time. At the moment it was inadvisable, since the concentration of German forces in the East made it necessary to take blows in the West without paying them back. In order to explain this to the people, Dr. Goebbels in the middle of August went to western Germany, where, according to the German press, he made himself interpreter for "the higher warfare" that concentrated all strength in the East. It was stated officially that the population had shown full understanding of the situation, but private reports on the behavior of the population during Goebbels' visit conflicted with this view. The regime was actually in a dilemma, for while Goebbels was the most unpopular man in Germany, he was also the only man clever enough to offer new excuses to the suffering population.

Varied Sentiments

Notwithstanding the relatively favorable development in the East at the beginning of the campaign, German morale showed a very marked decline during the summer. This was due partly to the air raids, but chiefly it was a natural reaction to the great hopes the public had been led to place in Rommel's victories. These factors and the continuous effect of the war on everyday life played their inevitable parts. With the specter of winter warfare about to make its appearance, morale declined faster. Developments in the East caused alarm. In the beginning results had been achieved relatively fast—but were they fast enough? Why didn't Stalingrad fall?

The day when Marshal Pétain capitulated, as *Das Schwarze*

Korps said in August, was the day on which all of us, with a few exceptions, believed the Germans to have been closer to the final victory than at any earlier moment. England seemed to be the only opponent left; and even the pessimists, who considered it necessary to conquer the whole island, figured that the war would last only a few more months. That the invasion did not materialize strengthened English morale and did much psychological damage to the Germans. In the background was Russia, and only the Führer and a few of his faithful followers knew what was concealed behind that frontier. "Today we have thoroughly prepared for war," said *Das Schwarze Korps*. "We realize well where we are and we have hung peace in the clothes closet with plenty of moth balls." But this was probably a wishful dream of *Das Schwarze Korps*.

That morale was declining revealed itself in many ways. An interesting symptom was the increase of rumors. They now dealt primarily with no less a person than the high chief of the German police. Some asserted that he was dead; others that he had been slightly injured on a flying trip between Norway and Hamburg; while a third group insisted that he had been forced by the General Staff to retire, after having drawn his revolver and shot a general in the presence of Hitler. That *something* had happened to Himmler in September seems possible. It is a fact that the bookstores in Berlin received a secret letter from the Propaganda Ministry, instructing them to remove all pictures of Himmler from display. But he seems to have been restored to his position shortly afterwards; at least he was functioning as usual later in the fall.

To counteract the decline in morale, the German leaders intensified their propaganda and sharpened police control. Propaganda had as its guiding slogan the difference between 1917 and 1942. In 1917, it was stated, the German nation was suffering from interior weakness and anemia at the top. Defeatism and a crippling fatalism were spreading; the German people lacked a will to victory. In 1942 the situation was different—they had acknowledged the war.

A telling argument was the outcome of the last world war. "Never again a 1918" was certainly the best propaganda slogan the National Socialists could have wished for. Further, they strengthened its effectiveness by pointing out that 1918 was child's play compared to what would now be in store for all Germans—without exception—should Germany be defeated.

The increased police control followed the usual lines: arrests, executions, espionage, etc. The German administration of law was remodeled by the appointment of Dr. Thierack as Reichsminister of Justice, with the Party fanatic Rothenberger as Assistant Minister. They were to be responsible for the enforcement of the consistent and total National Socialistic revolution.

It was generally expected that this task would be entrusted to Governor General Frank. But however faithful a National Socialist he may have been, he had nevertheless opposed despotic police rule. He had even had the audacity to give public lectures in which he had emphasized that the totalitarian system in itself was compatible with security under the law, and that the National Socialist state must not degenerate into a plain police state. The deafening applause which greeted Dr. Frank must have been a source of vexation to Himmler; and in any case, Frank didn't become Minister of Justice.

The active member in the Thierack-Rothenberger constellation was the latter. This fact became apparent to all the foreign press representatives in Berlin the day after the appointment. Dr. Rothenberger in Nazi uniform delivered a lecture to the journalists in which he said in almost so many words that he was the originator of the whole thing, that the changes had been made in accordance with a memorandum from Rothenberger to Hitler, and that he himself had drafted the powers of the Reichsminister of Justice. We heard that one result of this lecture was a scene between the Minister of Justice and his assistant, in which the chief used some pungent words.

A few weeks later, however, the foreign press in a body was made to feel that the atmosphere had become more tense. On September 7, it was announced that Dr. Brauweiler of the Propaganda Ministry wished to hold a special conference that afternoon with all foreign correspondents in Berlin. As there had already been rumors that stern restrictions were to be enforced on us, it was with forebodings of evil that we started out for the conference. These forebodings proved to be well founded. Dr. Brauweiler announced that the Reichs press chief had given out "new directions" for foreign correspondents in Berlin, because, according to the Reichs government, dispatches from foreign correspondents during the past few months had been harmful to the prosecution of the war. Two offenders, in fact, had already been expelled. The Reichs press chief, said Dr. Brauweiler, wanted to save the correspondents from any impairment in their working conditions—something that would necessarily result if censorship were imposed. "Untrammeled reporting" could be maintained only if regulations in force were "completed."

This "completion" brought about a radical change in the character of our work. All dispatches in the future had to be composed "in accordance with an authoritative source," and nothing but strictly official material would be regarded as authoritative. In other cases two copies of a written translation were to be turned over to a special control office which was to be established in the Propaganda Ministry. Newspapers and magazines in the territory of the Reich (including the Government General and the Protectorate) could, of course, be quoted, but they were not considered as authoritative sources.

The most interesting regulation, perhaps, was that all articles on foreign policy must have as *Tenor und Tendenz* what was said at the press conference in the Foreign Office. In this we could all see an attempt by First-class Envoy Schmidt to force us to express his opinions. The manner in which he leaned back in his chair with a triumphant smile was sufficient to dispel any doubt about his intentions. So far he had had the daily experience of seeing not one single line of all his tedious propaganda lectures reproduced in our papers.

Finally, Dr. Brauweiler emphasized that any deviation from the new regulations would be punished automatically by expulsion, and that the entire weight of the law would descend upon anyone violating the clauses against treason. One peculiarity of the Third Reich is that a foreigner, according to its laws, can commit treason against Germany. Even to inform our chief editors about these new regulations was an infringement of this law. The editors-in-chief of foreign papers, and of course their readers, were to be left in the dark regarding the reasons for the sudden change in the articles from Berlin. That was the German way of "avoiding the establishment of censorship." There was not a single journalist, of course, who did not by some means or other notify his chief of the new regulations. All the neutral correspondents were greatly distressed, and many, among them myself, thought of asking to be called home. We all felt that it would no longer be possible to come anywhere near giving an honest picture of what happened in Berlin. But our newspapers still wanted us to remain, at least for the time being. Brunhoff, in charge of the Scandinavian correspondents at the Foreign Office, also advised us to bide our time and suggested that perhaps it would in practice not be too bad. He was right, because in a few weeks we began to understand that the new regulations to a large extent were going to exist only on paper—consequently, nobody in the Propaganda Ministry knew where the new control office was situated, and when a stubborn colleague went to the Ministry and made up his mind that he was going to get a look at the new censors, he discovered that there was nobody but the old, familiar mail censor, who had merely been given a little more authority.

In practice the new regulations had the effect of making our work more difficult in various ways. We were no longer permitted to quote from foreign radio stations or to use the German newspapers in occupied countries. That was a handicap in our work, and the reports which we sent after September 15, when the new regulations went into force, were of a definitely lower quality than previously, but there was nothing to be done about it. Moreover, we lost another good news source when the German press, at the same time, was given a strict warning not to publish anything that could be classified as "malicious commentary."

The new regulations for journalists were accompanied by strict measures against other foreigners. The Foreign Ministry suddenly announced to the diplomatic corps that foreign diplomats were not to go farther than 50 kilometers from Berlin without the permission of the Foreign Office. Even foreign businessmen came to feel the increasing coolness of the atmosphere.

Hitler's speech for the Winter Help drive on September 30 had this time been awaited with greater suspense than usual. For that matter, people weren't sure to the very last that he would actually talk.

The meeting itself was like all the others. In a steady stream the leaders came in and were applauded by the hand-picked audience. Then suddenly arose a hurricane of applause—at Goebbels' entrance. We stretched our necks and wondered what in the world had happened—had Goebbels suddenly become popular? But in a moment the situation became clear; crafty Joseph had made the smart move of having Field Marshal Rommel with him. Rommel, after his unfortunate experience at El Alamein—which the German public was not yet acquainted with—was in Germany for a rest.

The two gentlemen went forward to the places of honor with terrific applause from the assemblage, which showed clearly whom they were cheering by calling "Rommel! Rommel!"

After a speech by Goebbels, whose only interesting point was a categorical denial that any leading National Socialists were sick, dead, etc., the Badenweiler march was played and Hitler appeared. He was surrounded by his staff and was accompanied by SS Chief Himmler among others. "So he's back again," people said to themselves, thinking of the rumors that Himmler was in disgrace. There was an impressive scene on the platform when the Führer greeted Rommel, who then sat down beside Himmler. "Rommel is well guarded," one of my Swiss colleagues whispered.

Hitler began with his usual ironical effusions about Prime Minister Churchill, and continued with a short review of the summer in Russia. The significance of the advance to the Volga was especially pointed out, and in this connection Hitler promised to take Stalingrad.

The British air attacks would be answered in their time, Hitler said, and he ended his short talk with a particularly urgent appeal to those at home to do their utmost. Every sabotage of the common good was to be mercilessly punished. All Germans should work together for victory or they would incur extermination together.

This last was a strong notice to those who thought that by some means they could keep aloof from National Socialism. The speech otherwise was given without the usual sparkle, and left an unsatisfactory impression on the listeners. This was stated openly during the following days by Germans of different categories.

The stage management was, however, in itself good, and a special effect was obtained by the singing in unison of *"Das Lied von Feldzug im Osten"* (The Song of the Eastern Campaign). The text was passed out before the meeting to all the participants, and the melody was extremely moving.

> *Wir standen für Deutschland auf Posten*
> *und hielten die grosse Wacht.—*
> *Nun hebt sich die Sonne im Osten*
> *und ruft die Millionen zur Schlacht.*

(We have been standing guard over Germany, keeping the eternal watch. Now at last the sun is rising in the East, calling millions into battle.)

A few days later came an amplification of Hitler's speech, when Goering spoke on October 6 to the German farmers. The Reichsmarshal in the beginning promised to give a clear exposition of the nation's condition with respect to food and other living needs. The situation during the past year was painted in gloomy colors. One could talk calmly now, however, of what had happened in the past, as this had been overcome and would not be repeated. We have conquered the most fertile districts in Europe, said Goering (obviously referring to the Kuban), and we are extracting the maximum from the occupied countries. The enemy is advised that if there is to be hunger anywhere, then at least it will not be in Germany.

With the public's applause, Goering then declared that he had ordered that the meat ration was to be raised by 50 grams a week in the districts under air attack, that he hoped to be able to give the German people as a Christmas present an extra portion of meat, flour and other essentials, and that from then on every German soldier on leave, as soon as he came to the German border, was to be given a package of provisions to take with him to his relatives.

Now naturally the enemy will say, continued Goering, that this is an attempt to get the German people to take the coming winter with fortitude—that it is a sop thrown to them. This sop will, however, be continued during the whole war and will become even greater. "I should consider it a crime for me today to predict anything for the German people that I am not certain I can fulfill. From today on the situation will become better and better."

An increase in bread and meat rations had already been announced, to begin October 19—the bread ration to the amount that had been in effect the preceding April; that is, to 5 pounds and meat to ¾ pound. The additional increases which Goering announced had been made despite strong protests from the person primarily responsible, Secretary of Agriculture Backe. The increases were considered, however, to be obviously necessary to improve the morale of the people, and besides there was reason to believe one could look for help to the farming districts in the East. Another measure taken even before Goering's speech was a great increase in disability allowances, widows' pensions and state contributions to the welfare of discharged soldiers, all of which had been shockingly low.

It soon became evident that Goering's speech and the measures taken to support it had produced a decidedly more cheerful state of mind. It wasn't so much that Germans now had a little more to eat, and some of them had more money to spend; it was rather that they had accepted Goering's thesis. The bottom must really have been reached, they said to themselves, or Goering wouldn't have been allowed to say so. Our leaders couldn't afford to make fools of themselves in public. . . . As late as January, I still heard favorable references to Goering's speech.

Germany's Allies, the Occupied Countries and the Neutrals

Relations between Germany and her allies during the summer and fall of 1942 were generally unchanged. It could be said, of course, and rightly, that the concealed opposition between the Germans and the Italians became sharper when the Italian troops gave such a poor account of themselves during Rommel's offensive in September. But the Germans and their foremost confederates had never loved each other, and the increased coolness between them was nothing of great moment.

German-Hungarian relations had become worse earlier, and this development continued during the second half of the year 1942. The German pressure became so strong, however, that the government in Budapest found it necessary to send stronger forces to Russia. They suffered, therefore, great losses. On Hungary's national day, August 20, Stephen Horthy, son and deputy of the Hungarian leader, died in the East under circumstances that have not yet been made clear. Probably his car was in an accident, but he was known to have had Anglo-Saxon sympathies, and that was enough to place the blame on the Gestapo.

At the Youth Congress in the beginning of the fall of 1942, Vienna saw a typical German-Hungarian incident. The Germans heard that the Hungarian youth leader General Béldy, chief of the largest youth organization in Hungary, had prepared a speech to the effect that Hungarian education was founded upon three factors: family, religion and patriotism. The German leaders requested that the word "religion" be deleted. General Béldy bluntly refused, and when the Italians and the Spaniards learned this they declared, with the support of the Finns and the Dutch, that they would not speak unless religion received its tribute. The German leaders then hit upon the ingenious idea of letting everyone speak in his mother tongue—the reports in the German newspapers could then be properly expurgated.

Germany's relations with the occupied countries grew increasingly bad during the summer and fall of 1942. There were serious disturbances in Norway, Holland, Belgium and France, although the German public at home heard almost nothing about them. All news of this sort was stopped at the German border.

Through a speech in early August by the acting Reichscommissar in Holland, Schmidt, it became known that representatives of the Evangelical and Catholic Churches in Holland had turned to the Military Commander, General Christiansen, and asked for a better treatment of the Dutch Jews, who were being taken eastward in increasing numbers. Schmidt stated, however, that the request would only stiffen the policy against the Jews. As the Dutch themselves were too softhearted, Germany had taken matters into her own hands, he said. Interestingly enough, he refuted the rumors concerning plans to move 3,000,000 Hollanders to the Baltic, declaring that the intention was to let 3,000 to 30,000 "pioneers" take over the management of certain farms and estates.

The situation in Holland grew more and more critical. At the beginning of August the Military Commander warned the Dutch against "favoring the enemy." The official warning awakened some suspicion and was generally linked with invasion rumors. The coastal provinces were evacuated about this time and new defense works constructed. Measures were taken to make communication between the Dutch people and London more difficult. One day, for example, all pigeons were ordered slaughtered and their feet with the rings on given to the mayors.

Some weeks later, German plans for the future of Holland suddenly came into the limelight. The leader of the Dutch Nazi party, Mussert, made a speech in Lunteren, directed against the SS, which plainly intended to make Holland a part of the German Reich under the slogan "Home to the Reich," Mussert declared himself instead as a supporter of the idea of a German alliance in which the chief of state in Holland must have the confidence of the Führer. Scandinavia would also enter the alliance. In a later statement, he explained that Holland had to choose between maintaining its present distrust of the Reich, in which case it would become only a colony after the victory of National Socialism, and freely and intentionally placing itself on Germany's side.

The speech caused much anger within the SS, the dominating faction of which did not acknowledge Holland as a free nation. But Mussert obviously had approval in higher quarters, where they understood the utter uselessness of inviting the stubborn Hollanders to come "Home to the Reich."

In Belgium, the Germans were deporting Jews to the East in mounting numbers. By the middle of August, the University of Brussels was closed, and at the end of the month, the opposition was dealt a death blow with the closing of *Caisse d'Avances et de Prêts*. This institution had been founded originally to repair war damages and grant loans to victims of the occupation. It had developed, however, into a supporting organization for the opposition, and the Germans accused its leaders of having put 40 million francs at the disposal of strikers.

The atmosphere in Belgium became increasingly embittered. This was especially true during the fall when the Germans began to deport workers to Germany. Again, when the German authorities in large numbers took to appearing as buyers on the black market, there was furious indignation. The German purchases on the black market increased the prices and diminished the supply of goods. Incidentally, the black market was almost the normal food market in Belgium.

During the latter half of 1942, the Germans began to take a more cautious attitude toward the neutrals. Turkey had of course always been strong enough to command courteous treatment, but it seemed now to be withdrawing farther and farther from Germany. Even Spain showed tendencies of pursuing a new course, and this caused anxiety. As a real blow came Franco's decision on September 3 to remove his brother-in-law, Serrano Suñer, from the post of Foreign Minister, and to put in his place the monarchistic Count Jordana.

Sweden was virtually unmentioned in the German press during this interval, but it was discussed all the more intensely at the private *Stammtisch* of Dr. Schmidt. An official statement was made after the Swedish elections. The increase in the Communist votes was greeted by Schmidt with poorly hidden delight, and was called "a European concern," something that Germany had accurately predicted. This naturally brought to mind rumors about the secret order to Swedish Nazis to vote with the Communists.

If Berlin generally was polite to Sweden, its tone to Switzerland during the fall of 1942 was noticeably sharp. On October 15, Schmidt named a great many Swiss newspapers which had been especially offensive, and Germany demanded "that neutrality should be maintained" in the Swiss press. One of the papers singled out, *Weltwoche*, had published an article in which Sweden's king and people were hailed in an ostentatiously anti-German manner. The Swiss government, however, calmly dismissed the German accusations.

Before the Invasion of North Africa

Hitler had explicitly promised that Stalingrad would be taken. During the first days of October, reports detailed the immense losses suffered by Germany. In spite of this fact, the amazement in press circles was great when it was officially announced that the Germans had ceased their furious onslaught and now relied entirely upon their artillery. It was reported quite plainly that this was done to avoid a new Verdun. The intention was to shell Stalingrad to ruins.

A week later, the Germans managed to take the Dzherzhinsky buildings, and we heard once more that the final battle was in progress. After a couple of days, it was declared that 24 of the 26 wards in Stalingrad were in German hands and that the Russian position was hopeless. But the days passed by and the expected announcement—that Stalingrad had fallen—could not be made. The autumn rain came pouring down, and the days grew colder. The change in the weather was especially calamitous to the German soldiers at Stalingrad, as they had no regular shelter and had to endure water rising in the fox-holes.

The rest of the eastern front was comparatively calm. During the fall much had been said about an impending offensive against Leningrad. Heavy artillery had been brought up and all preparations seemed completed. However, week after week passed, and no offensive started. Finally the heavy guns were moved back. It was later reported that it had been impossible to start the offensive because the necessary air support was lacking.

Other problems appeared. In the papers, the possibility of an Allied invasion was once more taken up for discussion in October. The British and the Americans made vague hints in which the African west coast played a prominent role. It seemed as if the Germans were taking these hints in their stride, but the French made preparations to frustrate an Allied attempt to take Dakar. German specialists stressed that their submarines would certainly be able to report in ample time each surprise maneuver from the Allied side. They would also know how to check such a maneuver. In other respects, the Germans were sure that the French would put up an effective resistance. Of course, no one in Berlin wanted to admit that Germany had taken a new attitude, passively calculating where the Allies would put in their blow. On the contrary, it was made plain from time to time that one could expect Germany to launch an attack in the West. "In the reasonably near future," said the *Dienst aus Deutschland*, "all the conditions will be present for a showdown with England." Threats were also made to cancel the Geneva Convention and begin an utterly brutal type of warfare against England by way of reprisal. But for the time being these were empty words. The only real threat came from the German submarines, and the importance even of these was overrated, both by the German leaders and the German public.

In the light of what happened later, it is surprising that the Germans did not take any steps to prevent an Allied attack against Morocco and Algiers. The truth is that this action came as a surprise and that the situation would have been quite different if the Allies had aimed their blow at French West Africa.

On October 24, the British began their expected attack at El Alamein. Forebodings were many. The Germans had received reports that concentration of British power had been going on. On the following day, it was obvious that the British attack had been made in considerable strength and that the enemy's air power was greater than had been expected. The battle increased in intensity and soon reached a fury hitherto unparalleled in North Africa. It went on day after day, as apparently the British wanted to wear out the German resources, relying upon their greater supplies and shorter lines of communication.

As early as October 24, there were rumors that Rommel was not present in North Africa, despite official statements. Only much later was this confirmed. When the battle took a serious turn, the Field Marshal arrived by plane and resumed the command. In spite of heroic efforts, he did not succeed in halting the English drive, and on November 4, he had to withdraw from the El Alamein position.

In international circles in Berlin, people asked themselves eagerly what could possibly have been the reason for the defeat—because it was obvious after some days that it was a defeat. When eyewitnesses arrived in Germany, they declared with one voice that the sinking of some big tankers had caused an acute gasoline shortage. This forced the commander to put his forces on small trucks and drive westward, after destroying his tanks and supplies to keep them from falling into Allied hands. The sinkings were made by British submarines which suddenly appeared in the Mediterranean in much greater numbers than the Germans had expected. Besides this, the eyewitnesses made the usual comments to the effect that the Italians had betrayed them. "They have gone over by the carload," said a German flyer some months later.

Another cause of the disaster was the German military command that functioned during Rommel's absence. Obviously it had not been first-class, or else it would have ordered retreat much earlier and avoided clinging to the far-advanced El Alamein position.

It was evident that the British had learned their lesson and that they were extraordinarily well prepared when they went into action. The British command functioned in a manner which made the memory of Tobruk fade away. Perhaps Rommel had even met his equal? General Montgomery knew his business, there was no question about that.

On the other hand, one could not help but respect the tactics used by Rommel. The retreat could not be effected it is true without sacrifices of rear guards detached from the main forces, but the British intention of annihilating Rommel was not fulfilled.

Responsible circles in Berlin were certainly fully aware of the serious defeat at El Alamein, but they tried to conceal this fact as much as possible in their propaganda. The hopes were that Rommel once more would be able to turn the tide. Therefore the Wilhelmstrasse on November 5 announced that it was only a British initial success lacking all importance, and that Rommel had taken with him the heavy artillery and the anti-aircraft guns.

From the jubilation in England it was nonetheless easy to conclude that the attack at El Alamein was part of a greater offensive. Nobody knew what it meant, but the answer was not long in coming.

VII

THE DOUBLE THRUST AGAINST THE AXIS

The Landing in North Africa

On November 7, a great Allied convoy was reported on its way into the Mediterranean. The report came from the Axis watchdogs at La Linea in Spain. Seen from the perspective of Berlin, the news did not seem of any great moment.

But November 8 told another story. I shall never forget the utter stupefaction with which Berlin received the published report of the Allied landing. Amazement was as great in the Wilhelmstrasse as among diplomats and journalists. Churchill and Roosevelt had certainly done a masterly job of camouflaging their intentions. Stalin's attack on the Allies for not creating a second front, the discussions on the subject of shipping losses in which prominent Englishmen were quoted as having admitted that these losses threatened to endanger the outcome of the war, the hints of an attack on Dakar and finally Eisenhower's trip to the United States— all this fitted beautifully in the general picture. In his last speech, Hitler had asked contemptuously what the idiotic Allies thought they were up to. Here was the answer.

He heard the news under circumstances that must have made it still more disquieting to a man of his type. On the night of November 7, Hitler had started out from his headquarters in East Prussia by special train to Munich, where he was due to speak at the anniversary of the Beer Cellar Putsch. The train's radio was not working. In order that Hitler should be informed of what had happened before his arrival, the German High Command sent word to Prague, through which city they presumed the train would have to pass during the night. By some error, however, it seems that the train was directed over another line, with the result that Hitler learned the news only in the morning, just before his arrival in Munich.

This did not prevent the Führer from delivering his speech, but

137

it is understandable that what he said was somewhat confused. It cannot have been pleasant for him to be forced to appear in public immediately after his enemies had made a bold stroke which had changed the entire situation overnight. It was significant that for once Hitler did not use one of his customary phrases: he did not say that what had happened "was not unexpected."

As can easily be imagined, the Wilhelmstrasse raged over "the brutal crime." On Monday morning both the Ministry of Propaganda and the Foreign Office were in a state bordering on panic. Telephones rang, messengers rushed in and out, journalists and officials crowded the conference hall. The Germans looked gloomy. After some time, Dr. Schmidt appeared. For once he seemed to have lost his usual poise. Heatedly he declared that the Wilhelmstrasse viewed the events with "icy and supreme calm," and that the German leaders would certainly act with promptness and determination. This he expressly asked us to regard as an official statement. Then he talked about the French, stating that they were resisting the invaders and that France "from a moral standpoint was drawn into the solidarity of the European countries." In his opinion it was still too early to make any announcement concerning Axis aid to France.

Finally, Schmidt commented ironically on the Allied refusal to tackle the steel line running from the North Cape to Biarritz, choosing instead a softer spot. Behind the irony was concealed something which others in the Wilhelmstrasse did not hide in those days—a raging fury over the fact that the British and Americans had flanked the Atlantic Wall which the Germans had built with so much toil and trouble. The thrust was aimed at the Axis from the South, hitting primarily Italy, about whose power of resistance no German harbored any illusion.

At the same time, it was strange to witness the obvious illusions concerning France. On November 10, it was stressed that France could put up a successful resistance. Private conversations made it fairly evident that the Germans did not fully realize, or wish to realize, that the France which could have put up resistance no longer existed. Even if the French at this time did not play a role worthy of their history, they did manage to do one thing— deceive the Germans. The attitude of the majority of the French must have been known by that time in Germany, but the Germans refused to believe that Admiral Darlan, known as anti-British, had gone over to the enemy. The same opinion was held about other

Frenchmen who had done a good job of concealing their sympathies. Often during those days I, too, had the impression that the Germans were doing some wishful thinking. They simply refused to admit that they had been duped.

Militarily, the German leaders did what they could. They dispatched planes and submarines to the Mediterranean, and sent some minor forces by air to defend Tunisia, in an attempt to salvage something at least. The Italians were raging mad. They told their partners that if the Italian claims at the armistice negotiations with France in June 1940 had been accepted, Tunisia would now be in Axis hands, and the whole Allied action rendered impossible.

The Axis achieved some results in their attacks on Allied ship concentrations. The Allied losses, however, were relatively small, since the whole fantastic enterprise was well under way and the landing effected before Berlin and Rome had realized what the Allies were up to. This was the German submarines' greatest fiasco, and an emphatic refutation of the opinion common in Germany and Italy that their submarines had taken such heavy toll of Allied shipping that the remaining tonnage was too small for a major undertaking. To a certain degree, the Allies had compensated for their limited shipping space by careful reduction of transported matériel—for example, by shipping dried instead of fresh eggs and vegetables.

From the German point of view it was logical for German and Italian troops to take possession of the unoccupied zone in France. This was accomplished on November 11, and the Germans tried to carry out the job in such a way as not to render mutual understanding between France and the Reich impossible. Relying on this understanding, they immediately declared that they regarded Marshal Pétain's protest as a formal gesture. It was noteworthy, on the other hand, that they did intend to leave Toulon alone. Maybe they wanted to support Laval, though as a matter of fact Italo-German troops controlled French harbors.

Laval had had to face a none too enviable situation. In Munich Hitler, using the most insulting language, had informed him that German and Italian troops had marched into the Vichy zone and that all Italian aspirations were to be fulfilled. France could expect to cede Corsica, Nice, Savoy and Tunis. Italy would thus be rewarded for declaring war on Britain and the United States. Nobody knows what Laval answered to this. Perhaps he was already wondering if it paid to collaborate. The Germans evidently still had some illusions concerning Laval himself. A well-known specialist on France in the Wilhelmstrasse solemnly explained to a journalist that Laval in his opinion had the French people 100 per cent behind him.

The Germans had never lost hope of making France their new ally. On November 17, the Wilhelmstrasse announced that the actions taken by the French Government signified that "the Axis and France are resolved to organize a joint defense."

The reorganization of the French Government, announced shortly after the Allied attack on North Africa, was viewed in Berlin with interest hardly in proportion to its importance. With suitable modesty, Dr. Schmidt declared that this affair was naturally none of Germany's business. "It is not our method," he said, "to meddle with the formation of government in other countries. That is each country's own sacred privilege." Schmidt made this statement with an air of solemnity and even pathos. The faces of his listeners were worth watching.

After some time the Wilhelmstrasse decided how the French problem should be treated. They continued to pay court to Marshal Pétain, gave their confidence to Laval and showed their contempt for all who had "betrayed France," above all for Darlan. They thus went on maintaining the pretense that an official France still existed as a sovereign state, even with the modifications arising out of the armistice. They continued to pretend that this France could be used in the game against the "traitors." Furthermore, the Nazis speculated on the conflicts between the British and the Americans in North Africa, noting with open relish every sign in this direction, and siding with America. Such malignant delight as that displayed by the Germans when Willkie made his criticism of the British Empire and when his statements in *Time* and *Life* became known, I for one have seldom witnessed. Privately one heard what was behind this delight: "If we perish, at any rate it won't be the British who get the credit for defeating us." This attitude may be regarded as one of the leading motives behind the Nazis' war policy. Hitler and his advisers could face an American or Russian victory with comparatively light hearts, but a British victory would drain the cup of bitterness to the dregs. This might seem an unrealistic political attitude, but Nazi Germany has departed a long way from realistic political attitudes. The Nazis look upon England today as they once looked upon their political adversaries at home.

The attitude toward France remained unchanged even after
Hitler and Mussolini decided to complete the occupation and have
their troops march into Toulon. Of peculiar interest is the letter
written by Hitler to Pétain and made public on the day of the
occupation of that city. It was a strange document, significant for
a future analysis of Hitler's personality. The letter was written
as if intended for Germans instead of Frenchmen; it began with
a long history of Hitler's lengthy and unbroken peace strivings
and his efforts to create friendly relations with France. There were
no arguments that could possibly make any impression upon
Frenchmen. In the Wilhelmstrasse, it was stressed that this letter
showed how magnanimously the Führer had treated Germany's
hereditary enemy. "That," a grim colleague whispered to me during the press conference, "is the Nazi idea of magnanimity."

From a military standpoint, the occupation of southern France
played a minor role. It could not be compared to the Allied conquest of Morocco, Algiers and French West Africa. If a real
counterattack was to be planned, the only choice was between
Turkey and Spain. These two states came into the limelight in due
time.

On November 12, German troops had reached the French-
Spanish border. During the following days, unusually strong troop
concentrations were made in this region. The Spaniards in Berlin
grew uneasy and declared that they foresaw an invasion of Spain
itself and an Italian occupation of the Balearic Islands. Major
Sommerfeldt made some statements, hinting that something of
that kind was probable. On November 13 and 14, he said that
within a week the state of affairs "would be totally changed" and
that "quite a new situation" would have to be dealt with. Late in
the evening of November 14, an official declared in private that
the invasion of Spain, along the whole border, was only a matter
of hours. The reliability of this statement has been verified by
other spokesmen. At the last minute the order was canceled, nobody knows why. It has been said that General Franco let it be
known that Spain would fight under any circumstances, even if
he did not take command.

Immediately after November 15, it was fascinating to observe
how the interest moved from the western to the eastern Mediterranean, from Spain to Turkey. The cause of this change we
cannot judge. From November 20 on, the Turks in Berlin prepared themselves for the worst. They did not conceal the fact that

they expected a German invasion before long; to give weight to their assumption they cited troop concentrations in Bulgaria, on the Aegean Islands, which they said were being reinforced by air at night, and in Greece. They also pointed to the anti-Turkish agitation in Bulgaria and to the attitude in that country as a whole. There was, however, one well-informed Turk who told me that many factors would prevent the Germans from taking such a step. At a moment like this, it could only be a measure of desperation, not something that could decisively change the fortunes of war. Rommel's position at the time did not encourage hopes of a pincers movement against the Near East.

Field Marshal Rommel held an unenviable position. He had lost both matériel and men and, up to the end of November, he had received only one division of reinforcements other than the garrisons he had been able to free during his retreat. He had continually called for help, and on one occasion was said to have asked for 16 divisions to turn the tide to the advantage of the Axis.

Before we learned that the Germans and Italians would be able to hold the bridgehead in Tunisia, Rommel's position looked almost catastrophic. A "Dunkirk" from Tripoli would have resulted in disastrous losses.

Rommel managed, we know, to carry through the retreat by fighting delaying actions. But his position was precarious, and it was announced on November 13 that Tobruk had been evacuated. The Ministry of Propaganda in Berlin was anxious to point out that the evacuation was "voluntary" and not caused by British pressure. All supplies and matériel were either brought out of Tobruk or destroyed, but there is no denying that reports of the evacuation were evil tidings for the Germans. Although the German press began to make acknowledgments of the British victory, Major Sommerfeldt had instructions to keep up appearances as long as possible. On November 15, he announced that Rommel had reached his "assembly positions," which had been prepared long in advance and were equal in strength to those at El Alamein. On the following day, however, he had to acknowledge the retreat. Our military commentator was obviously not feeling too comfortable.

On November 15 came Berlin's announcement that Italian and German troops had landed in Tunisia. The public had known this for some time. The moment the acknowledgment was made, both the official spokesmen and the newspapers connected the battles in Cyrenaica with those in Tunisia. That Rommel did not defend Tobruk was perfectly natural, claimed Major Sommerfeldt, for the simple reason that the Field Marshal had acquired an excellent supply base, Tunisia, from President Roosevelt.

The battles in Tunisia grew in violence, though so far both sides had only minor forces in the field. Clearly, both were devoting time and effort to getting themselves properly armed for a show-down. By early December the Germans had evidently received such strong reinforcements that the British and American attempts to drive them into the sea could be made very costly. The Allies had to gear themselves for a systematic conquest that in all likeli-hood would take a long time.

The Russian Attack

During November the eastern front had been relatively quiet, the German attacks having gradually petered out. As autumn moved into winter, a Russian offensive appeared as a possible pros-pect. Every now and then strong Russian troop concentrations were reported. The German position caused some anxiety.

In private, hardly any German military authorities concealed their belief that the German positions at the end of the great sum-mer offensive were about as bad as they could be. The Führer's determination "to make the impossible possible" was responsible for the German failure to take both Stalingrad and the Caucasus. In private conversations people were admitting quite frankly that if the Russians made a strong thrust, it would be impossible to hold the German lines north of the Caucasus. At first, this statement was generally combined with one of hope that the German offensive would be resumed in November and lead to the definite conquest of Stalingrad before the beginning of December. In such a case, the whole territory from Stalingrad along the Volga to Astrakhan, and from there along the coast of the Caspian Sea to Makhach, would fall into German hands. This would make a winter line fairly tenable. But once the people realized that German offensive strength had ebbed, they began considering the alternative of a general retreat to better positions.

To those capable of following Hitler's mentality so far as mili-tary matters were concerned, little doubt remained that he would choose the solution that had been possible the previous year—in other words, that he would mark time. Now, however, conditions were different.

The German public had no idea what to expect. The press emphasized only that Germany was far better prepared for a winter war than it had been in 1941, and that it could contemplate the immediate future with calm. Out of the 1941 improvisations a defense system emerged in 1942. Those territories in which communications had been disorganized during the preceding year now presented an entirely different picture. (Strangely enough, nothing was said of the territories conquered in 1942, where the communications were much weaker than in the districts conquered the year before.) Finally, the press laid emphasis on the Wehrmacht's good winter equipment, and on tactical improvements.

If Hitler had contemplated a retreat, he delayed it too long. On November 19, the Russians opened the attack. The starting points of that attack were at Stalingrad and the central Don. In Berlin, the Germans wrapped themselves in silence, but in the face of Russian reports of great victories, it was privately conceded that the enemy had had certain successes. At Stalingrad, this had been possible mainly because two Italian divisions suddenly fell back, thus exposing the flank of their German comrades. On November 23, it was officially announced in Berlin that the Russian offensive at Stalingrad was formidable and that certain "local breaches" had been made. Even in the Don bend, the Russians had achieved some gains. Here they had utilized the bridgehead on the south shore of the Don at Kletskaya, a town they had held in spite of all German efforts. Moreover, they skillfully took advantage of the fact that the Germans had been forced to entrust the defense of the central Don to Italians and Rumanians.

To make their own offensive simultaneous with the Allied action against North Africa, the Russians, according to Major Sommerfeldt, had obviously started it earlier than they had originally planned. The Russians, moreover, had been favored by the autumn fog, which had prevented the German air force from taking any strong action.

On the 24th, a most peculiarly worded announcement was made to the effect that the Russians, through ruthless expenditure of man power and matériel, had broken through at the Don, and that counteractions were in progress. The purpose of these actions was said to be not a restoration of the status quo, but an attempt to convert the battle into a Russian defeat. The phrase "counter-action," not "counteroffensive" was used. The Germans had thrown new weapons into the battle. Among these were a machine gun, or rather a combination of machine guns, with a firing capacity of 3,000 rounds a minute, and a tank equipped with a fire-thrower. But the anxiety in the Wilhelmstrasse, and in circles usually pretty well informed, was real. Could the Russians possibly be stopped? They were not at all sure. As one German militarist said to me: "The Rumanians run like rabbits, and the Italians are little better." Then he added that German troops had been rushed to the central Don to replace the yielding Italians and Rumanians. By the end of the month, the German lines were holding, and the atmosphere grew a little calmer.

Simultaneously, on the central front a terrific battle was in progress. A Russian force had smashed its way through the German lines at Kalinin and Toropets, but it was cut off and, so the Germans claimed, annihilated. At any rate the Germans were holding their positions in this sector with unexpected success. A month earlier, a noticeable nervousness had prevailed in Berlin because of Russian troop concentrations at these very places—Kalinin and Toropets. Privately, an officer had explained that the High Command had no idea where these troops had come from. He added that the line between Velikiye Luki and Rzhev was not an easy one to defend because it could be attacked from two directions.

Despite the favorable turn of events in the Kalinin sector, the general situation on the eastern front was extremely serious, mainly because of the great danger at Stalingrad. Even then some people believed that 22 divisions had been cut off and trapped.[1] Berliners were still waiting for the great German counteroffensive. But all through December the only word they heard concerning it was the announcement that the heavy winter reserves had been thrown in. "To attack or merely to hold the lines?" people wondered.

One condition necessary for a successful German counteroffensive was weather permitting full use of air power. On the other hand, it was not at all certain that the Luftwaffe had the strength to deal the Russians a crippling blow. It had diminished both in relative fighting importance and in quantitative strength. A prominent German scientist specializing in these questions estimated that at the end of October Russian airplane production was 1,200 planes

---

[1] *The two Russian armies attacking northwest and southwest of Stalingrad had actually met on November 23, surrounding the city.—Tr.*

a month, and the total Allied production at least 5,200, while the Germans could turn out only 1,600.

A medical factor also had a negative influence on the problem. Some months earlier, Germany's foremost surgeon, Professor Sauerbruch, mentioned privately that it was a mistake to believe that the German soldier could stand this winter better than the preceding one. The reduced and irregular diet, the physical strain among those who had been in Russia in 1941 and the lower quality of the youngest and oldest draft-age groups combined to produce the opposite effect. The physical weakening also tended to reduce the soldiers' spirit; with their nerves on edge, they were naturally more susceptible to the influence of the extreme cold.

Another unfortunate circumstance was the Germans' inability to cope with the partisans, who hampered every movement of the Wehrmacht and dislocated their communications. From Leningrad all the way down to the Caucasus, these partisans were mounting in number and growing in audacity. We also heard that the partisan war was shifting toward the West.

Hordes of partisans were now appearing in the Ukraine. In Poland, they were moving slowly westward. Even the Poles themselves, according to a report from Wartheland, had started partisan action. As for the Baltic countries, the partisans there were more of a menace to the Germans than anywhere else. Even small groups were in communication with the Russian command, and when their situation threatened to become untenable, Russian flyers were summoned by radio.

All reports agreed that German troops had found no way of dealing with the partisans. By day, these people were Russian laborers in German employ, while at night they were soldiers. To separate the sheep from the goats systematically was impossible; the goats were too numerous.

The New Political Situation—"The Apostasy of the Neutrals"

The Anglo-American landing in North Africa and the Russian thrust accelerated a development in foreign policy which had begun some time ago: the attitude of the neutrals toward Germany underwent a marked change. Even during its early stages, many people in these countries were convinced that Germany would lose the war. Moreover, the sympathies of an overwhelming majority were with the Allies. But the moment the British and Americans revealed that they were capable of more than standing up to the Axis, confidence in the Allies increased by leaps and bounds. Automatically, the neutrals adopted a more determined attitude toward Germany.

A similar tendency prevailed all over Europe. The Germans were at last beginning to realize to what an extent Nazi policy was responsible for German isolation and for the loss of all sympathy in both occupied and unoccupied countries. The battle for sympathy, which, according to Dr. Schmidt, Germany had won, had now been definitely lost.

"The apostasy of the neutrals"—which was how one prominent German characterized the situation—did not pass unheeded in Berlin. Even the neutral press felt this reaction. Berlin political circles were especially incensed with Swedish and Swiss newspapers, which were regarded as barometers of these nations' feelings. Berlin correspondents for these neutral papers, said the Germans, had assumed an insolent attitude. One day in early December, at a press conference, the most important Quisling editor—or Q-man, as we called him—raised the question of flights of British planes over Swiss territory. The question was a "plant," as everyone knew. As a rule, foreign correspondents ignored the fact that certain questions were "planted"; but on this occasion a Swiss colleague, the correspondent for Die Tat, lost his temper. His paper printed his dispatch as follows: "The correspondent for the Norwegian Government press (Quisling) asked today what was to be said about Allied flights over Swiss territory. The question, which apparently was welcome, gave First-class Envoy Schmidt the opportunity to make a statement." The following day Schmidt was in a fury. He read excerpts from the article, declaring that he protested "against such unparalleled defamation of the press conferences." Gundersen, the Norwegian who had started the whole business and who was known as "The Admiral," did his best to express his resentment. But Schmidt, who knew Gundersen's ability to cast ridicule upon himself by his bombastic tirades, cut him short with a curt: "The affair is dismissed."

Some days later, the Swedes felt the lash. Foreign correspondents in Germany, said Schmidt, had been availing themselves of "doubtful sources," rather than reporting what they heard at the press conferences. "Several correspondents," continued Schmidt, "seem to have considered it their most important duty to communicate with the American journalists in Stockholm, and supply the American legation there with material for its bulletins. Once more, I want to emphasize that the business of the press conference is to decide *Tenor und Tendenz*. I urge you to avail yourselves of the possibilities of the conferences, either by active participation, that is, by asking questions, or by passive participation, that is, by attending. You are not to follow the example of the Swedish journalists, who send only one man to the press conferences and expect him to pass on information to the rest." Dr. Schmidt ended with a threatening remark to the effect that Berlin could manage very well with fewer foreign correspondents.

It was true that the Swedes were conspicuous by their absence at Schmidt's conferences. The main reason was that, from a journalistic point of view, we very rarely benefited from them. Once the questions were over—and almost all questions of interest remained unanswered—the conference leaders would read out "received information." These readings, which could have been interesting, developed into endless propaganda sermons which many of us had neither the time nor the inclination to listen to six times a week.

The Swedish press and its Berlin representatives were not alone in causing annoyance to the ruling circles in Germany. There was some reason to distrust even the Swedish government. The mobilization in December raised the question: Against whom is Sweden mobilizing?

The changes in Spain, Portugal and Turkey were more serious for Germany than the fact that Switzerland and Sweden had assumed a more determined attitude. In Madrid, the Germans actually did obtain sympathy, and apparently influenced Spain's policy. During the late fall of 1942, however, the Spaniards began slowly but surely to free themselves from their ties with Berlin. "We have passed from being nonbelligerents to being neutrals," said our Spanish colleagues. Germany had been careless enough to work against the restoration of the Spanish monarch. As monarchist feelings grew in strength, popular opinion in Spain became more anti-German. When General Franco, in his speech on December 9, hinted at the possibility of re-establishing the monarchy, the German press carried not a word of it in their news columns.

Toward the end of the year, well-informed quarters in Berlin decided that Spain was lost. As for Portugal, it expressed its general anti-Communistic attitude and paid ostentatious tribute to England

—an important gesture which made it suddenly clear that Germany had nothing to hope from Salazar.

The invasion of Turkey, expected by many at the end of November, did not materialize. The German press repeatedly carried information from Ankara about Allied attempts to make capital out of the events in North Africa. Complaints were heard that the official Turkish telegraph bureau, *Agence d'Anatolie*, had sided with the Allies in its news coverage. The Turkish radio, too, had assumed a definitely pro-Allied flavor. The *Essener Nationalzeitung* lamented the Turkish government's failure to take action against these deviations from neutrality. These incidents, however, had no political consequences for the time being.

Of the partners, only Italy suffered directly from the Allied action in North Africa. Even in 1940, Italy had wanted to occupy Tunisia, but this move did not fit the German plans at that time. Now, suddenly, the Italians realized that the war was moving toward their immediate neighborhood. Hitler's abrupt announcement to France that all Italian aspirations on French territory would be fulfilled was possibly a form of apology on his part. At the same time, it was intended as an encouragement. The effect of the announcement in Italy naturally could not be so strong as it would have been earlier, since by this date there was general doubt about Germany's ability to fulfill her promises.

For some time influential quarters in Italy had been of the opinion that the country should "jump off the train." There were reports of demonstrations in favor of the royal family and peace. Toward the end of 1942, there were discussions as to the possibility of Italy's capitulation, but they offered no practical hints as to how Italy could extricate herself from the situation. Only the initiated knew what Myron Taylor, Roosevelt's special envoy to the Vatican, was empowered to discuss with the Pope. Whatever it was, he had to return, his task uncompleted.

Even if Italy were not ripe for a "peace offensive," it was significant that the country tried to disengage itself from the military undertakings which hitherto had been Mussolini's pride. Italian divisions left the Balkans in mounting numbers. Even in Dalmatian coastal fortifications—that is, in districts formerly Italian—Italian soldiers were replaced by Germans. Increasing nervousness was reported among the Italian forces in the Balkans. At a social gathering in Zagreb, the Italian military attaché was said to have declared that the war was lost and that Hitler would have to carry on alone. The Italian minister in the Croatian capital had his furniture and personal belongings sent home.

The Italian situation influenced Germany's remaining partners in southeastern Europe. Hungary prepared for the worst by strengthening her own defenses along the Carpathian border.

The situation in Croatia grew more and more confused. Ever since the summer of 1941, vast portions of the country had actually been controlled by the partisans—a term here applied to all the factions in revolt. Rivalry certainly existed between General Mikhailovitch's followers, who were regarded as regular troops under the command of the Yugoslav government, and the Communist insurgents, who looked to Moscow as their headquarters. Both groups co-operated, however, against the Ustachis in Axis pay.

The foundation of the revolt lay in the fact that 1,800,000 of the inhabitants of Croatia were Serbs. If the new Croatian regime had treated this section of the population with a little tact, they might, perhaps, have kept quiet for the time being. But the terror exerted against the Serbs, especially by the Croat irregulars, the Ustachis, gave everyone the feeling of unbearable tyranny. Nobody had anything to lose by armed resistance. The Serbs in masses took to the woods, where they set about organizing themselves. At first, they answered the Croatian terror with murder and plunder, but before long they established a more systematic warfare.

Towards the end of 1942, the partisans in Croatia were encouraged by the Allied landing and even more by Rommel's retreat. They were in constant communication with Cairo; at times they even ran a daily courier plane. Partisan tactics, no doubt improved by influences from outside, grew really dangerous to the Germans and their partners. Catholic churches and members of the clergy were unharmed; the partisans even tried to come to an agreement with them. Furthermore, the partisan administration in Croatia was organized within the controlled territories. A Croatian officer once told me that a priest, a friend of his, witnessed the occupation of his parish by the partisans. When the priest fell ill, the local chief of the partisans gave him a week's pass to Zagreb for treatment. Again, when members of the partisan command seized all the available medical supplies in a small town, they presented the pharmacies with genuine receipts, and returned a few days later to pay. Such reports spread like wildfire through the country.

One reason why partisan activities spread so rapidly in Croatia was the ambiguous attitude of the Italians. This also affected Serbia and Montenegro, where the partisans were far less active than in Croatia. The intentions of the Italians were never quite clear. It may be that they wanted to buy peace. In any case, the partisans received from them both weapons and supplies.

The chaos prevailing in Croatia was intensified by the fact that Pavelitch managed to offend the Catholic Church after the archbishop of Zagreb had delivered a sermon condemning the Nazi treatment of the Jews. There were rumors that Pavelitch would be forced to resign. The Germans, however, protected him stubbornly, as they have protected all their stooges. But Pavelitch was already a political corpse. Privately, people who pretended to be his staunchest supporters expressed their joy that Dr. Krnyevitch, a Croatian and a member of the Yugoslav government in London, was becoming more and more influential.

In Rumania, the Allied landing in Africa came as a serious blow to the pro-German faction. In that country the German influence had been far stronger than in Hungary, and Rumania had retained —and still does—a special position in Germany's favor. Even so, there were important forces whose great desire was to see Rumania freed from subservience to the Nazi regime.

The Slovaks, too, were growing suspicious. They were merely awaiting the opportunity to withdraw from the game when Germany's fate seemed to be sealed. In Finland, the Allied action had caused a government crisis. All down the line it had shaken confidence in Germany's invincibility and seriously undermined the whole Axis system of alliance. It had also strengthened the neutrals in their efforts to follow a political line of their own.

As for the Japanese, their pessimism had so increased that their diplomats were rumored to have advised the Germans to change their policy toward the people in occuped countries. They pointed, it was said, to the success Japan had achieved by appearing reasonably tolerant. The Germans answered this by showing concern over the long-awaited Japanese advance. They advised the Japanese, in turn, to make some agreement with China at any price, so that they could throw their forces against the Soviet Union. The German press showed great interest in the Japanese "peace offensives" toward Chungking, and unofficial Germans expressed disappointment over its failure.

New Hope for the Occupied Countries

November 8, 1942, is a day occupied countries in Europe are not likely to forget. That day fanned the flame of resistance and was more than a hint that the hour of liberation was near. This impression was strengthened by news from the eastern front.

One occupied country was directly influenced—in fact, its entire situation was changed—by the Allied invasion. That country was France. In reality, "Vichy" broke down, losing all resources on which it had built its intermediate position between the Allies and the Germans. By Vichy's passivity during the critical days, the French lost their chance of rehabilitation. Some people have since insisted that Marshal Pétain, together with General Weygand, should have flown to North Africa and there taken up the fight on the side of their former allies. Actually, Weygand was seized by traitors before he had a chance to leave France. And so, with folded arms, Vichy witnessed the German occupation, and the newly organized French armistice army, *l'armée nouvelle*, had not the opportunity of firing a shot before it was dissolved.

It is, of course, dangerous to believe that the Germans did not realize that the whole pretense of co-operating with the Germans was a hoax. Nevertheless, some time elapsed before Berlin was convinced that Germany could not trust a single Frenchman—not even Laval. Even after they were convinced in theory, in practice it was to the German interest to play the game with "official France," and this was the line the Wilhelmstrasse chose. On November 21, Dr. Schmidt declared that Laval and Marshal Pétain "deserved the high esteem of every European patriot," but that the only people upon whom France and Laval could rely were the German and Italian generals. When it became clear that the Germans could not compel Laval to declare war on England and the United States, the official tone sharpened. Privately, the Wilhelmstrasse did not hide its bitterness over what it regarded as the unscrupulous manner in which the French had cheated the Germans, and the reputation of neither Pétain nor Laval remained untarnished in Berlin. A significant statement about Marshal Pétain, attributed to Schmidt, was quoted widely: "That old fool doesn't know up from down after nine o'clock in the evening."

The German press didn't take long to express its dissatisfaction. First the provincial press and then the Berlin newspapers sharply criticized the French attitude. Only energetic action, they said, could rouse the French people from their lethargy. Even Laval, they maintained, was surrounded by people bent on counteracting his influence. At the end of November, the *Westdeutscher Beobachter* reported that Darlan's treason had caused amazement in Germany because the Germans had a strong sense of honor and were accustomed to assume the same in others. "We looked upon Darlan," continued the paper, "as an officer traditionally anti-British. We imagined that as soon as he realized what the defeat meant, he would place himself in the service of the New Order." But in the eyes of the average German, a Frenchman is either a victim of prejudices or entirely blind. He may be pleasant and polite, but his word of honor counts for nothing. If he declares himself a collaborationist, he gives the impression that he is conferring a favor. No matter how convincingly Laval may speak, the average Frenchman does not believe a word he says. "In himself," the paper concluded, "Laval is no more a friend of Germany than is Pétain. He is simply cleverer."

On December 10, the organ of the German Foreign Office, the *Berliner Börsenzeitung*, stated that Pétain's favorite subject was "the eternal France" which had risen out of the ashes, but that the sober German observer could see only the ashes and no sign of the phoenix. According to this paper, the French military collapse had been followed by a moral disintegration which still had not reached its lowest ebb, and the French people were a formless mass with no will power whatever.

Some days later, another bombshell came from Joseph Berdolt, Vichy correspondent of the *Danziger Vorposten*. This man pictured the Vichy government as involved in surreptitious dealings with the British and Americans. He described how Darlan had been loaded down with suitcases when he left by plane, ostensibly to visit his sick son. Vichy, he said, had published bulletins about "heroic resistance," bulletins written and tucked away in drawers before the "defense" could have possibly started. The troops in Algiers had stayed in their quarters while their officers went down to the harbor to greet the Americans. Though Darlan was negotiating with the Allies, Berdolt maintained that on November 8 Pétain sent him a wire expressing his greatest confidence. Next day the Minister of Information in Vichy issued those "war reports" which had been tucked away in the drawers.

Despite all this, official Berlin continued to uphold the fiction that "the Vichy government" was a worthy partner in negotiations. Every imaginable judicial subtlety was employed to make it appear that the relations between France (i.e., Vichy) and Germany were still operating according to the armistice agreement. Correspondents noted that there was a tendency to treat the occupied zone with greater leniency. Nobody knows whether this tendency was caused by a sudden fear of the consequences of terror, or whether it could possibly have been related to protests from Japan.

Actually, this change of front was most apparent in the East. When the Lithuanian deputation arrived in Berlin in December, it was welcomed with kindness. As for the poor Poles, who had been treated worse than animals ever since 1939, they began to receive hints that maybe they were human beings after all. The first indication of less brutal treatment for the Poles came early in December, when bread rations were increased by 8 ounces a week. At the end of the month, a still more remarkable thing happened. Gauleiter Arthur Greiser made a speech in Poland in which he seemed to be announcing a new policy toward the Poles. He declared that they would have a chance to carry on "a materially safeguarded life" as wards of the German State (*Schutzangehörige des Deutschen Reiches*) if they loyally complied with the unconditional German claim of leadership. The Polish workers, claimed Greiser, are at their best and feel at their best when living under the inspiring leadership of the German people. The Poles, he continued, had been given a new social insurance, a new hospital system and two new sanitariums for tuberculosis. But the real sensation came when Greiser made public the formation of a Polish "Elite group" (*Verband der Leistungspolen*) consisting, as he said, of "some of the Poles willing to work." Members of this organization were to be allowed to carry a special badge entitling them to favor in purchasing and in dealing with officials.

Denmark, of course, suffered least. There Dr. Best continued to carry on his moderate occupation regime, and to everyone's surprise the new government did not include any representatives of the Nazis. In Holland, however, the pressure was undiminished. On November 21, it was announced that 15 Dutch saboteurs had been executed, and that in the future the Germans would hang such offenders. In December, the occupying forces gave greater power to the Dutch Nazi Party by making it more influential in the administration. Dr. Max Blokzijl, Mussert's propaganda chief, complained about the conservatism of the Dutch people. Workers, farmers and teachers, he said, are impossible to whip into shape. Only the young people know what the New Order means.

There were rumors in Norway that Quisling would be thrown out. With their Norwegian policy, the Germans were getting nowhere. Germany's representative, Reichscommissar Terboven, had managed to make himself so hated that not even the stiff and impossible Seyss-Inquart could compete with him.

From Alsace, some German nationals were expelled for bad behavior, and Gauleiter Wagner predicted even more stringent measures for Germans who acted irresponsibly. He urgently exhorted all Reichs Germans to set a good example in Alsace, and added that they had aroused annoyance because they behaved as if they lived in a conquered country, whereas all Alsatians had been conscripted into the German army.

It was clear from Wagner's statement that the Allied invasion had made an impression in Alsace. He reported that there were "fools who believed the Americans would come to Alsace." The *Strassburger Neueste Nachrichten* complained in December that unknown persons had begun scratching "1918" on the walls.

Efforts to Make a Separate Peace

The Allied invasion in North Africa and the Russian victories in the East brought with them a moral crisis in Germany of a much more serious kind than "the winter crisis" in 1941. I shall deal with this crisis later. Here it is sufficient to state that in November 1942, it was evident to a great number of Germans that their leaders, whose technical efficiency had been unchallenged, were showing themselves inferior to the Allies. Hitler, in spite of all his boasts, had been taken by surprise, and his Russian campaign had brought the German war machine into a critical position.

In early December appeared an announcement which was an omen to many a German. It was made known that the man who had been looked upon as the brain of the German army, Colonel General Halder, had been replaced as chief of the General Staff by another. The new chief, Zeitzler, was totally unknown, not only to the German public, but also to a majority of the officers; in January 1942, he had been only a colonel. How Hitler even found him is a mystery. When the picture of the new chief of the

General Staff, with his round and jolly face, was shown, more than one German came to the conclusion that a great deal of trouble must have been taken to find someone courageous enough to take the responsibility for Hitler's strategy after the resignation of the internationally known Halder. On January 31, 1942, Zeitzler was made major general, and after that, in rapid succession, colonel general, general, and finally chief of the General Staff. This was an unparalleled career for a man who only six months before had been a 47-year-old unknown colonel. Hardly a soul believed that General Zeitzler would dare to differ with the Supreme Commander on the question of tactics. The change therefore must have meant that Hitler intended to exert even more personal influence than hitherto, and this caused uneasiness even in faithful Party circles. Halder was not the only one to be relieved of duty. General Jodl, for a long time Hitler's personal counselor, also gave up the struggle.

Even before November 8, ruling circles in Berlin had obviously been aware of the seriousness of Germany's position. In October, Dr. Goebbels had called in a number of the top-ranking newspapermen and told them frankly that Germany had lost the war. "Only a miracle can save us," said Goebbels. Awareness of the actual situation was widespread. It grew increasingly difficult for officials to look unmoved while uttering well-known propaganda phrases before the foreign correspondents. Stories circulated about pessimistic pronouncements by high officials. At quite a large gathering, the wife of Reichsminister Funk was supposed to have said to Frau Frick: "The Führer is leading us headlong into disaster."—— "Yes," came the answer, "the man is insane."

The general impairment of the situation seems to have compelled the German leaders to make a number of serious attempts at establishing an acceptable peace. As a point of contact with the Western Powers, Spain was most often used, but without any apparent result. An effort was also made to open communication with the British. The British traitor, Amery, broadcast to England a typically German argument that only the United States could gain by an Allied victory. England, however, was not impressed.

During the whole Russo-German war, there has been an even flow of rumors about a separate peace between Germany and Russia. Mostly, they have shown signs of German wishful thinking, but in some cases there is reason to believe that the rumors were founded on more concrete evidence.

Thus, it is fairly certain that the Japanese, especially during the fall of 1942, tried to act as conciliators and establish a separate peace between the two countries. There was one basis from which to start: namely, that those two powers carried the heaviest burden of the war. The Germans pointed out to the Russians that the position of England and the United States would be uncomfortably strong if the two continental powers continued to wear each other out. It is probable that the Russians felt a certain appreciation of this argument. They were also able to share Hitler's often-expressed opinion that the Allies intentionally delayed the opening of a second front. The step was too long, however, from agreement on these two points to a definite break with the Allies.

Nor would it serve the German purpose if Russia, in accord with the Allies, agreed upon an armistice with Germany and then renewed the fight some months later when the German people had presumed that the war in the East was over. That would indeed be a hard blow for Hitler and one which would have serious repercussions, particularly inside Germany.

Be this as it may, the Germans believed that they could justify certain hopes during the late fall of 1942. The furlough cards given to the soldiers on the Russian front instructed the holders, in the event of an armistice, not to return to the front but to report elsewhere. There were also rumors that von Papen had met Molotoff and held a preliminary discussion. But it was soon clear that all efforts had failed.

Even so, there was still another alternative. After the initial Russian successes in November, I was told that one of the highest Party men had declared that if the situation in the East became hopeless, the Nazis would under no circumstances allow the British and Americans to win. This, according to the spokesman, was also Hitler's intention, and he referred to what the Führer had once said: "If I fall, I shall drag the whole world with me." This, they declared, would not be difficult. All Hitler had to do was to let the Russians enter Europe on a broad front.

When I asked how this could be done from the military point of view, I was told that it would be conceivable for Hitler to strengthen all fronts against the British and Americans, but weaken the eastern front and withdraw before Russian pressure. The psychological preparation for Bolshevism in Germany could be brought about by the discovery of an actual conservative plot against the Führer, followed by the execution of about 50,000 "traitors" among the bourgeoisie. Immediately, terror would break out and Bolshevism walk in. Hitler himself would naturally disappear, to die eventually on the eastern front. With the Führer out of the way the Leftists within the Party, led by Goebbels, would go over to Stalin, and before the German people had time to realize what had happened, the Russians would be in the heart of Europe.

I must admit the idea was a nightmare. The more one contemplated it, the more likely it appeared. One had to presuppose that Hitler and those who wanted to follow him on this road of despair would, until the last possible moment, camouflage their aims. But who, for that matter, could resist them? The wing-clipped German generals, who were already living under the strictest Gestapo supervision? I had to admit that, from a psychological point of view, nothing stood in the way of the idea. Goebbels' part would be just what one would expect him to play. As for Dr. Schmidt, wouldn't it be just like him, with the same cocksure haughtiness, to stand for a Bolshevized Germany under Stalin? It was easy enough to say that none of these gentlemen would survive the Bolshevist regime, that both the Russians and the Germans would see to that. But who could be absolutely sure? Who knows what the attitude of the Russians would be? Couldn't Stalin be counted on to give the more adaptable Nazis a chance? Could one imagine him refusing to accept what, in reality, would be a capitulation to *him*?

Among the lower functionaries within the Party, this idea was spreading. If the worst came to the worst, many of them were clearly counting on saving their skins by adopting the hammer and sickle. "We would be good Bolshevists," one of them told me. I do not doubt it.

Recent events, however, do not support this theory. Perhaps the whole thing was a bluff to scare the conservatives into continuing to fight for Hitler.

ᴨᴨᴨᴨᴨᴨᴨᴨ **VIII** ᴨᴨᴨᴨᴨᴨᴨᴨ

THE WINTER OF 1942-1943

The Catastrophe at Stalingrad

A GERMAN counteroffensive had been expected in the East, but instead it was the Russians who, after pausing in the middle of December, again took the initiative and directed a violent thrust against the German lines on the middle Don. A spokesman for the German High Command had to admit on December 21 that the Russians had made a breach 60 miles deep and 40 miles wide in the German positions. It would be closed off like a leak in a ship with watertight compartments, said Major Sommerfeldt; but despite the reassuring comments made by other persons in the Propaganda Ministry, it was quite clear that the situation had taken a sudden turn for the worse. The bad weather paralyzed air activity, and the great mass of armament on the Russian side could be flung without hindrance against the Germans, who were considerably inferior in strength.

On December 27, it was announced that the Germans and their allies had begun a counteroffensive. We heard during the next few days that they were gaining ground, but Major Sommerfeldt denied this story by implication, explaining that no important change had occurred. At the beginning of January 1943, the cold grew more intense and temperatures of 20 and 25 below zero were registered in the war zone. There was no let-up in the fighting. The Russians showed that they were familiar with the terrain, and they used the snowstorms as a screen behind which they brought forward their tanks. Their skirmish lines moved swiftly on snowshoes. Concern for Stalingrad increased in Germany. The offensive that the Germans themselves had started southwest of the city ended in a complete fiasco, and the great Russian advances made the majority suspect that General Paulus had in effect been cut off.

By crossing the Don above Rostov, the Russians had directly threatened the communication lines of the Caucasus army. Quietly during the first days of January the Germans began to withdraw on the southern front, although the only retreat they

admitted at the time was the evacuation of Elista. Since this was
the only important stronghold they had on the bleak Kalmuck
steppes, its surrender was a sign that the Germans had begun a
general retreat to the West and intended to leave Stalingrad to
its fate.

For a retreat of this sort to be successful, the German troops
on the lower Don would have to check the advance of the Russians
from the North, so that the hinge at Rostov would remain in
German possession. And so it did, for the time being, but the fact
remained that the Germans had been forced to withdraw southward and westward, that Stalingrad was cut off, and that the
retreat in the Caucasus continued so fast that no one could say
with any certainty whether or not the German troops would be
able to escape from the Russian grasp. Once more the Russian
offensive had revealed that Hitler had underestimated the strength
of his opponents, that the Russians could take full advantage of
the terrain, and that the weather continued to be Stalin's foremost
ally. It also revealed that Russian leaders were successfully using
tank tactics borrowed direct from the Germans.

Toward the end of January, interest in Berlin centered more and
more on the hopeless struggle that General Paulus and his troops
were waging in Stalingrad. His only contact with the outside world
was now by transport planes, which could still land on the constantly shrinking area within his defense lines. We heard that the
Russians by the end of January had thrown in 30 divisions against
Stalingrad. Inch by inch the Germans were pushed back to the city,
and block by block it was wrested from their hands. Arms, ammunition and food began to run low. Toward the end of the month,
the Russians seized the last airfield, and the only way to bring in
supplies was to drop them from low-flying planes. They fell into
Russian hands quite as often as they reached the defenders, but each
clip of cartridges was valuable and equally so was every loaf of
bread.

In Berlin we were told that the Russian losses were many times
greater than those of the Germans and that the delaying action by
General Paulus was worth while. But there were those who pointed
out that the Russian matériel was superior to what the Germans still
possessed at Stalingrad, and that Russian heavy arms must have had
greater effect on the defenders than the relatively light arms of the
latter could have on the attackers, distributed as they were over a
wide area.

It seemed that everybody in Germany was arguing about whether or not it had been necessary to keep the Paulus group at Stalingrad. The well-informed would have it that Paulus himself, Mannstein, Keitel and even the new chief of the General Staff, Zeitzler, had been opposed to the idea, but that Hitler in a burst of rage had ordered Paulus to hold out to the last man and see to it that he himself did not fall into the hands of the enemy. Early in January, Paulus had come by plane for a visit to Hitler's headquarters and had offered to bring home his encircled forces with a 50 per cent loss. Hitler refused to listen.

Many Germans, however, said that it had been necessary to sacrifice the Sixth Army in order to safeguard the retreat of the troops in the Caucasus, considering the general situation at the beginning of January. Still others answered that the Paulus group could have done still more to protect its comrades in the Caucasus if it had been allowed to retreat from Stalingrad intact and if it had been as well supplied with weapons as the rest of the German armies.

On January 26, Major Sommerfeldt told us that the Germans at Stalingrad were fighting without hope of escaping with their lives. The next day we learned that the remains of the Sixth Army were still among the ruins in a hell of blood and iron. It was in these last hopeless days that Paulus was made a field marshal. Apparently the Russians forced the final battle in order to announce the fall of the city on January 30, the tenth anniversary of Hitler's accession to power. Through exerting themselves to the utmost, however, a few smaller German groups managed to hold out until February 2, when "Cease firing" sounded at last. Paulus and eight other generals had been taken prisoner on January 31. We heard on good authority that Hitler gave vent to his rage when he learned that his newly promoted field marshal had fallen into Russian hands.

Moscow reported that 91,000 prisoners had been taken at Stalingrad from January 10 to February 2. The original strength of the German and Rumanian forces, according to the Russians, may have been 331,000 men and this figure was not much above the one I heard from well-informed German sources. We heard that the High Command was less disturbed by the loss of man power than it was by the loss of 60,000 trucks, which the Russians in the Stalingrad sector had destroyed or captured from November 19 until the fall of the city. All in all, the Germans are said to have lost 120,000 trucks in the East during this time, besides 7,000 tanks and 5,000 airplanes, transport planes included.

The effects of the defeat at Stalingrad were both military and political. They penetrated deep into Germany.

One of the military effects was that the greater part of the summer's conquests in the Caucasus had to be relinquished, the very ones that had been hailed with joy in Berlin. The German armies moved north and west of the Don, except for a smaller force that was ordered to hold a bridgehead on the Taman Peninsula in order to safeguard the Kerch Strait and therefore the Crimea. Incidentally, the fact that this bridgehead was held until the early fall of 1943 is among the most extraordinary performances of the German military forces. But besides losing Stalingrad and the Caucasus, the Germans also had to evacuate the greater part of the Donets basin. On February 14, both Voroshilovgrad and Kharkov fell, and well-informed persons in Berlin were forced to admit that the situation had taken another turn for the worse, since the Russians were massing all their available strength for a thrust to the Dnieper; nothing seemed to stop them. Even before the danger had reached its peak— and later it was described by a soldier correspondent as enormous —Hitler had apparently suffered a complete collapse. Field Marshal von Mannstein, one of Germany's foremost military experts, was now at the helm. He had the help of Colonel General Halder, who offered his services in the new situation. Both men seem to have ruled quite despotically until the middle of March, when we heard that Hitler had again assumed command of the army.

Very soon we saw the results of competent leadership. On February 20 came the first of a series of German counterthrusts that set the wheels turning in the opposite direction. While the Russians were slowly pushed back along the Donets, and while the German lines above the Sea of Azov were anchored on the Mius River, there were other decisive moves far to the North on the Moscow front. The Germans had a salient there projecting far northeastward to Rzhev, but the task of keeping it supplied had proved extremely difficult. It was now evacuated, but not before all buildings, roads, railroads and bridges had been destroyed and the population carried away.

On most of the front, the situation was now considerably more favorable for the Germans, although there was still a serious threat from the Russian forces around Kharkov. This was eliminated, however, by Mannstein's swift advance, and on March 12 Kharkov was recaptured. Everything had changed so quickly that Ritter von

Schramm, the German military writer, was hardly exaggerating when he spoke of "the miracle on the Donets."

When it became evident that the Russians were attacking with considerably larger forces than anybody thought they had at their disposal, the Germans began scraping the bottom of the barrel in their search for man power. This new mobilization was placed under the command of General von Unruh, who was given dictatorial powers to draft men for service at the front. In a special train he traveled back and forth through Germany at headlong speed. All officials had to obey his orders. Both the civil service and Party organizations had to release any men he called for, and there was practically no appeal from his decisions. Unruh refused to be impressed by the lists of "key industries" and "essential workers" presented to him by the Party bosses. Their henchmen were marched out in droves and they could not protest. People became terrified at the mere mention of his name. He might come suddenly in the middle of the night, and for anyone to betray his schedule in order to warn Party comrades was a crime against military secrecy and hence was high treason. It was said that Unruh's adjutant was named von Wirbel; giving a rough translation, you might call them General Anxiety and Adjutant Whirlwind. At any rate their actions suggested lightning out of a clear sky.

Besides having full authority to draft those who had so far escaped military service, Unruh also descended on the German home guards and sent whole garrisons to the front, replacing them with elderly reservists. Women began taking the place of men even in barracks and police stations as the men were shipped off to the East. People differed about the results of his ruthless campaign. Leading Nazis would have it that he succeeded in scraping together no less than 2,500,000 men, but probably the number was considerably smaller; experts have placed it between 1,000,000 and 1,500,000. Even at that, the results were amazing.

The quality of the new recruits, however, did not match the quantity. In the Party and among officials, Unruh found a few superb physical specimens, but most of the men he drafted were those who had previously been rejected because they lacked one or more fingers or had weak hearts or other physical disabilities. Despite all the efforts of army doctors, a large proportion of them had to be discharged before they had finished their training, and even the others were well below the average for the German army. Officers who had the none too pleasant task of converting these wrecks into soldiers within three months (after this period those without prior military training were usually sent to France to serve in garrisons while completing their training) complained bitterly about the physical weakness of the recruits. The mental attitude also left much to be desired—especially in the case of men who had so far managed to escape army service.

Meanwhile German youngsters were undergoing forced training. When the fifteen- and sixteen-year-olds of the Hitler Youth were ordered into the anti-aircraft defense service, there were signs of protest all over the country. Some of the fifteen-year-olds were killed during an air raid on Berlin. Everywhere you heard expressions of bitterness and despair. "It's the end," many people said, "when children are killed like soldiers."

The SS troops and the Wehrmacht were rivals in claiming these younger classes. It was the SS that had the upper hand early in 1943, and with Hitler's permission they started a campaign for the "voluntary" enlistment of Blackshirt Guards in schools and factories. So much pressure was brought to bear that it took great moral courage on the part of Hitler Youth to refuse and enter the regular army instead. Out of the 1925 and 1926 classes—that is, the eighteen- and seventeen-year-olds—the Wehrmacht is said to have received only 30 per cent, while the Blackshirt Guards took the rest. Goering was also trying to start his own little army, but it seems that he had relatively little success.

Stalingrad and the Home Front

At the end of 1942, the Germans were in a mood of doubt and self-examination. In their family circles and among friends—wherever they could talk without too much fear of the Gestapo—they held lively discussions of the Russian offensive and the landing in North Africa. All sane Germans realized that, as a people, they stood completely alone. Hope of victory had almost disappeared; it was now the fear of defeat and its consequences that was the strongest motive for continuing the fight.

There were many expressions of this changing attitude. Even people without special sources of information began to think about what they would do in case of a final collapse. Nobody had any notion of how or when this would come about, but many made minor preparations for it, like investigating the possibility of sending their families to stay with relatives in some quiet corner of the country. Another evidence of the changing atmosphere was the almost open loathing aroused by official bulletins of victory and by all the insignia of the Nazi regime. As soon as the ordinary German felt that he could rely to some degree on those present, he abandoned his reserve and began talking about the "carpet eater," referring of course to Hitler's nervous attacks of rage.

The police had to resort to stern measures in order to prevent open criticism of the regime; all their controls were tightened. For this reason, foreigners in Berlin were surprised in December when letters from abroad began arriving without the censor's stamp. It turned out that the background for this was a gigantic espionage affair within the censorship, which till then had been under the High Command. Some 30 people were shot and military censorship was abandoned. A new censorship bureau was organized under the Gestapo, partly with such of the old personnel as was considered reliable. Meanwhile a number of Jews were executed. The charge against them was that they had revealed figures of production and industrial secrets obtained from the saboteurs inside the military censorship.

There was no sign in the press of the private discussions about the failure of German leadership, except possibly the absence of the usual tributes to the great commander. People noted, however, that when *Das Schwarze Korps* discussed the invasion of North Africa, it left it to history to judge whether the German command had been taken by surprise. In other words, it came as close to admitting that they had been surprised as one could expect from an SS organ.

In December, you began to notice more and more evidence of sheer physical exhaustion. After six months, the results of lower food rations had begun to show. You heard stories in business circles about workers collapsing at their machines; when the factory physician examined them, it was "the same old trouble." They were sent home to sleep, they perhaps received some extra rations (which the factory sometimes procured on the black market) and then they had to go back to work again. As a matter of fact, it was amazing that the health of the German people was not more deeply affected. Physicians declared that their resistance to infections was extremely low, and yet there were no great epidemics.

One gleam of hope was the extra rations that Goering had promised. Minister of Agriculture Backe—after much figuring, we heard —had balanced the available supplies and had worked out a weekly ration consisting of about 9 ounces of meat, 4 ounces of fat, 2 ounces of cheese and a little less than 2 ounces of coffee, besides a pound of wheat flour and a quarter-pound of caramels (although by Christmas time these last had become practically inedible). The increased rations were not granted, however, to the millions of foreign workers in Germany, nor did these workers receive the extra food that was given to Germans for heavy physical labor.

At Christmas time Berlin had a somber air, even though all the amusement places were filled with temporary visitors and soldiers on leave. Most Berliners who could do so stayed home for an extra day or two of sleep, for by this time there was no longer any Christmas holiday.

With the New Year, Germany was flooded with proclamations; nearly every Reichsleiter and Gauleiter had one of his own to issue. In general their contents were stereotyped. Goering said that all Germans looked forward to 1943 as "the year of victory and peace." Hitler declared to the army in his order of the day that Churchill and Roosevelt had taught Germany to hate. Gauleiter Grohe addressed the people of Cologne in a mood of desperation. Every man, woman and child knows that Germany *must* win, he said, "because otherwise it will not even have a chance to exist."

In January 1943, Dr. Goebbels set the tone for the new propaganda that would offset the invasion of North Africa and the defeats in the East. For once the Propaganda Minister had groped for some time before finding the proper line of attack. Distrust of Goebbels personally and of German propaganda in general had greatly increased, and soldiers everywhere were jubilant when they heard his work derided in any way. The author of a comedy then playing in Berlin had dared to insert an apparently innocent but very eloquent scene. Eight men charged with guarding supplies are sitting around a radio to which none of them listens. The radio voice says, "This war has shown that the German soldier realizes that he is fighting for higher values—yes, that in cold and snow he is defending the heritage from Beethoven and Bach." A pause. "Now follows the next program, Beethoven's Eighth Symphony, played by. . . ." Spontaneously the eight soldiers jump up to turn off the radio.

About this time I first heard the story about Rudolf Hess that was repeated all over the country. Twenty years after the war, a man comes out of the Hotel Adlon and meets little Joseph Goebbels selling newspapers. "How are things going?" he says. "Very well, thank you," answers little Joseph. "I'm keeping my head above water." "And what about Goering?"——"He's in business too; he's selling medals and decorations."——"Ah yes, indeed. And don't you recognize me, Joseph?"——"No."——"Think again. I am Lord Hess."

Goebbels' new line had really been suggested at the end of December by that excellent barometer of all German propaganda tendencies, *Das Schwarze Korps*. This weekly wrote that the last reservations must be abandoned if the German people wanted to win the war. In spite of everything that has happened, it said, we Germans are standing with one foot still in peacetime. Everybody knows this who has observed the hunt for knickknacks in the shops at Christmas time and the long lines that formed outside ticket booths. "In a total war there is only a total victory. This war will not end like a shooting match. It concerns our very lives. We cannot win it halfway, or even three-quarters of the way. We can only win a total war."

The core of Dr. Goebbels' article in *Das Reich*, where the new campaign was launched in the middle of January, was an appeal for total mobilization of German resources. The struggle involves all or nothing, Goebbels said, and it must not be impeded by the private citizen who wants to preserve as much peace as possible for himself. At home we must work "totally"; at the front we must fight "totally."

The *Völkischer Beobachter* said that German civilians had so far acted as if they were privileged to devote their spare time to sport, the radio, taverns, theaters and the movies. That must be changed. Stalingrad, North Africa and the British bombing raids against the Rhineland and northern Italy have demonstrated the increasing efforts of the enemy to spread the world conflagration. Before we are consumed by it ourselves, let us throw overboard some of our comforts. . . . The article went so far as to mention the contributions of Englishwomen to their nation's war effort as an example to be followed. Another German newspaper recommended the use of force against "the shirkers and stand-to-one-siders."

We heard from competent sources that the new mobilization would gradually but definitely put an end to all luxury—not for the leaders, of course, but for the people—and that the closing of all unessential shops would mean a saving of man power, gas, light and raw materials. There was, however, another object too, just as there had been another object besides increased production in the rationalization campaign of the preceding winter. The German public was to be kept so busy at home that it would forget about the defeats in Africa and Russia.

It was generally assumed that the outlines of the new campaign would be announced on January 30, which was the tenth anniversary of Hitler's rise to power. Everybody expected the Führer to deliver one of his long orations, and all the Party leaders were preparing to gather in Berlin. We began to notice an air of uncertainty, however, and two or three days before the anniversary we were told that Hitler would not speak. The requisitioned Adlon suddenly had all its rooms free and the sleeping-car trains to Berlin threatened to run empty, although a few days before it had been impossible for anyone except a high official to get a berth. The big party to which Dr. Brauweiler had invited the foreign correspondents "on the eve of the tenth anniversary of the assumption of power" was postponed "for technical reasons."

There was feverish activity at Promi on the 29th. We were told by those in the secret that Goebbels had been given practically unlimited authority to conduct the new campaign for a total war effort. The correspondents wondered what he would do, considering that all through the ten years' rule of National Socialism he had never displayed any qualities that would fit him for this particular task. At any rate, his program was to be explained in the speech he would give in the Sportpalast, at three o'clock on the afternoon of January 30.

Goering was to speak at eleven in the morning to the military forces; most of the correspondents planned to hear him by radio. At eleven o'clock they heard the new air-raid alarm signal, the "pre-alarm," which meant that single planes might be expected over Berlin, that there was some risk of bombs and shell fragments, but that the people should continue about their business without seeking the air-raid shelters. "The English are punctual," everybody was saying. Goering's speech was delayed for a full hour while the radio blared out martial music and the announcers declared at intervals, "The Reichsmarshal's speech has been delayed for a few minutes longer." The few British Mosquitoes that soared over Berlin didn't take the trouble to drop any bombs, being there out of pure mischief.

At the press conference in the Propaganda Ministry, we learned that Dr. Goebbels' speech would be delivered before the scheduled time, in order to forestall interruptions from the troublesome Britishers. We were waiting in the Sportpalast when little Joseph arrived at 3:30. The audience was about the same as usual—we could recognize the guards from the ministries and the stenographers from various bureaus of Promi—but the general atmosphere was dispirited. Goebbels himself tried to give the impression that he was in a warrior mood by coming dressed in a leather jacket like the one he used to wear during the years of street fighting. His speech was a disappointment from the start. Though its theme was total mobilization, he said nothing about the special measures that would be adopted; indeed he offered nothing but a rehash of the old Nazi phrases.

By the standards of former meetings in the Sportpalast, the applause seemed hesitant and without conviction. Still worse for Goebbels was the character of the "spontaneous interruptions from the floor." At former meetings, these had the air of being carefully rehearsed and worked like clockwork, but this time they were awkward and even hostile. When Goebbels said that the German people from this moment must give their all for victory and must show themselves worthy of the soldiers at the front, a powerful voice cried, "It's about time." A murmur swept through the vast auditorium and Goebbels paused for a moment. Once or twice the interruptions sounded like pure sabotage. Someone roared "Out with the Jews" at the wrong time and set the audience to laughing.

We wondered whether the British planes would come at four o'clock, when the speech had been scheduled to start. The prospect of bombs in the Sportpalast was not inviting. Goebbels himself seemed to be nervous and spoke at a galloping tempo. Almost at the stroke of four, a little boy in a Nazi uniform handed a slip of paper to the speaker. Goebbels glanced at it, and a moment later his voice began booming like thunder through the loud-speakers. There was another rumble outside—that of anti-aircraft guns, as we afterwards learned—but we heard no sirens. They had been disconnected on Goebbels' orders.

The Propaganda Minister rushed through the rest of his speech like a train making up lost time. After chugging to a halt, he read a proclamation from Hitler, which as usual began with Adam and

Eve and came down through the ages. Not even the most fanatical Nazi could find anything new in it. At the end of the proclamation, the little boy handed Goebbels another slip of paper. He read it with relief and began to speak more slowly; the air raid had ended. I happened to glance at Himmler, who was hastily mopping his forehead. Perhaps Goebbels felt that Hitler's message had been disappointing, or perhaps the impertinent British planes had caused him to omit some passages of his own speech. At any rate, after the danger was over the audience was amazed to find him delivering what was practically a new address. It was, however, merely a re-hash of what he had said at first, and Goebbels clearly had trouble finding an effective peroration. At last came the familiar slogan, "Führer command—we follow!" like a minister's Amen at the end of a long prayer. I went home with the impression that the days of jubilant boasting were over and that this was perhaps the last big meeting for a long time to come.

Afterwards it turned out that Goebbels had succeeded in fooling the German public and the RAF about the time of his speech. It had gone on the air exactly at four o'clock, as announced.

Despite his poor speech, Goebbels was the man of the hour. At Promi there was general rejoicing over the important position its chief had received, as well as over the opportunities now at hand for taking the Foreign Ministry down a peg or two. One of Goebbels' first measures of total mobilization was to close the greatly appreciated Foreign Press Club in the Fasanenstrasse. For two hours First-class Envoy Schmidt sat pleading with Goebbels to spare the club, where he himself had an apartment that was his principal field of operations. Goebbels was implacable. It was only after Schmidt had mobilized the foreign press attachés that he succeeded in making the Propaganda Minister revoke his decision.

It was not long before the anticipated closing of shops became a reality. In Berlin a number of the better-known luxury restaurants went out of business—among others, Horcher's, the Taverne and Zum Alten Schweden. The majority of antique, jewelry and furniture shops had to close, and perfumery shops, beauty institutes and dress shops saw their last days. It was also announced that a number of newspapers and magazines would be suspended.

Behind the scenes there was a violent tug-of-war about individual restaurants. The gossip was that Goebbels arranged to have "indignant citizens" throw stones at certain luxury restaurants that were owned by men of influence in the Nazi Party, so that he could point to these public demonstrations as an excuse for putting them out of business. There was also a rumor that Goering, after a bitter struggle, had succeeded in rescuing one of them for his officers.

The closing of the shops aroused more bitterness than had been expected among the German people. It was a measure that deeply affected the middle classes. Despite many official assurances that these would be compensated after the war, most of those concerned had a feeling that this action had been taken not so much to advance the war effort as to appropriate a large part of the supplies still on hand—partly for the personal use of the Party bosses. It was at any rate the general assumption that these had not neglected the opportunity to feather their nests.

During the next few days, Goebbels' speech at the Sportpalast was forgotten in the universal mourning over the catastrophe at Stalingrad. Every German home was full of dejection, but the grief was most acute in regions where it was known that local units belonged to the Sixth Army. In Vienna, which had a whole division in Stalingrad, there were pitiful signs of despondency. On streets and in trams one could see faces drawn with worry or paralyzed by sorrow.

Along with the grief went bitterness over what had happened. There was hardly anyone who looked upon it as an unaccountable natural catastrophe; it was plainly the result of bad leadership, and everybody had a clear idea of who was responsible.

More and more stories about Hitler's condition began to circulate. At the beginning of February, we heard on good authority that he was completely isolated and was guarded by his deputy, Martin Bormann. A prominent person had to make an official visit to the Führer. He was told that Hitler under no circumstances was to be told what was happening in Russia.

What seemed like a public refutation of these rumors was the announcement that all the Reichsleiters and Gauleiters—in other words, the big men of the Nazi bureaucracy—had visited Hitler at his headquarters, and that he had expressed to them his firm determination and inexorable will to victory. The *Völkischer Beobachter* called this "a political demonstration of the greatest magnitude." About its propaganda value we were somewhat dubious, especially when we saw the published photographs of the fat and bloated Party bosses. Hoffman, the court photographer, had wished to put forward his corpulent son-in-law, Baldur von Schirach, and had therefore shown all the heavier men in the foreground; there were actually lean ones too, but they were hidden.

After some of the Party leaders had returned to Berlin, we heard more about the meeting. Hitler was supposed to have said that the summer of 1943 would show whether or not he had been "the greatest visionary of all times." That didn't reassure Germans who were worried about what was coming.

Even though Goebbels' propaganda obtained some success, the feelings of the German people were leading toward direct political action. It became necessary to undertake new raids and arrests. In Siemensstadt alone—the great factory section adjoining Berlin— 600 persons were arrested. There was also a purge in the Foreign Office. Two of those arrested were Under Secretary Luther and his right-hand man, Councilor of Legation von Buettner. The formal charge against them was that they had used their position to deal in real estate.

Strange stories came from the provinces and especially from Munich. At the end of January, Gauleiter Wagner had called together a group consisting of the foremost Party bosses in the Bavarian capital, as well as representatives of the Reichswehr and state officials. In the speech with which he favored them, he was said to have declared, in part, "If we win this war, it is the Party that wins it; if we lose, it is the Wehrmacht that loses." A military man, wearer of the Knight's Cross, then came forward and, according to the story, gave the speaker such a box on the ear that Wagner had to go to the hospital with a broken jaw. I have not succeeded in verifying this story, except for Wagner's remark about the army. A well-informed German told me that the young officer had not hit Wagner but had only marched out of the room; probably this is what really happened. In Munich, however, there were disturbances and student demonstrations. When the Deputy Gauleiter made a stern speech before the young men and women students of Munich, whom he accused of studying merely to escape essential war work, some rose and left the hall. After a moment of silence, the other students also rose and left the amazed Nazi leader alone on the platform. Some bold students even made public a proclamation against Nazism, and the result was a raid with many death sentences.

Dr. Goebbels doubtless had the feeling that his own appearance

on January 30 had been far from successful and that the German
people needed a more powerful stimulant to get through the
winter. On February 18, he made a new appearance, wholly unexpected. Before a hastily summoned but carefully selected gathering in Berlin he made what was undoubtedly one of the memorable
speeches of this war. Persons who were present—I heard it by radio
in Vienna—assured me that Goebbels had never before revealed his
power over the masses in such a masterly fashion. Their reaction,
too, was close to hysterical, something that was conveyed even
by the radio.

The speech was consistently marked by its emphasis on the class
struggle and its appeal to the lowest human instincts. Many said
afterwards, "One more speech like that and the Communist program will have been proclaimed." It was not without interest that
the Propaganda Ministry insisted on reminding the foreign correspondents that Goebbels had always belonged to the left wing
of the Party and had always been a socialist of the purest dye. We
wondered if the National Socialists had decided to stake everything
on the card, "social revolution."

As a rounding out, Goebbels proposed a plebiscite of all those
present; he wanted to prove that the audience was representative
of the German people. He shouted out nine questions that were to
be answered with a resounding Yes, plus one to be answered No;
but in the haste even this one got its thundering, thousandfold Yes
and therefore had to be restated.

Many extraordinary things happened at this meeting. Even
Goebbels' statement that Germany up to this time had tried to wage
war "with the left hand" carried one's thoughts in a definite direction. The sharp anti-Semitic trend foretold a new action against
the Jews—"Hang the Jews!" was a frequent shout from the floor—
but perhaps the most significant of all the slogans was, "All power
to the Party!"

The speech was a skillful performance from the standpoint of
mass suggestion. But when its spontaneous effects had vanished, the
German public began to reflect upon Goebbels' urgent tone and
the sharpness of his words. People also began to ask if a catastrophe
threatened in the East. A neutral observer could notice other points,
such as the strong appeal to women to enter war work. In spite
of everything Germany is far behind England in the contribution
its women have made to war activities. One thing is very noticeable.

While queens and princesses have served as nurses at the front and taken their careers seriously, there has been no move in that direction by Frau Goering, Frau Goebbels or Frau von Ribbentrop.

This new appearance of the German Propaganda Minister led people to ask more questions about Hitler: Where was he and what was he doing? The rumors spread and increased. An attempt to answer them was made on February 23, the anniversary of the founding of the Party. Under Secretary Esser was sent forth to read a proclamation from Hitler, who, it was explained, was prevented by circumstances from being there in person.

It now became more widely known that the German generals had succeeded in stabilizing the situation in the East and even in making successful counterattacks, with the result that the general atmosphere in Berlin improved a little. But many Germans who, as late as January 1943, had believed in National Socialism, were greatly shaken by events. The relative improvement, too, lasted only until the Royal Air Force began a new series of attacks.

The Winter War Against the Western Allies

In January, Rommel had to continue his retreat from El Agheila toward Tripoli. The Germans in Tunisia, however, were able to make a quick thrust against the lines held by the Americans. It caught them in the midst of preparations for an offensive, and therefore caused heavy losses of matériel. Axis troops reached the border of Algeria.

The U-boat warfare continued with more and more intensity. At the end of January, High Admiral Raeder was replaced by Admiral Doenitz—"the lion," as he was called by his subordinates —and this was taken as a sign that Germany was to devote even more attention to the U-boat campaign. Possibly there was another reason, too, for this change in leadership. It was stated—though I was never able to verify the rumor—that there had been an attempt at organized anti-Hitler opposition in navy circles and that Raeder had failed to take a firm stand against it. The story was that 80 naval officers had been shot.

Doenitz was said to be responsible for the new U-boat tactics that were leading to much heavier Allied losses at sea. The official German statistics about enemy ships sunk present interesting problems that only specialists can solve. For years, neutrals in Germany have felt that the German claims in this field were as exaggerated as those they gave for Russian prisoners taken. One explanation may be that the Germans have been misled by the British, who are masters in the art of camouflage and who sometimes change the names of their ships—for example, they have been known to give a 1,000-ton vessel a name listed in Lloyd's Register as that of a 2,000-ton vessel. There is, however, no reason to suppose that the Germans have any more prejudice against dressing up their statistics of ship sinkings than they have against changing any other figures, if they think it will serve their purpose.

Far more intensive than the actual fighting in Tunisia and on the Atlantic was the diplomatic tug-of-war between the Allies and Germany. At the end of January, everyone in Berlin seemed to know that a meeting between Churchill and Roosevelt was imminent. Dr. Schmidt spoke with heavy irony about the fact that the British Prime Minister had gone to Washington to get instructions and to hear his master's voice. When it later turned out that the two statesmen had met in Casablanca, Schmidt was unperturbed. He claimed a new exploit for the German information service, which had reported quite accurately that the gentlemen were going to meet in the White House—in Spanish, the Casa Blanca.

The Wilhelmstrasse realized that the meeting in Morocco had laid plans for resuming the Allied offensive. But Stalin had not been present at the conference, and this was the point on which Dr. Goebbels chose to concentrate his heavy guns.

Immediately after Casablanca, the Germans had another painful shock; it was Churchill's visit to Turkey. At once the spotlights swung back to the Dardanelles and the Germans began to be really worried about a possible invasion of the Balkans. Nobody really thought that Turkey would become an active belligerent. On the other hand, there was no telling how the Turks would react to a British request for the privilege of sending troops through their country.

Ambassador von Papen, during his visit to Berlin after the Adana meeting, presented a highly pessimistic report. The English were making themselves more at home with every passing day. A mass of English weapons had arrived, to be stored in depots under the guard of English military personnel. The matériel designed specifically for the Turks was controlled by English "instructors." A number of roads were being built for military use, signposts in English were being put up and railway building went along at top speed under the direction of Allied technicians. English and American commissions with numerous personnel were installed in Ankara and Istanbul. Airfields in large numbers were being laid out—for whom? There was scarcely one modern Turkish military plane for each field.

The Nazi leaders to their enormous chagrin had to register the fact that Churchill's Adana conference meant a powerful political offensive on the part of England in the Middle East. Until now the Party had found comfort in thinking that although things had gone wrong for Germany, they were going even worse for Britain, which was yielding one position after another to the Americans. Now, however, everything pointed to the fact that Churchill, at least for the moment, was bringing home the spoils. As yet Russia was out of the running. Her ambassador in Ankara had asked why all these war supplies were being delivered there, but the only answer he received was that they were designed for the Turkish army. The influence of the United States in Turkey had decreased considerably. This was partly because it was thought in Ankara that the Americans were considering the possibility of sacrificing the Dardanelles and the Bosphorus to Russia; but the Turkish-American bonds had also been weakened because the Turks suspected that the United States wanted to acquire the Dodecanese Islands and thereby gain a permanent position in the Mediterranean. A controversy about the Bagdad line did not make matters better.

It was not only in Turkey that fortune favored the British. From the Arabic-speaking countries, and above all Saudi-Arabia, came reports of increasing British influence and a great interest in English plans for an Arabic federation. I was told by someone who knew how matters stood that Ibn Saud had begun to have misgivings because of the vigorous fashion in which American scientists and commissions had begun to investigate the natural resources of the country. Behind all this the Arabs suspected Wall Street.

The Nazis had good reasons to be enraged at the attitude of Turkey. Nor was it any better after Turkish Premier Saracoglu on February 21 ostentatiously hailed Britain as his ally. German questions were answered politely but evasively by the Turks. The German policy in Bulgaria was a nursery game compared with what the Allies resorted to in Ankara. Neutral correspondents began to hear angry words about Turkish hypocrisy. Dr. Schmidt declared to his faithful that the Turks were 80 per cent illiterate, were on bad terms with all their neighbors and had reason to be on their guard. Statements like this were certain to reach the ears of the Turkish ambassador, for everything Dr. Schmidt said at his *Stammtisch* was common knowledge next day in the whole foreign colony.

As late as 1941 such negotiations with Britain under the very nose of Germany would have been met with a lightning attack early some morning and a Hitler proclamation that the Turkish Government had broken its promises. Even now it seemed as though some Berliners were playing with this idea, but I doubt that it was taken seriously. The impossibility of getting any action out of the Bulgarians made action difficult. At his *Stammtisch* Dr. Schmidt did not conceal his disappointment. This was the big chance for Bulgaria to take part in the war, he said, but she was unwilling. The Bulgarians were a contemptible little people without a heroic myth and they didn't even know how they became a nation.

The general situation in the Balkans was hazardous from the German point of view. During the winter months Rumania had lost from 200,000 to 300,000 men, and the internal crisis was deepening because of the quickly spreading inflation, which could not be stopped despite all efforts. Things were seething in the country. It was no secret that an influential group, headed by the vice-president of the Council of Ministers, Michael Antonescu, was making efforts to get in contact with anti-Nazi factions.

In Serbia and Greece, partisan warfare flourished. Greek guerrillas now and then kidnaped high German officers; formerly they had confined such activities to the Italians. Thanks to liaison officers with the guerrilla armies, Allied headquarters in Cairo were well informed about the increasing difficulties of the Germans in the occupied Balkan lands.

On February 5 came a real political sensation: Mussolini dismissed his son-in-law, Ciano. A number of rumors about this event were flying around. The anti-German attitude that Count Ciano had adopted of late was well known in Berlin. It was said that he was dismissed by German request, when the Reichs Government showed proofs that he had tried to negotiate a separate peace with the Allies. If this was true, the Germans could hardly have been soothed when Ciano got the pleasant post of Ambassador to the Vatican. Shortly afterwards Archbishop Spellman of New York paid a visit to the Holy Father.

It can be categorically stated that there was an attempt to get a separate peace for Italy in the middle of February. Just as during the visit of Myron Taylor, all negotiations failed because the two sides could not agree on conditions. Some good prospects must have been at hand, for later we could notice a still more marked coolness in German-Italian relations.

It was, however, the situation in North Africa that created serious misunderstandings between the Axis partners. Tripoli was evacuated in February. This retreat had been agreed upon in German-Italian conferences, but at the last moment the Italians changed their minds and demanded that the city should be defended. There were heated arguments with mutual accusations of cowardice, and the outcome was that a considerable Italian force remained in Tripoli and allowed itself to be captured almost without protest; this was the heroic defense. The Germans became still more embittered when they heard that the Italian administration in occupied Libya had promptly placed itself at the disposition of the Allies.

Heavy German reinforcements were continuing to land in Tunisia. At the end of February there seemed to be plans for a prolonged defense, although the Germans must have known all along that they would be forced sooner or later to surrender the whole bridgehead. Churchill's words about Hitler's master hand, which had planned the attack on Stalingrad and prepared the German armies there for the catastrophe, would be confirmed once again in Tunisia.

At the end of February, the English began to intensify their air warfare. Essen and a whole group of West German cities were the objects of devastating raids; then, on March 1, it was the turn of Berlin. The big squadron that attacked the city was not stopped by the anti-aircraft defenses; it dropped an enormous number of heavy bombs and incendiaries. As the wind increased toward nightfall, the flames spread with raging speed. When the Berliners came up from their shelters, the horizon was bright red and there was some fire in almost every block.

This March 1 raid was the hardest blow that the German capital had so far experienced. A great depression prevailed during the next few days, even though Goebbels tried hard to combat the spirit of defeatism that was spreading through the capital. It was easy to understand why the Propaganda Ministry was exerting itself, considering the central position of Berlin on the German home front. A number of honors were conferred upon Berliners for bravery during the raid and the newspapers were full of hymns of praise to the bold citizens. That the capital had stood the test was the verdict everywhere. Goebbels himself appeared in a steel helmet at the Breitenbach Platz and dealt out chocolate bars to the children. That happened immediately after the raid, but during the next few days neither Goebbels nor any of the other leaders put in an appearance. The reason was that the mass of Berliners had shown their discontent in an unmistakable fashion. Crowds shouting the old slogan, "We thank our Leader," had greeted the Nazi bureaucrats. In one block, 30 people had been arrested for "treasonable comments." Stories like this became a commonplace: "Where did you get your black eye? Is it something you owe to the British raid?"——"Well, yes, indirectly."——"What do you mean indirectly?"——"It happened this way. When I came up to a good friend in Stieglitz [one of the sections that suffered most from the bombing] and found him looking at the ruins of his home, he gave me the black eye."——"But for what reason?"——"In my haste I happened to greet him with 'Heil Hitler.' "

My Trip to Vienna

At the beginning of February, I received a longed-for holiday of four or five weeks, which I planned to spend digging into the government archives in Vienna. Full of anticipation, I stepped into the sleeping car one night at the Charlottenburg Station, on my way to a city that has had a peculiar charm for me ever since my wanderings in student days. To be sure, I had often revisited the city on the Danube, but how can one renew old acquaintanceships during a visit of one or two days?

What I had once known was the Vienna of the years before the Anschluss, a city that lived in hardship and poverty, but with memories of a proud past, and one that exercised a peculiar fascination over the stranger. I shall always count it my good fortune to have lived there, not as a luxury tourist or a man who has to count his minutes, but as a student with little money and time unlimited. You have to see Ottakring and the outlying districts where foreigners seldom go in order to round out your impressions of the Graben, Am Hof, Schönbrunn and the great imperial palace, the Hofburg.

I had made a few short visits during the years from 1939 to 1942, but I had not stayed long enough to realize the great changes that had taken place. What I saw this time was a Vienna stamped by the war. A number of hotels had been requisitioned and converted into hospitals. There was one field hospital in the Hofburg and another in Schönbrunn. On the streets you heard all the languages of Europe, but especially Ukrainian and Croatian, for there seemed to be even more foreign workers in Vienna than there were in Berlin. The sick and wounded strolled through the streets in their uniforms. The trams were even more worn and creaking, the taxis even more rattling and the railway stations even dirtier than last time. On public buildings the plaster was flaking, and the façades of the houses clearly revealed that for years they had not been cleaned.

The shops still had a little more to offer than did those in Berlin, but the markets were just as empty. The food in restaurants, however, seemed fairly divine to a person just arrived from Berlin. At the old, stately Sacher they still served *Palatschinken,* the familiar thin pancakes that tasted just as good as in old times; the soups were excellent and were without chemicals; and the bread was considerably better than in the German capital. In small restaurants they still served their "specialty of the house," prepared with great care. But everybody said that the food was continually getting worse, and soon it would be just as bad as in Berlin. I saw a street vendor selling what I thought were roast chestnuts. I gave him a coin and cannot forget my disillusionment when I was handed a fire-baked potato covered with soot.

At first I was disappointed in the Viennese. Where was the old amiability that made such a great impression on northerners? One day a good Swedish friend told me that in some way I would have to show people that I was Swedish, because otherwise, through my German accent, I would be taken for a Prussian and treated accordingly.

I learned very soon that he was right. At a place where I was accustomed to eat and where I had so far had been treated rather coldly, to say the least, I unfolded an old copy of *Svenska Dagbladet.* The headwaiter came up, cast a long glance at the newspaper and said, "Is the Herr Doktor Swedish?" Just the fact that he had changed from "Herr" to "Doktor" told the whole story, but to make matters quite plain he apologized and said he was sorry that he had not known this earlier—"*I'h hätt' Sie jaa gaanz aanders behaand'lt,*" he said—"I'd have treated you very differently." Afterwards he took my order, asked if he might add a carafe of wine and then hurried away. With the dessert, the proprietor turned up and he, too, offered excuses; until then he had taken no notice of me. He hoped I didn't mind, he had no idea, etc., etc.

I ate my next meal at a hotel where I happened to have had a heated argument with the waiter the day before. The same scene was repeated almost exactly, with the sole difference that this time even the director of the hotel appeared, offered his formal apologies and graciously assured me that in the future it would give him the greatest pleasure to see that I had one of the best tables.

I was a bit embarrassed by the obvious favors that were shown me everywhere, as soon as I identified myself as a Swede. Finally I found that the best plan was simply to show my press card to the proprietor. In some instances I was a little frightened by the turn that matters took. I remember the time when I sat down at a table where a typical Prussian officer was waiting impatiently for his dinner; I ordered and got my food twenty minutes before he did.

But soon I fully understood the reasons, especially after I had witnessed a little scene. I had decided to have lunch at one of the better-known restaurants in Vienna. The only seat I could find was at a table where a North German—apparently an official—was finishing his main course. Catching sight of the headwaiter, he called out to him that he had been given only 50 grams of meat, although he had surrendered ration points enough for 100. The headwaiter made an investigation, decided that the German was mistaken, and came back with the report that it was unfortunately too late to do anything about the matter; he was, however, extremely courteous. The German official lost his self-control and pounded on the table till the plates and glasses jumped; then he said—no, shouted—that he would teach them what the Prussians meant by order, that this damned Austrian sloppiness, this *Schlamperei* would cost them dear. Everybody could see that he was wearing a Nazi Party emblem. Two German colonels at the next table writhed in discomfort and tried to catch their fellow countryman's eye, but in vain. As he shouted, "These slovenly people," and, "We'll beat order into your heads," you could see people clutching the edges of the tables to keep their self-possession.

It was my bad luck to have him sputter in my face. I wiped off the saliva with a napkin, asked for another table and went out into the hall to wait for it. Soon the German rushed out as if shot from a cannon, gave me a murderous glance and disappeared without leaving a tip for his hat and coat. I gave a coin to the old woman in the checkroom. Soon the headwaiter came out and apologized for the scene. "You know what they are like," he added with resignation. "That is why everybody loves them."

It was by no means only in restaurants that one noticed the animosity between Austrians and North Germans. During one of my first days in Vienna I saw a policeman studying a map of the city and looking up at the street signs. It seemed strange, for a policeman ought to know the streets he is patrolling. Later I heard another policeman in the Operngasse ask a lady where the Operngasse was; he spoke in a typical North German dialect. From the spot where he was standing there were no street signs visible. To my amazement the lady said quickly and firmly, "You must go to the left and then turn into the third street on the right." The policeman thanked her and went to the left. I looked at the lady who noticed my surprised glance, reddened a little and hurried off.

When I told one of my old friends about this episode, he laughed and said that not a single policeman in Vienna knew any of the streets. The old honorable Vienna police had been sent to North Germany on account of their "unreliability" and had been replaced with *Pifkes*—a nickname for the Prussians that has caught on everywhere. My friend added that no Viennese loses an opportunity to show a policeman the wrong turn.

A few days later I was sitting in a G2 tram when a policeman stepped in and asked the woman conductor if this tram went to Hohe Warte. I happened to be going there too, but I still was not sufficiently acclimated and therefore was surprised when the sweet conductor said, "Oh no, you'll have to take a B2 tram." The policeman stepped off and the tram rattled on. There were smiles on the faces of the passengers and the woman conductor also smiled happily. I afterwards learned that the B2 tram turns to the East and runs directly away from Hohe Warte.

As I glanced around I saw that many of the passengers undoubtedly must have been Reichs Germans. The next day I asked an Austrian how anyone dared to do things like that when there are so many Germans in Vienna. He answered with a smile that at such moments not one of them had the courage to identify himself. Possibly they might report the matter afterwards, but the conductor could always plead that she had misunderstood the policeman's North German accent.

In the shops, too, one could make interesting studies of the general atmosphere. I happened to be in Vienna when it was announced that the big stores were about to be closed and when the supplies of the smaller shops in general were being quickly exhausted. Any Austrian and any foreigner got what there was to be had, while the Prussians learned that everything was sold out—*ausverkauft*. The shopkeepers hardly bothered to keep up appearances, but pretended that they could understand only the Viennese dialect, forgot to wait on Germans or brought forth some wretched stuff and declared with blank faces that this was something "extra fine, made in Berlin."

All other languages were easily understood in the Austrian shops. Croats, Czechs and Hungarians would speak their own tongues and be served politely. When the versatile clerks had a chance to speak French, they did so with joy. Even English was often heard. With a good friend and highly esteemed colleague, I went into a large antique shop. When the clerks saw our trench coats, resembling those of British officers, we were addressed immediately in perfect English. When we went out—after having seen the very best there was on hand—everyone stood at attention, while two German ladies patiently waited to be served. In other shops we were pressed to buy, with the comment, "It is a pleasure to sell to you. Otherwise the *Pifkes* take it all."

It was obvious that the Austrians were trying to alienate themselves from everything German. It was not so much National Socialism they disliked as things German in themselves. "We" meant the Austrians, and "the Germans" meant those from the old Reich —in case one wanted to be polite. Otherwise the word was *Pifke*. The German language was called *pifkesisch* or *pifchinesisch*—that is, "Pifchinese." There was a fine of 70 marks if the police caught anybody using such terms.

With all this bad feeling, the Germans began to feel ill at ease. During a later visit in May, I noticed that there was a real "staring-out campaign" against them. I also heard then that careful Germans had sent their families back to the Reich, fearing that in Vienna there would be a night of the long knives. Once I experienced something that I supposed took place only in anecdotes, namely that a German in a shop said, "I am a Rhinelander and a Catholic." He received more polite treatment.

The deep animosity against everything German was greatly deplored by my Reichs German acquaintances in Vienna, who had many a hard word to say about the Austrians, with their fickleness,

Schlamperei and insulting manners. But some Germans admitted that there was nothing to do about the matter, because it was impossible to prevent the Prussian Germans from making pigs of themselves. From both Reichs Germans and Austrians, I heard that all private contacts between the two groups had ended, but these had been none too lively even in the heyday of the Anschluss. A German who had lived in Vienna since 1938 and had retained a cordial and even friendly relationship with his Austrian colleagues —several of them were Party members—told me that he had never yet been in any of their homes. "Oh, yes," he added, "just once, and then the group was made up of three or four Germans and the host. The hostess had gone to the country that day."

The hostility extends through Austrian society from top to bottom. A shoemaker whom I have known since 1936—he is an old dependable Social Democrat—told me that a year ago he had to mobilize the whole family and threaten to put his only daughter out of the house because she wanted to marry a man from Hannover. But finally the old man tricked the unwelcome son-in-law into "showing himself in his proper colors." How this was done I never learned, in spite of my discreet questions, but obviously there had been politics mixed into the game.

Vienna is a seething mass of anti-Hitler opposition, though it is hard to say how much of it is idle talk. In the Viennese fashion, part of the battle against the Nazis and the Germans is waged with anecdotes, each of which has an obvious political point. The calling of elderly men to the colors called forth a story about Methuselah, whom the Good Lord sent down to earth to restore order. Soon afterwards Methuselah came back. "Shortly after I reached Germany," he explained, "I heard that Adolf Hitler had called men of my age to the colors and so I didn't risk staying."

In a group there were two generals, one from Prussia and one from Austria. The Austrian complained that all German-speaking people were held responsible for what the Prussians did. "Yes, but remember," said the Prussian, "that we are also held responsible for everything the Austrian paperhanger thinks up."——"That, my dear friend," said the Austrian, "is our revenge for the defeat at Königgrätz."

A teacher in a public school was giving his class its daily ration of Nazi propaganda. "Who is our father?" he asked. "Adolf Hitler," said the children in chorus. "Who is our mother?"——"The German Reich."——"What do you want to be?" Most of the children gave answers like "pilot," "bombardier," "tank driver." But little Max from Vienna said, "I want to be an orphan."

Nazi decorations were the subject of much ridicule: for example the Oak Leaf, *das Eichenlaub*, was called the Corpse Leaf, *das Leichenlaub*. The swastika was called the "tarantella." When the Viennese wanted to talk about Hitler, they referred to Haschek; Mussolini was Maschek and Stalin Staschek. Churchill, on the other hand, kept his own name. In Austria he enjoyed a popularity that was quite fantastic. One day at a party I heard a newcomer greet the hostess and then say, "How is he today?"——"The latest communiqué sounded hopeful," was the answer. After one long minute it dawned on me that they were speaking of Churchill, who then, as I recall it, was just recovering from his siege of pneumonia.

In many other ways the atmosphere in Vienna was made clear. Prisoners of war were treated strikingly well. Now and then someone handed them cigarettes and food—munificent gifts when you recall how scant the rations are. There were also interesting little outbursts in the classified columns of the Vienna newspapers. I saw, for example, "Will exchange skillet, because of fat shortage, for a Hitler portrait"; and, "Anything useful as food in exchange for a large number of portraits of the Führer." You could not fail to notice how much solidarity prevailed among the Austrians. If any German got into a dispute with an Austrian, there were always witnesses to support the latter; there were never witnesses for a German.

At the time of my visit, the opposition was becoming active. By night on the streets there were flying police patrols, armed to the teeth, but now and then there were still cases of sabotage. Against the Communists, the Gestapo acted with utter ruthlessness. In one day there were 60 death sentences in Vienna, and there were usually from 250 to 300 people waiting for their death sentences to be confirmed in Berlin. Apparently there had been no riots of any size. A few minor disturbances took place but these had been easily suppressed. Sometimes the Nazi bosses came out from a meeting to find their tires slashed. In Grinzing a German soldier was killed by 30 Austrian women. He had said that the Germans lost Stalingrad because the Austrian units there had been afraid to fight.

In their disappointment over the regime and their war weariness, the Austrians forgot that many of them on March 13, 1938, hailed these same Germans at whom they are throwing stones. Five years have passed and now they know them all too well. Austrians of all classes have met Germans of all classes, and the result is a crushing blow to German hopes of preserving a great united empire. It was by no means an easy task in the beginning to reconcile the honor-loving Austrians to the idea that their land was to become a small German province. For an effort like that to succeed requires tact and still more tact on the part of the larger nation; and tact was never one of the Germans' virtues. In Vienna you saw them acting almost as they did in the conquered countries.

Everything of value has been drained out of the land, from food supplies to works of art. The collections in the museums have been plundered and sold to antique dealers abroad. Where the Nazis have advanced like a swarm of locusts, no grass grows. Yet the plundering has played a smaller part than the systematic, grinding pressure. It is as if there had been a deliberate attempt to hurt the feelings of the Austrians. Despite the fact that sensible officers have tried to be impartial, the Austrians in general have received shabby treatment in the German army. They have seldom been formed into homogeneous Austrian units, perhaps because the Germans are afraid of what they might do if they were together. In German units, Prussian subalterns—and also the new Party officers—have tried to teach the Austrians their place; and since the Austrians think they know their place already, conflicts are always flaring up. I don't know how many soldiers I met who complained that they had been called "Austrian swine" and had been selected as a matter of course for the details sent to empty the latrines.

Many decisions of the German government have caused bad blood in Austria. When the precious Gobelin tapestries in the Hofburg were sent to Hitler's new Chancellery in Berlin, every Austrian felt it was a blow to his national pride. It was another blow when the imperial regalia were taken away, and also when the remains of the Duke of Reichstadt were transferred to Paris. Public opinion has been most affected, however, by little daily irritations. The Nazis are waging war against the very concept of Austria. It has come to the point where the Lower Austrian dairy— *Niederösterreichische Molkerei*—has been forced to change its name to the Lower Danubian Dairy. For a time Austria was known as Ostmark, but now even that term is forbidden. The next step in the process of assimilation has been reached. Austria is now called *die Donau- und Alpenländer*, "the Danube and Alpine Lands."

In March I returned to Berlin with a strong conviction that Vienna was lost to the Third Reich. From reliable persons I have heard that the rest of Austria has shifted in the same direction. Graz, which used to be a stronghold of Nazism, wishes it had never heard of Hitler. But Linz, Hitler's birthplace, is one town that still remains faithful to him—or at least it stood firm last February.

SPRING, 1943

The Campaign in Africa and the Allied Offensive Against Italy

THE Axis forces lost the temporary advantage they held in Tunisia in February, partly because of the fury of the Allied attack and partly because General Montgomery's formidable Eighth Army was approaching from the South. The Italians openly admitted that this army was the best in the world. Meanwhile the Germans and the Italians found it increasingly difficult to maintain connections with Italy. For some unaccountable reason the Italian fleet was not in operation, with the result that the British were almost unmolested at sea.

During the latter part of March the Eighth Army attacked the Mareth line, where Rommel's troops had halted on their way northward. Some of the British forces flanked the line, while other strong formations pushed forward in a frontal attack. Because of the great numerical superiority of the Allies and their absolute control of the air, it was not long before the Axis command had to yield the whole Mareth line and withdraw in the direction of Gabes. The Americans, attacking from the West, had penetrated deep into regions controlled by the Germans. A few German units had to surrender when the Mareth fortifications were overwhelmed. The retreat of the others naturally took place "according to plan."

The reverses brought Italy into the limelight. Immediately, German newspapers began offering long explanations, insisting that any separate peace by Italy was preposterous. "Italy," commented the *Frankfurter Zeitung*, "stands nearer to us than ever before." And they followed this up by stating that Sicily, Sardinia, Corsica and the Italian south coast comprised one long well-fortified wall of Fortress Europe.

Gradually, however, as the news grew worse, German military groups began to complain bitterly about the slackness and defeatism of Italy and to advance their theory that it might even be better to occupy the country rather than tolerate the current situation there. Travelers from Italy reported that there was a definite weakening of morale, and that Mussolini's position was no longer secure. But most Germans still believed that the Italian dictator would always remain loyal to his partner.

In April, the Allied offensive forced a decision. On the 6th the Eighth Army attacked again, at Shott-el-Jerid, and the very next day Major Sommerfeldt had to admit that once again Montgomery had succeeded in breaking through the German lines. Suffering great losses, the Axis troops were thrown northward, escaping encirclement by the skin of their teeth.

By this time British groups began to speculate on the relatively weak German-Italian command. For weeks, a rumor had been circulating in Berlin that Field Marshal Rommel was seriously ill and that he had been forced to leave the front, a fact later confirmed. Slowly General Montgomery advanced, forcing the Axis troops to continue their retreat northward. At the same time, strong Allied forces were attacking from the West, and the whole Tunisian bridgehead began to contract like the German lines at Stalingrad.

Even before this, the situation had become alarming. Air activity against Italy had increased in intensity, and Malta was now prepared as a base for offensive action. Further and further the fateful shadows began to fall over Italy. Journalists in Berlin were therefore not surprised by the announcement that a meeting between Hitler and Mussolini had been arranged. There was the usual official demand for great secrecy, and Braun von Stumm (Schmidt himself was considered so important that he always attended a meeting of this kind) once again reminded us of the regulations. But, once again, there was a leak. On this occasion the newly organized Trans-ocean-Europa Press released a telegram. The Foreign Office, foaming with rage, demanded the head of the offender on a platter. I don't know if they got it.

The meeting between Hitler and Mussolini—the penultimate one, as it later turned out—was noteworthy insofar as the comments on it must have struck terror into the hearts of even the most faithful Nazis. For the two statesmen, ran the report, "after careful consideration of all eventualities, had decided that the Axis could win only by means of a total and uncompromising contribution of all strength." Nothing like that had ever been said before. Never before had it been even suggested that victory was not certain.

In Berlin it was assumed that Hitler and Mussolini had decided to evacuate the Tunisian armies under the protection of the Italian fleet and the Luftwaffe. In the middle of April it would certainly have been possible to withdraw a large number of troops from Africa. Although any such measure was inconsistent with the mentality of Hitler, I cannot say if it was for this or some other reason that the two dictators decided to fight on.

The "narrower bridgehead," which the Axis troops held after their retreat had temporarily halted in the neighborhood of Enfidaville, was still fairly strong; everyone assumed that it would hold for weeks. Up to this time, progress had been at a surprisingly slow pace in North Africa. The German-Italian command also had the advantage of inner lines, a point that was emphatically stressed in Berlin.

And then the Allies sprang their last surprise in Tunisia. Since there had been an attack along the whole line near the end of April, with no positive results at first, Berlin had been explaining that the Eighth Army drive had been launched with weak forces, owing to the losses suffered by this most famous of British armies. In reality, a strong body of troops had been detached from the Eighth Army and transferred to the central sector. Because the Allies had command of the air, the Germans and Italians were apparently unaware of this movement. They kept large forces in the South to meet an attack that didn't come.

There were a few calm days at the turn of the month. Then, early in May, after an artillery and air bombardment that probably had no equal in this war, the Allied infantry moved forward like a battery of steam rollers. Very soon the whole Axis position gave way. After Mateur had fallen to the Americans, Berlin admitted that the Axis troops were in retreat and that the whole situation was extremely grave.

It was openly admitted the next day that Tunisia was lost. Major Sommerfeldt naturally had to be more cautious, so he pointed out that the German-Italian troops were still offering resistance not only on the Cape Bon peninsula, but also in isolated hedgehog positions. "The Axis troops," he claimed, "will fight to the last cartridge." Then, on May 11, Sommerfeldt did admit that the British had penetrated deep into the peninsula and that the situation was hopeless. Two days later, all was definitely over.

Practically nothing of the Axis armies in Tunisia could be saved.

Losses at sea during the last month of the campaign had also been considerable. As for the number of planes brought down by the Allies, it was nothing short of terrifying. In one day there had been 90, although this figure was an exception. The defeat was all the greater because the annihilated or captured units belonged to the best of the German forces. Rommel's legendary Africa Corps had ceased to exist. The Hermann Goering division had suffered tremendous losses.

Tunisia was another Stalingrad; there was no doubt of that fact. But the final struggle in Africa was not the same heroic epic as the last battle of Field Marshal von Paulus among the ruins. The German and Italian soldiers had fought valiantly even during the last stage of the Tunisian campaign. But in the face of unprecedented pressure from ceaseless artillery and air bombardments (without corresponding support by their own forces) and against continuous enemy attacks from fresh troops, the Germans and Italians were worn out. They collapsed, in fact, just as the French had under the lightning attack of the German war machine.

In the main, the officers held out to the end and tried to prevail on their troops to resist to the last man. Officially, they were told not to surrender before all ammunition was gone and the supplies destroyed. But, oddly enough, the men did not agree to this. Time and again they did surrender, thereby abandoning considerable supplies. Prospects of a British prison camp did not seem terrifying to them. The situation in Stalingrad had been very different.

Moreover, the British in their turn had known how to use masterly propaganda. A German military surgeon told me that the last vessel to leave Tunisia was a hospital ship. It was overtaken by a British destroyer and ordered to Bizerte, which was then already occupied by the Allies. On its arrival it was searched with the greatest care, but since everything was in order the British commander offered excuses and said that the vessel (which had some 2,000 wounded and also the highest German sanitary staffs on board) could proceed at once. The search had been so thorough, he explained, because a couple of Italian hospital ships had carried gasoline and therefore had been sunk. Before the German hospital ship departed, British doctors came on board and distributed whisky, cigarettes ("the first decent smoke the Germans had had for weeks," said my informant) and chocolate bars. Then, since the ship's medical equipment was by this time running low, the

British bandaged the wounded and put large supplies at the disposal of the German doctors. When the ship departed, it was escorted to the Italian coast by the same destroyer that had seized it. Naturally, there was not a word about propaganda.

In a few days, said my informant, this tale was the topic of conversation among all the German troops in Italy. The wounded, as they were landed in Naples, exclaimed: "If that is supposed to be the enemy, then you can count me out of this war." Of course the majority understood the propaganda behind the whole incident. But it had all happened so spontaneously, cheerfully, quietly, above all so unobtrusively, that crew and passengers on that ship were flabbergasted. When a German wounded officer had refused to accept cigarettes, the crew had actually made a protest.

Even before the final struggle, incidents had occurred to give the German command trouble. An Austrian élite regiment, led by its officers, had gone over to the enemy. When this became known, Himmler himself went to Vienna to conduct the job of putting all relatives of the men in that regiment into concentration camps. He also saw to it that this story was spread throughout the whole of Austria.

The German propaganda machine had been prepared for the fall of Tunisia. By his earlier emphasis on the bridgehead there, Goebbels had questioned the strategic value of the Allied landings in North Africa on November 8, 1942—that is, so long as the British and the Americans had not succeeded in capturing Tunisia. But by April, in good time, he was launching a new tune for his propaganda orchestra. With no direct suggestion that the bridgehead might collapse, the emphasis was shifting to the strength of the southern European fortifications and to the fact that the Allies' strategic goal—the opening of the Mediterranean to Anglo-American ships—could not be reached merely by an occupation of the Tunisian coast.

That Italy was directly threatened by the Allies was now clear to every German. The press, however, reflected extraordinary caution. Count Hans Reischach wrote that life was tough and full of sacrifices, tears and worries, but that Fascism had taken over the task of mobilizing "the last strength of the country for victory." Nevertheless, all Germans who had been in Italy, or who had firsthand accounts of the general sentiment there, were pessimistic. Anxiety increased when it became known that Italian workers were to be sent home from Germany. "But it was here that they were making their only contribution to the war," said Berliners.

In order to conquer one must have Russian arms, English food, Italians as enemies, and Hitler as the Unknown Soldier, ran the tart comment. But in May the majority of Germans seemed to have the impression that Hitler would make sure of there being no "jumping off the train"; also that the German troops in Italy were so powerful that a defense could be organized independent of Italian co-operation.

The more serious the situation in Africa, the more the authorities tried to belittle Allied victories. After the Tunisian campaign was over, the German press declared that the Axis powers had suffered a surface wound, but that the resistance in Africa had postponed an invasion for "decisive months," which in turn had given the Axis both the time and the opportunity to strengthen its southern front and assemble reserves. But the German people did not react as they were expected to. The outcome in Tunisia was interpreted as a real defeat, not a "reverse," although it seemed less bitter than Stalingrad. Above all, the fact that the captured sons of Germany were now in American and British camps, instead of facing an uncertain fate in Russia, sustained morale. Despite all the Nazi propaganda against the "plutocracies," and despite the air raids, it was plain that the attitude toward the Western Powers was wholly unlike the attitude toward Russia. Time and again I heard such comments as this: "Now at least our boys will get decent cigarettes"; and once an acquaintance of mine said dreamily: "It wouldn't have been so bad to have been captured in Tunisia."

And then, in one day, all the talk about the African war stopped. Dr. Goebbels had found another trick to make the public forget what was happening on the battlefields.

Public Sentiment in the Spring of 1943

For a long time we had been hearing that German food rations would be reduced, a step that had been postponed as long as possible. The situation was really serious. Even now, after ten years of Nazism, it is still possible to dupe the Germans, but not one of them could have forgotten Goering's speech in 1942 in which he made a definite promise that the rations, then increased, would remain fixed or be increased even further. Now suddenly, on May 10, it was announced that for the next allotment period the meat rations would be cut back again to only 9 ounces a week. Violent discussions broke out. Anger and bitterness ran high and in a flash the memory of Tunisia was completely blotted out.

The technique of killing one piece of bad news with another even worse can be very effective. As the fury gradually subsided, and the summer came with a few more vegetables for the table, no one even thought of Tunisia. But naturally the atmosphere was far from satisfactory. In fact, toward the end of the spring the Germans, particularly Berliners, began to reveal war weariness on a scale hitherto unknown. By and large, there were two reasons for this: even the inveterate optimists began to question the outcome of the war, and citizens in the German capital were suffering more and more from its discomforts.

I have already mentioned the general pessimism. Intensified during the spring, it still remained but a passive phenomenon, with little direct opposition. In fact, of late one symptom had actually disappeared, doubtless because of the weariness: the characteristic Berlin pun was now languishing. If there was any joking during the spring, it was either "gallows humor" such as, "Enjoy the war, because the peace will be terrible," or some old worn-out stories. One story that refused to die dealt with a man who was bombed out of his home and who with a ration card went the rounds of the tailors in search of a new suit. He couldn't get one anywhere. At last he burst out: "And all this on account of one single man." Of course he was brought promptly before Pontius Pilate, who asked what he meant. The culprit then answered, "Of course I meant Churchill. Whom did Your Honor mean?" Another joke was about the optimist and the pessimist. The former says: "It is simply terrible—we're going to lose the war." And the pessimist replies: "Certainly, but *when*?"

Goebbels did everything in his power to counteract this defeatism. He wasn't very successful, but it was amazing to see what could be done with the simplest of means. Complaining Berliners, for instance, found themselves caricatured in the persons of a Herr Bramsig, a tall and melancholy man, and Frau Knöterich, who was plump and cheerful. They appeared on posters all over Berlin, and under them were printed ironic little verses, expressing their sins—particularly the sin of listening to the radio. With the following verse the poster shows them tuning in on London:

Hier meldet London "welch' ein Glück,
Die deutsche Front zieht sich zurück!"
Und hinterher noch "welch' ein Fest,
In Kiew herrscht die Leichenpest! ! !"

("This is London speaking! How fortunate that the German front is in retreat! Not only that, Kiev is being ravaged by the plague!")

Both Herr Bramsig and Frau Knöterich, of course, repeat this bit of news, and gradually the story spreads. Naturally, no matter what the story or the sin, the final poster always shows a couple of hefty cops escorting Bramsig and Knöterich to jail, there to contemplate their sins. Although no open opposition broke out during the spring of 1943, everyone knew that it was only a matter of time before people began to act. One striking symptom was the increasing hatred of strangers. Well-dressed foreigners were attacked, diplomats' cars had their tires slashed, and those who carried parcels were the object of angry stares. Crime increased. Ration cards were stolen, often by half-starved workers who did not stop short of murder to get some paltry bread coupons. Foreigners receiving food supplies from abroad had to pay heavy duties.

The food problem went from bad to worse, and I often wondered how housekeepers managed to scrape together enough for their families to eat. For hours they had to stand in line to buy, say, a few radishes. The markets usually carried only three kinds of vegetables, and as often as not the supplies were so miserable it wasn't worth waiting in line. All hope of living on non-rationed food, obtained through regular channels, had long since disappeared. Even the largest stocks soon petered out. German household reserves were coming to an end. Fish one might get once a month, provided one watched the markets carefully.

The black market naturally assumed increasing importance, and its thriving business was one more sign of the flagging morale. Before I left Berlin, practically everything could be had on the black market, provided you could pay the fantastic prices. In the spring of 1943, coffee cost 150 marks or more a pound, butter 60 marks, and cigarettes anywhere from 50 pfennigs to one mark apiece. An acquaintance once told me that a stranger in a subway snatched a cigarette from him, thrust one mark into his hand and before he could say a word rushed off with the words, "Excuse me, but I simply must have a smoke." In order to buy black-market liquor, you had to be a very rich man. A friend boasted to me that his French cognac had cost him only 250 marks a bottle.[1]

The black market has its wholesalers just like the normal trade. Though the big syndicates keep themselves in business by paying bribes and observing great discretion, members are occasionally caught, and if the offense is sufficiently serious, it can cost their lives. The Nazis have issued a booklet of wartime regulations. "Anyone trying to get some private, sordid gain from the suffering of the Fatherland is a bloodsucker and a parasite," runs one comment. "He can expect neither sympathy nor mercy."

The risks are great, but the prices correspondingly high. Many of these people keep on the right side of the law by a scrupulous study of the fixed maximum prices in all shops. Everything, of course, has to be strictly formal, but the transaction is not the less lucrative for that. If, for instance, someone has two bottles of cognac and wants some coffee, he may get 3½ pounds of coffee for the liquor, which is "debited" to a value of 1.20 marks per pound of coffee—in other words, about 4.20 marks. The owner of the two bottles of cognac in his turn "debits" the peacetime price, a sum of perhaps 5 marks a bottle. The transaction ends as the coffee seller ceremoniously hands out the difference, in this case 5.80 marks.

During the first six months of 1943, the disintegration of morale was so great that hardly a German remained entirely law-abiding. Everyone had some small private blot on his conscience, either for some slightly "shady" trading in a store, or for buying at black-market prices. The value of money had fallen so enormously that no one could be blamed for such practices. In spite of increased taxes, there was cash in abundance, but no matter where one went there was a shortage of goods. Because the state was trying its hardest to hold the excess cash and help each owner to invest it in something of practical value, there was a constant battle between the two interested parties. That battle, in most cases, ended in victory for the individual, since the law, despite all its efforts, could not block every loophole. Berliners bought almost anything simply to get rid of their money. The trouble was there was hardly anything to buy. A man in Berlin today doesn't ask: "Do I need

---

[1] Or $100 at the pre-war rate of exchange, which was about 40 cents per mark.—Tr.

this or that?" or "What does it cost?" but simply: "What is there for sale?"

The black market received considerable supplies direct from the armed forces—one more proof of weakening morale. Gasoline came mostly from the army; sometimes we even saw the army gasoline coupons with which sales were made.

In the military forces there was a wholesale trade in automobiles. For instance, a commission consisting of one officer and two civilians was dispatched to an occupied country with an order to buy private cars. They bought twelve cars and paid, roughly, 50,000 marks. On their return they accounted to the authorities for only six cars—the other six were sold privately to eager speculators for 75,000 marks. Other commissions went even further, bringing back a diversity of goods for a lucrative turnover on the black market.

The increase in the length of the working day—ten hours was about the minimum and eleven to twelve hours was the average—added to the innumerable difficulties caused by the war, and resulted in sharp wear and tear on human beings. Often I had occasion to reflect on the fantastic tenacity that the Germans displayed: their endurance seemed only short of the miraculous.

Let us follow a German civil service employee of the lower middle class through one of his days. Since only a few are able to live in the center of Berlin, we may assume that he lives in a suburb. The workday begins early. The alarm clock goes off, say, at 6 a.m. At 6:45 Herr Müller has a hasty breakfast of bread and a little ersatz coffee or tea. At 7 he walks to his bus stop, which, at best, is ten minutes away. With good luck he gets on his bus at 7:15. Without such luck, the bus goes past without stopping, full to the last seat, and then it may be a long time before another comes. After a half-hour ride, he reaches the center of Berlin. Then an additional ten-minute walk brings him to the building where he works, perhaps an old public school. It is already eight o'clock. The workday has begun.

After Herr Müller has put in four hard hours, lunchtime arrives. If he can do so, he ignores this break. He has smuggled in some sandwiches which he will eat stealthily—to all appearances Herr Müller has not taken time out for lunch and he will get this time at the end of the day. But if Herr Müller is a bachelor or for some other reason does not carry a lunchbox, he must rush out at noon to try and find some food somewhere. What he gets will be little enough—unless the proprietor, looking far ahead to reliable post-war customers, favors him with fatter portions. He must stand in line for a table. He must sit long and patiently until he is served. He must hastily devour his food, for he has little time left. His meal consists, say, of potato soup, a meat course, warmed-over potatoes, a salad and—if our Müller is a brave man with a strong stomach—a chemical dessert, "real IG Farben." The meat course, it must be added, is something he can afford only occasionally, since the ration of 250 grams (about 9 ounces) allows only five meat meals of 50 grams each, per week—that is, 40 grams net with bones excluded. For a healthy man, it is scanty enough fare. With the noonday meal, however, comes a little gleam of light in the form of some weak beer. Now it is late, and he must hurry back, or else his assistant will get no food at all—after one o'clock there is usually not much left.

Müller plods on and soon he has put behind him ten hours of work. At 7 p.m. Müller is finished and goes after his bus, where he finds a seat or stands. With good luck—buses stop running at eight or nine o'clock—he arrives home at eight for a dinner consisting largely of boiled potatoes. After that he can attend to his private affairs until bedtime.

Generally, Saturday is a half-holiday, work ending at one or two o'clock. A total week must comprise at least 54 work hours. On Sundays, as a faithful Party comrade, Müller has his air-defense courses. Sometimes he also stands special guard duty at the office, in exchange for whatever free time he may have had during the week.

Müller's lot is pretty drab and sad. He hardly ever goes to the cinema and he seldom enjoys any kind of amusement whatsoever. If he has energy left for reading; it will more than likely be a news-paper. He may occasionally listen to the radio—Deutschlandssender, for Müller is loyal. When you see these petty officials and weary German workingmen, it is hard not to sympathize with them, and it is equally hard to know how they manage to survive their tasks. But when you see Herr Müller on his job, authoritative, confident, industrious, you get an opposite impression. Then he is *Herr Beamter*, a person of some importance.

One of the most difficult problems in Berlin is housing. If you have an apartment and are not dispossessed by the military forces, SS or a state organization, life is relatively smooth; not having an apartment means staying in a hotel or a furnished room, though the hotels are overcrowded and furnished rooms, as such, have disappeared. In recent years it has been practically impossible to rent an apartment. In the autumn of 1941, when I was looking for a place and thought I had found it, I was told that I could not rent it after all. No less than six generals and admirals were on the waiting list.

Air raids have made the problem still worse. Rigorous attempts were made in the spring of 1943 to house people who had been bombed out. The authorities circularized all homes, demanding declarations as to number of rooms, number of persons living there, etc. In principle, only one room to a person was permitted. If you had more than one room, you would have to take in lodgers. Everyone tried to dodge this rule, usually by the device of listing names of people who were dead or in the army, but the authorities knew all the tricks. Their answers were brusque: "If you won't take someone in, we will see to it that no one takes you in when your house is bombed." Also resistance is described as "a crime against the community spirit," and every German knows what penalties that involves. The threat of lodgers, however, worked well for foreigners, because they were eagerly sought as guests. Germans naturally preferred to have a well-paying foreigner in the apartment, rather than a bombed-out and destitute family.

One Nazi remedy for the acute housing shortage has ceased to function—the Jews. Once apartments occupied by Jews were requisitioned "according to demand." Now that is over and a somber chapter is ending. The last of the Berlin Jews are being shipped to the East. After Goebbels' March 1943 speech, there was a new wave of deportations. Under the most brutal conditions, Jews were picked up even on the streets, were herded into synagogues, then sent to Poland. From the synagogue in the Lewetzow-strasse you could hear the wailing of these unfortunate people. Just opposite was an SS barracks, and the young soldiers would lean out of their windows to watch the fun. Once I happened to be close by when a truckload of elderly Jews drove up. I heard loud peals of laughter from the barracks.

During that spring we witnessed many "shipments" of Jews. It was an appalling sight. The faces of the prisoners revealed such hopeless despair that even Germans were affected by it.

One day as I drove off from the Swedish Legation, I happened to come up behind a large covered truck, open at the back. After a while I looked up and saw the truck's freight—about 30 Jews. I followed it through half the city, wanting to find out where it was going. Suddenly I noticed that they were waving me off. Through my mirror I saw that a police car was behind me. I turned off at the next crossing and the police car went on.

At the beginning of May the last Jews were evacuated from our part of the city. A Jewish family had lived opposite us and we had always found their apartment friendly and cozy. One day it stood empty. The kitchen curtains had got caught outside the window, and they hung that way for weeks. Then the usual truck came to carry away everything movable and fixed, including the curtain poles. My wife once visited a Jewish home and there she got to see an evacuation at close range. The men did not speak to her. They worked calmly and methodically; everything was catalogued, packed and taken away. Both apartment and furniture were desirable enough. After a week another family had begun to put up curtains.

I do not know if Berlin has gotten rid of all its Jews by this time. Most likely the Nazis would have announced the fact if it were so. But when I left, it was assumed that no more than 4,000 remained. They were the sort the Germans were not eager to send away, for most of them were at work removing the fuses from delayed-action bombs, clearing up bombed houses, cleaning out garbage cans and carrying out other disagreeable tasks.

The more extreme steps met with some opposition. Prominent Nazis tried to convince the authorities that it would be better to stop the persecutions than to risk the possible resentment of the German people. There were even a few cases of armed resistance when Jews were being rounded up. In one house in the Fasanenstrasse, near the Foreign Press Club, all the tenants staged a protest when two Jews were taken away. A thirteen-year-old German girl was shot. Several prominent men ordered to divorce their Jewish wives committed suicide. One famous instance was the triple suicide of the well-known author, Jochen Klepper, his Jewish wife and her daughter by an earlier marriage.

There were many signs that the German people were becoming concerned over the brutal treatment of the Jews and were asking what had happened to them on the way to Poland and afterwards. One of my last memories of Berlin is associated with a painful incident. As I was entering the police station in Sächsischestrasse to "sign off," I noticed that "green Minna"—the fearful green police car—was parked outside. Suddenly an old woman was brought out from the police station and bundled into the car, her face paralyzed with fear. As the car started, an older German woman rushed up and tried to open the door, crying hysterically: "But she isn't a Jewess—I have known her for thirty years!" Even after the car disappeared, she continued to scream. Finally she went up to the official I had come to see and implored him to save her friend, with whom she had lived for 30 years. "I know she is not a Jewess," she sobbed repeatedly. "*Herr Beamter*, you must help me."

The official squirmed uncomfortably. Nothing, he assured her, would happen to her friend. The woman would not be quieted: "I know what they do to the Jews," she kept saying. When the official finally noticed me, a foreigner, he instantly sent her out, telling her she was lucky not to have been taken along with the Jewess.

There was a silence while he accepted my application for departure. But just as I was going, he said half to himself: "We really can't help it."

Far from easing up on their campaign against Jews, the Nazis planned throughout the spring to shorten the whole business, and included in the schemes even *die Mischlinge 1. Grades*, that is, half-Jews. So far the Nazis have not gone beyond removing half-Jews from their jobs. Apparently the High Command has objected even to this measure, but the High Command has often been overruled in matters of internal policy. I should judge that the best these new victims can hope for is a reprieve, not a pardon.

The Intensified Air Warfare

During the spring of 1943, the air war became more of a strain. The increasing devastation caused by the bombings created new organizational problems, indirectly affecting the war effort. But the bombings affected the war effort directly as well. A German journalist stated that one-third of the Krupp works in Essen were destroyed as far back as March. That is, one-third of the surface area was so hard hit that, for all practical purposes, it was wiped out.

The damage to heavy German industry was, however, proportionally small. Before the dynamiting of the Mohne and Eder dams in May 1943, foreign observers estimated that the average loss in West German production was not much over 10 per cent.

Afterwards the percentage rose. The attack on the dams was of enormous significance—indeed, it is no exaggeration to say that these bombings have been among the most telling blows struck against Germany so far. Not only were masses of people drowned, but the tax and census system of whole regions was disorganized—the floods carried away church records, police registers and other valuable documents. The blasting of the dams had important military consequences as well: the electric current supply was disrupted, the water supply in the vital canals decreased. As a consequence, barges had to carry lighter cargoes, with the result that shipping schedules were completely disrupted. Even if the dams could be repaired, it would still take a long time to refill them. From a military point of view, these bombings and those of the western industrial section were of far greater significance than the Berlin raids. But although the raids on Berlin were unimportant from a military standpoint, they had profound psychological meaning. Not only was the capital of Germany hit, but the symbol, as well, of National Socialism.

Many of the foreigners who visited Berlin in 1941 and 1942 expected to find the city in ruins. In fact, they had to search even to find traces of the raids. The war had indeed ravaged Berlin, but it is a big city and in the central districts the effects of the bombings were slight. Besides, the repair services worked with incredible speed. Within a few weeks, all traces of damage from a big raid were completely wiped out. During those first war years the authorities in Berlin spared no effort to conceal bombing damage. Money, materials and labor were lavishly expended. From the view of propaganda, it was important to demonstrate that the British raids were only pinpricks. When repairs were out of the question, planks were put up before the damaged property, with posters announcing that the building was in the hands of a contractor. Strangers in Berlin often marveled at the lively building activities.

By degrees the scars deepened, and as early as 1942 extensive repairs were no longer made. The more devastated streets were closed, the glass and gravel were removed, but otherwise things were left as after the raid. Since then the appearance of Berlin has drastically changed, especially after the heavy raid on March 1, 1943. With one blow it made Berlin a war-ravaged city.

The later raids in March and April were on a far smaller scale, but some sections were seriously damaged. In April the Gestapo began to circulate rumors that the British would observe Hitler's birthday, April 20, with a raid that would make the earlier ones seem amateurish. Berlin attics were feverishly emptied of everything inflammable, and those who could do so left the city on the 19th.

The 20th brought a reinforcement of the motorized anti-aircraft defenses, and Berliners packed their shelter bags in readiness for the alarm. Some time after midnight it came. Berlin defenses burst into action, but only a few bombs fell before we heard the "Danger past." Most of the populace waited on, believing that the British would surely come again. The British airmen, however, had other plans that night.

The next day I got news that threw a different light on what had happened. An acquaintance of mine suddenly received lodgers —soldiers from Stettin who made no secret of the fact that practically all the mobile anti-aircraft defenses from Stettin and Rostock had been sent to Berlin. It was apparently just what the British had wanted, for as soon as their secret service radioed the report, Stettin and Rostock were raided, and catastrophic damage was visited upon Stettin particularly.

With May began the almost daily visits of British Mosquito planes, their chief object being to annoy and wear down the Berlin populace. There were so many raids the authorities stopped announcing that there had been an air alarm, as they had done until that time. It would be a mistake to ignore the effects of these raids on the physical endurance of the inhabitants. There were times when the British, though they dropped only a few bombs, hung around Berlin so long that everyone was forced to spend several hours in the shelters, losing most of his night's sleep. At the start, trips to the shelters had been treated as sport. Those who would not go down justified their attitude by citing the slight effects of the bombings, or offered the very opposite excuse—that the shelters were so flimsy they threatened to cave in and bury everyone alive.

That Berlin was not better protected is difficult to understand, considering that work of this nature had been started there earlier than in any other city and that for years arrows had directed the way to shelters. The air-defense measures were on a far wider scale than in London or Stockholm, but the fact remains that, even according to the demands of those days, this protection was inadequate. The reason is, presumably, that no one had seriously expected large-scale raids on the capital.

Later, because of labor shortage and lack of material, there was no improvement, with the result that today Berlin shelters cannot be compared with those in Sweden. The Berlin shelter usually consisted of a cellar with the rubbish cleaned out and a couple of supports put in. In Sweden, proper cellar support is obligatory. In Berlin, this has been supplied on only a limited scale. And so those who have to sit in the German cellars, with water-pipes under the ceiling, gas-pipes in the walls and drains running from ceiling to floor, find in these conditions more than ample cause for depression. Moreover, the inhabitants know that the ceiling is weak and has no power of resistance should air pressure cause the building to collapse.

Not until 1941 did they begin to construct subterranean corridors and open up passages between one house and another, so that, if people were trapped, they might have a better chance to escape. But even with this precaution, inhabitants ran a greater risk of being suffocated or buried alive than of being hit by bomb splinters or burned. When two apartment houses near our home in the Zähringerstrasse collapsed, some hundred people were buried under the ruins. A few were dug out, but many died of suffocation.

Rescue work is highly complicated, since mechanical equipment can be used only rarely. Often, in fact, the work has to be done entirely by hand, as when a wrecked house is removed stone by stone. On one occasion a narrow carpet was inserted through an opening dug out of a coal pile, whereupon the victims were pulled out, one by one, on the carpet.

When the alarm is heard the inhabitants, with few exceptions, go down to the shelters, however weak those shelters may be. They carry gas masks as protection against dust, in case the building crumbles. Those who remain above ground have to reckon with splinters and fire. Anti-aircraft projectiles, sometimes splitting into small needle-like pieces of steel, can not only go straight through a human body, but even pierce a hard roof.

By the summer of 1943, damage in Berlin was pretty evenly distributed. The western sections had suffered least. Unter den Linden had been badly hit, although some buildings had been repaired. The Opera House had to be rebuilt, since only the bare walls remained. The University and the famous Prussian State Library were functioning. On the other hand, no attempt had been made to repair St. Hedwig's Cathedral. Minor damage was visible at the Hotel Adlon and the Café Kranzler, while scaffoldings still half-concealed the Swedish Travel Bureau, which is located a few yards from the completely demolished Deutsche Bank. Shortly after my arrival in Berlin a bomb fell near the Hausvogteiplatz, completely destroying a large department store. Next morning, to my horror I saw a mass of bodies lying on the street, covered with sheets. A man walked up and kicked the pile. I was on the point of protesting when I discovered that the bodies were wax mannequins.

In almost every raid the British tried to hit the Friedrichstrasse railroad station, but their bombs had fallen on practically everything in the vicinity except the station itself. The only real damage done there was caused by a bomb concealed by a saboteur.

The blocks round the Wilhelmstrasse had gone almost unscathed. The Ministry of Communications on the Wilhelmplatz had its top story destroyed, and Goering's ministry was hit by a well-placed air mine that ruined offices in 27 of its departments. But so far the Goebbels' ministry stands unscathed.

In the South of Berlin and especially in the Southwest, damage is terrific. A drive down the Potsdamerstrasse and the Hauptstrasse in the Schöneberg section reveals whole rows of houses wholly or partly wrecked. In the suburbs of Zehlendorf, Lichterfelde and Dahlem, many large homes, including those of prominent people, no longer exist. Some SS barracks in these regions have also been hit. Where the Kronprinzenallee and the Königin Luise Strasse meet in the suburb of Dahlem, a number of villas are in ruins, but the barracks there escaped uninjured.

West Berlin, above all Wilmersdorf, is a shambles. The Prager Platz and the Motzstrasse are devastated to a degree unparalleled elsewhere in the city. It is a gruesome experience to drive through these blocks at night, when the moon shines through glassless windows and roofless houses and there is not a sound to be heard. The nightmarish silhouettes of ruins against the sky suggest a stage set rather than reality.

Other seriously wrecked streets in the West of Berlin include the Nachodstrasse, the Bambergerstrasse and the Aschaffenburgerstrasse—all three, when I was there, temporarily closed. Further west, toward the Fehrbelliner Platz, where the British had so far failed to knock out the gigantic palace of the High Command, the

Zähringerstrasse, for one, was badly damaged. Many of this section's large garages, with their innumerable automobiles, went up in flames. One of the larger public schools in Münstersche Strasse was also hit one night. The municipality made temporary repairs: loose bricks and splinters were removed and paper put up in the gaping, empty windows. But in bad weather the paper blew away and there was nothing to do but definitely suspend the schoolwork, much to the delight of the children.

The Kurfürstendamm, even in the spring of 1943, had been exceptionally fortunate, but near the Halensee Station were some bad scars; while beyond this station, in the Grunewald, house after house has been burned to the ground. In the North of Berlin, a lot of damage had been done around the Putlitzstrasse Station and in the workers' district of Siemenstadt. Eastern Berlin had come off lightly, Neu-Köln being practically untouched.

The raids at the end of August 1943 hit the Memorial Church (Gedächtniskirche), and the Zoo and Charlottenburg Stations; but I was not there to see the extent of damage done.

Although there are military objectives in Berlin, I don't think much harm was done to them while I was in the city. A number of factories were destroyed and some barracks hit, but on the whole the attacks have taken a heavier toll of stores, private and apartment houses, churches—all of which are only indirectly essential to the war. The Germans claim that the British and Americans have purposely dropped bombs on civilian objectives. For a neutral observer it is very difficult to take a stand on such a question. Often while watching raids, I had the impression that the British fliers took great care as to where they let their bombs fall. On other occasions, fire bombs seemed to have been dropped indiscriminately.

It must be said, however, that no action against Berlin is carried out under favorable conditions. The anti-aircraft defenses are strong and well placed in and around the city. To prevent enemy fliers from putting these defenses out of commission the Germans have built towers (the largest of which is in the Tiergarten) with powerful units of night pursuit planes near by. Again, camouflage and "mirage" constructions have played their part in deceiving Allied pilots. But the importance of this form of defense should not be exaggerated. To begin with, many of Berlin's large establishments and their precise locations are known to the British. Secondly, building is at a standstill today for lack of both materials and labor;

and no camouflage can last indefinitely. The so-called "mirage" constructions in the North and South of Berlin may, however, be the explanation for the theory held by the British that the Potsdamer Station was hit. What they actually hit may instead have been a "mirage" station in some of these camouflaged sections. Fliers over Berlin, after all, have only a limited time at their disposal and it is for this reason that Berlin could not be bombed so systematically as the towns of Westphalia, which are hundreds of miles nearer England. Nor has any precision bombing of the capital been possible. Mostly the British have used explosive and fire bombs of average weight. The phosphorus bombs are especially terrifying. They can flare up a week after they have been dropped and they are very difficult to extinguish. Occasionally, time bombs, air torpedoes and air mines have been used. The British flares present a fantastic sight as they slowly descend, throwing a warm, red glow over the city.

Even though Berlin may not have endured what other German cities have been through, it is no child's play to experience a raid there. On the whole, the inhabitants have suffered the hardships of these raids with great courage, but not with the heroism that Dr. Goebbels celebrates in his speeches. Let no one cast stones who has not himself experienced an air raid. The ghastly howling of the sirens alone is enough to strike fear into the average man or woman. For a year we lived in furnished quarters in the home of a middle-aged woman who became hysterical at the first sound of the alarm.

Let me try to give some idea of what a raid on Berlin was like. In the darkness, we all grope our way down to the shelter. With us we take clothes, valuables and enough food for a day or two. As a rule, the majority don't dare use the elevator on the rare occasions when it works, for fear of getting caught between floors when the electric current is shut off. At the entrance to the cellar, a crowd has already gathered. We have to move carefully in the dark, so as to avoid falling over bundles and luggage. Suddenly the darkness is studded with blinding flashes of light. Anti-aircraft shells are exploding in the sky. The air reverberates from the roar of the guns —and children begin to scream. At last we manage to push our way into the shelter. Our party is made up of eight, including our little girl. The cellar is light and warm. Each of us has his or her own place, on old sofas and garden chairs, and we make ourselves as comfortable as we can. The atmosphere is tense, but not too unpleasant. The children, feeling safe, begin playing together. We grownups try to occupy ourselves—the greatest problem in a shelter. Simply to sit still and wait is extremely bad for the nerves.

I used to sit with my typewriter on my knees and write something to send to my paper on the following day. The Italian colleague who lived in the apartment below us used to play Patience, or a game of cards if he could find a partner. Others would read or sew. The older women talked incessantly, eager not to let themselves think. I often felt like telling them to shut up, for they had a passion for gossiping about those who had been wounded or killed in the previous raid.

Suddenly their conversation would be interrupted by whistling sounds from outside—it is the splinters raining down. Crash! That was a bomb. The house above us shakes, and the pipes in the ceiling groan. Now there is silence. Where will the next blow strike? There it is, but it's weaker. Thank God, the plane is leaving.

It's odd what trivial thoughts run through men's minds in a shelter. I often remember thinking to myself: "Thank heaven, I managed to put through my call tonight." As though it would have mattered, had my family perished from a bomb, whether or not my dispatch to the *Svenska Dagbladet* ever reached that paper! But that's the way one's brain works in a shelter. A good friend of mine, a Swede, told me that through the whole of one night he sat thinking how awful it would be if his splendid supply of wine were destroyed. Another friend had left his wallet in his apartment with 1,000 marks in it, and he kept arguing with himself whether or not he should venture out and fetch it.

The only thing that can be said in favor of "shelter life" is that it is both an equalizer and an unmasker of men. Common fear makes all people, even Nazis, human. When the bombs come crashing down, off comes the Nazi mask; and the moment the "all clear" sounds, on it goes again.

Air raids are a two-edged sword for the attackers so far as morale is concerned. Some people react with extreme bitterness, and are all the more ready to fight; others relapse into a state of utter hopelessness. I think it is a common belief that the morale of a people is strengthened rather than weakened by air raids. But if air raids come when there are political or production jobs to be done, then the contrary is the case.

Air raids, therefore, play an important part in the industrial production of the country attacked, in that they affect the workers physically and psychologically. Even though not a single factory is hit, the production results are affected because of the increasing physical weariness. An air alarm of two or three hours in the middle of the night is a great strain; what is lost as a result of it cannot be replaced by trying to get more sleep the next night; for the next night may be a repetition of the one that went before. Life itself becomes one long alarm—in all senses of that word.

Many Berliners have formed the habit of not undressing until about two o'clock in the morning, while others experiment with the system of retiring at eight o'clock in the hope of getting five hours sleep before an alarm sounds. But not even an "alarmless" night gives complete rest. It is as though the subconscious remained in a state of continual tension, prepared to have sleep disturbed by the sound of the sirens.

Military and Diplomatic Activity on Other Fronts

After Kharkov was recaptured from the Russians in the middle of March 1943, and the battles in the East had died down, it looked as though Hitler had once again assumed control of the armed forces. His photographs began to reappear in the German papers, and the space they received was evidence that everybody was expected to bow down before the Führer.

However, it was clear by now that Hitler's prestige as a military leader was at very low ebb. The most hair-raising tales were being circulated about his interference in military matters. He was utterly indifferent to any army formality and was said to issue commands to companies and battalions, over the heads of their superior officers. This attitude was characterized in a story of General von Bock, who was asked by the world-famous conductor, Furtwängler, why he had been relieved of his command. "My dear Furtwängler," replied the general, "if the Führer could play the mouth organ, you too would conduct no more in public." Hitler's bad reputation as a military leader was not improved when Colonel Scherff wrote another of his articles proving that he was one of the greatest commanders of all time, a man who acted from an "inner sense of duty."

To those who could read the Scherff article and ignore its propaganda aims, it was not without interest. During the most critical days, said the writer, Hitler could not remain calm; he suffered too much with his soldiers; such is his passionate temperament—and without passions, Mommsen once said, there can be no genius. It was quite natural, therefore, that Hitler's passionate desire to overcome crises should find passionate expression. To enforce his will upon a weakening eastern front, the Führer needs human greatness and all but superhuman sternness. Fate does not ask the Chosen Ones to fulfill the accepted idea of a commander. A genius selected by Fate must not be "censured by criticism." He is censured by Fate itself, concluded Scherff. This is as near to the truth as a Nazi can get when he starts writing history.

For some unknown reason the Memorial Services to the Nazis who fell at Kharkov was postponed a week. Then, for the first time in months, Hitler appeared in public. He looked older. He spoke with marked seriousness, in a voice hoarser than usual. People who didn't attend the meeting but merely heard the speech by radio spread the fantastic rumor that Hitler hadn't appeared at all but that the speech had been delivered by one of his deputies. "It wasn't Hitler's voice," they said.

Politically, the spring was dominated by German peace feelers and a growing interest in the Balkans and Turkey. Dr. Schmidt, of course, denied that there had been any suggestion of the Nazis suing for peace; he reminded us that for Germans, "the word 'victory' must come before the word 'peace.'" Some of his colleagues, however, made it known that there had been attempts to get in contact with the British direct, but that they had failed. Efforts to negotiate through a third power had also come to nothing—although Spain, highly interested in the results of arbitration measures, did all she could to further them.

For a long time it did look as though Hitler might try to negotiate for a separate peace with Russia. According to Berlin, the appearance of the Russian Quisling, General Vlassoff, in the spring of 1943, had some connection with a peace move. Supposedly well-informed circles claimed that Vlassoff commanded no fewer than 700,000 men, though only a small portion of this force could have been sent to the front. The strengthening of Vlassoff's position, however, did look like a typical attempt to find something to put into the scales during the talks with Russia.

A still clearer indication of German policy was the affair of the murdered Polish officers whose bodies were said to have been discovered in mass graves in the Katyan Forest (the Germans called it the Katy Affair). The charge that they were killed by the Russians was Nazi propaganda that, for once, had its desired effect. Regarding the truth of the charge, I am not in a position to judge. Unfortunately it does not seem completely incredible that the Russians might have executed thousands of Polish officers. It is, however, absolutely grotesque for the Germans to hold the Russians up to obloquy, when everybody knows that millions of Jews and Poles are rotting in far larger mass graves, and that their deaths were ordered by the same government that was declaiming against the Russians.

But the Nazis knew just what they were doing when they brought up the Polish question at that moment. For this problem continues to be a secret bond of union between Russia and Germany, both having laid their hands on what they could of that unfortunate country. The relationship is not unlike that which formerly prevailed between Prussia under Bismarck and the Russia of the Tsars. When Moscow suddenly broke off diplomatic relations with the Polish Government, German foreign propaganda recorded its first great triumph in a very long time. This time Goebbels had nothing to do with the case. It was Ribbentrop who had managed to force a wedge between Poland and Russia and create tension between Russia and the Western Allies. His success created favorable circumstances for preliminary peace discussions between Moscow and Berlin, in which it was hoped they might reach a decision to divide Europe between them.

Despite the undeniably favorable start, the German efforts failed. The increased tension between the Allies and the Russians, however, remained a fact, and one which the Germans were to use later in another drive for peace.

In the middle of April, the German press took up the subject of Turkey. Almost every day the newspapers—particularly the *Essener Nationalzeitung*, which had an excellent correspondent in Ankara—published extensive reports about Turkish developments. They were soon taking a specific line. British infiltration and the increasing orientation of the Turks toward London were treated lightly. Instead, these reports emphasized British intrigues in Turkey. They maintained that the British, by a war of nerves, were trying to prevail on Ankara to change its policies. But the Turks, so the newspapers said, had refused to compromise themselves in the eyes of Germany.

Slowly the tone against Turkey sharpened. When a member of

the Turkish Parliament declared that the Germans were the first to bomb large cities, the *Völkischer Beobachter* answered curtly that this was "unfathomed insolence." Then came a more violent attack on the Turks from another source in Berlin. Dr. Schmidt announced that a lecture would be delivered at his Tuesday *Stammtisch* in the Foreign Press Club. When members learned that the subject was Turkey, they turned up to a man. Even non-members were highly excited.

That evening was remarkable in many respects. One of the editors of the Slovak newspaper *Grensbote*—who had just returned from Ankara—made a speech. He declared that Turkey actually was infiltrated with British and Americans, that the Turkish resistance to them was weak, but that it still lay within Turkish power to prevent Allied influence from increasing. Dr. Schmidt jumped to his feet. "No," he said, "you are mistaken." And then, to the stupefaction of the audience, the Chief of the Press Division of the German Foreign Office proceeded to explain that Turkey had become "one single British airfield," that the British had laid out roads, piled up supplies by shipping them through the Dardanelles to warehouses on the Black Sea, and finally that they had so consolidated their position that militarily, politically and economically Turkey was more than ever in the power of the Allies. "Turkey believes," continued Schmidt firmly, "that she plays a part in world politics, but actually she is only a tool. It should be in Ankara's interest to remain neutral, but the British have apparently convinced the Turks that the only way to escape Russian troops at the Straits is to let in the Allies."

This was a bombshell. But Schmidt's audience was even more flabbergasted when he began to emphasize the interest that Bulgaria took in Turkish policy and to dwell on the strength of the Bulgarian army, which stood ready to march.

As late as 1942, anything like this would have been followed by a summons to a special conference at five o'clock the following evening, with Ribbentrop there in his Foreign Office uniform to announce that still another country had been invaded. The fact that this did not happen gave the impression that there must have been a very different motive for such extraordinary statements— and just what that motive might be was the only topic of conversation for the next few days. Why all these threats? It was not like the Foreign Office to put all its cards on the table if immediate action were intended. Naturally, the Turkish Embassy knew all about the threat almost as soon as the astounding words were out of Schmidt's mouth. The Turks, however, were not in the least frightened. They knew that the days when Germany could afford to attack new countries twice a year were now in the past.

NAZISM

The Leaders

I⊤ is still too soon to draw up a balance sheet of the Nazi regime. For decades scholars will busy themselves with the question: How did it come about that such a movement, headed by such men, succeeded in usurping control of the strongest nation in Europe and setting the whole world on fire?

Research will concentrate upon the men in the movement, for they—and not the ideas—have conquered Germany. The ideology of National Socialism is by no means original, and in practice it has undergone great modifications. What is left today, for instance, of the once loudly proclaimed economic theories of Gottfried Feder? The Nazi leader corps, however, has held together in spite of all inner conflicts. This fact has been its great strength and is partly an explanation of its triumphs. The outward harmony has been dictated at one and the same time by a community of interests and by a fanatical faith in the National Socialist idea, represented first and foremost by Adolf Hitler.

But behind this unified front is hidden a muddle of clashing interests, an unprecedented tug-of-war between situations and persons, which Hitler seems to have encouraged in order to retain his place as supreme judge. He has also been able to keep the struggle within permissible limits, that is, within the framework of the Party. Those who tried to break away were immediately seized and some of them were shot.

It is wise not to speculate too much on the political effects of the many clashes within the Nazi Party. Every leader knows that a dire fate awaits him at the moment when this combination of individuals is dissolved. The desire to jump off the bandwagon is held in check by fear of the consequences.

Some of the clashes have a more general interest. Perhaps the most famous of them is the one between Goering and Goebbels, but it has become less obvious in recent years, and in many instances the two former enemies have united against common opposition—

for instance, against von Ribbentrop. The corpulent Reichsmarshal cherishes an antipathy for both the person and the policies of the Foreign Minister. But Ribbentrop in his turn has a powerful ally— the new Minister of the Interior, Himmler—who in turn likes to collaborate with Hitler's deputy, Martin Bormann. The two have repeatedly tried to remove Goebbels by using items of scandal from Ribbentrop's files; but the Minister of Propaganda has proved to be indispensable, and he has been able to lean on Hitler himself.

In some other matters Himmler and Ribbentrop are also fierce rivals. The Chief of Police belongs to the groups that have championed the use of Quislings, a policy opposed by the Foreign Office. Moreover, the Foreign Office is often supported by the High Command, to Himmler's great displeasure.

In the midst of these complicated intrigues, turns of fortune come swiftly. Early in 1943, Goebbels, for instance, became the man of the hour, but after a few months he had sunk back to his former place. Then Goering disappeared from his high position— how often this had happened before is unknown—and near the end of the spring we heard that he was in half exile in Graz. In August, something mysterious happened that brought him again to the fore. Although it has often been said that the Reichsmarshal was the choice of the military, there are signs of distrust on one side and the other. Nevertheless a situation can arise for the Reichswehr when something quite simply needs to be done, and Goering at such a time may be the man to do it. This may have been the case last summer, when he returned to governmental power. That Himmler became Minister of the Interior about that time is a fact pointing in the same direction, for the appointment seems to counterbalance something else. But what? Was his promotion a measure directed against Goering, and is Himmler for the present Hitler's favorite? Only the observer on the spot has some chance to find an answer. But this much is certain—Himmler at one and the same time is Hitler's indisputable tool and is completely dependent on the Führer.

The foreign observer in Berlin usually has a chance to see Hitler only during his rare public appearances. Watching him speak, one is impressed by the striking inconsistencies in his nature. Hitler's bearing seems stiff, without ease or dignity. When he steps out on the rostrum, he looks like a petty tradesman trying in vain to play the part of a great statesman.

He begins to talk in a loud voice, usually telling the by now familiar and completely boring tale of how he rose from being an unknown soldier to becoming the leader of the German Reich. By degrees he warms up, and suddenly one sees quite another man, a bundle of nerves, highly passionate. His phrases fall like hammer blows, and a glance reveals that the whole audience follows every word with gaping mouth and goggling eyes. You have to pinch your arm not to be swept along by the mass hypnosis. Then suddenly the spell vanishes, and what you see is only the little man trying to convince others and himself of his greatness. One looks in vain for any moral exaltation. There is seldom a manly or chivalrous word about his opponents—only a paroxysm of burning hatred. When Hitler slips down into the nether regions of his own personality he is merely common, in the worst sense of the word.

Superficially, his foreign policy seems to be colored by a cynical realism. But the truth is that his emotions and his personal attitude have played a far greater role than is imagined by many outside Germany. It is no secret in Berlin that something on the agenda may lie waiting for weeks, since the councilors do not dare to bring up any painful or difficult matter until some moment when Hitler is in an unusually good frame of mind. Many times his personal rancor may determine the policy of Germany. This irrationality is the terrifying feature of his regime. Some fine day he may give an order that will lead to the invasion of still another country. Unless his councilors succeed in changing his mind, Germany will have taken some new initiative that cannot be justified from either a political or military point of view.

As for the military command, no one can deny Hitler's ability to make magnificent plans. But he also has a passion for details, a trait that has irritated the military enormously. His Chief of the General Staff may be called 30 times in a morning to explain the meaning of operations that should be the business of the commanders in the field. Hitler may also delay the approval of some new weapon, declaring that he wants to check all the details personally, a process that may take weeks or months.

To have a commander-in-chief so conscious of his power and yet so lacking in military education must be among the greatest trials of the German General Staff. Nobody would deny that political and military decisions for a nation at war must, in the last analysis, be made by the same man or group of men. Yet the statesmen of other countries have solved the problem of retaining a decisive influence over the conduct of the war without interfering at every moment with the military leaders. This is something that Hitler has signally failed to do. He wants to be a soldier as well as a statesman—in fact the greatest soldier in history—and he hasn't the necessary equipment.

In different connections I have tried to describe his personal contributions to warfare. During the past years they have had disastrous effects for Germany. Perhaps the best explanation is the motto he has followed all his life: "To make the impossible possible." In the political field that principle has produced brilliant results. Against the expressed advice of the generals, Hitler ordered the remilitarization of the Rhineland. Against their advice he marched into Austria. Against their advice he "solved" the Czech question. How could all these political triumphs fail to give him the impression that his military judgment, too, was infallible?

It was this policy of realizing the impossible that Hitler sought to follow when he invaded Russia. The violent offensive against Moscow, the summoning of all resources to strike an irresistible blow—all this carries the imprint of Hitler's personal conception. But it was a conception that failed to include such military factors as reserves, transport, the weather and the fighting spirit of the Russian people. Because Hitler has misjudged such factors, his military authority has collapsed on the Russian steppes and in the North African deserts.

During the past two years Hitler has changed, as is apparent to all who have seen him at infrequent intervals. He has grown older. In his eyes is a more tense and harassed look. He gives the impression of a man who knows that the sands in the hourglass are running low.

As for his health, only the initiated know his real condition now. I shall not attempt to list the many collapses that Hitler has suffered from time to time; it is enough to say that he has not been un-interruptedly in power. Sometimes for weeks or months, the political and military control has been in other hands—the political usually in those of Himmler and Bormann, the military in those of the High Command. But one wonders if Hitler, even at the height of his vigor, really learned the truth about the situation. It is natural enough to dress up the facts when they have to be presented to a stern master. Today Hitler lives in complete isolation and sees very few persons.

As the day's strife fades into the background, history will appraise his career and try to solve the riddle of his personality. Perhaps the clues will be found in physicians' reports and in some events of his youth—his leaving the Austro-Hungarian army in 1914 and his service in the First World War. Why have so few of his officers and comrades from that period made themselves known? Problems like these must be left to the future.

Hermann Goering has boasted of being Hitler's foremost paladin. At times circumstances have pushed him aside for others, but he now seems to be restored to his old place. In the present critical circumstances he has one trump card in hand—he has been formally named as Hitler's successor in case something should happen to the Führer.

Originally Goering was used by the Nazis as the broom for the first rough sweeping. But even for the more complicated problems later under his control, such as the organization of the new air service, his zest and energy have been a vital asset. All opposition was overwhelmed. A German industrialist has given me a vivid account of how Goering cleaned house if the least protest was made against his economic powers. The results were brilliant and all objectives were realized on paper—but was it a victory? The cost of carrying out the plans was not included in the reckoning of accounts. Even if National Socialism in its earlier stages claimed to be indifferent to questions of high finance, there still should have been one matter to make the Nazis think twice—the waste of energy. If Goering had listened to the advice of his leaders in industry, many a fiasco might have been averted.

It is strange that this man whose personal brutality exceeds that of the other leaders has come to represent the human side of the regime. His interest in uniforms and medals, in childish display and good hearty food, was something that the Germans recognized as a national characteristic and that made him their favorite. His popularity has waned. In the face of grim necessity no one now looks tolerantly on his fondness for luxuries. He is no longer called "our Hermann," though he is still relatively popular in comparison with the other Nazi leaders. However, more and more stories have been spreading about his liberal conception of mine and thine. Many are inclined to judge Goering more severely than Goebbels, primarily because Goering was an officer in the Kaiser's army, chief of the Richthofen Squadron, and holds the Pour-le-mérite for his exploits in the air. One of the many stories about him reflects the general attitude. At a reception a guest was admiring a handsome chandelier. A general passed by and said to the host, "Be careful or Goering will see it."

As an orator Goering is weak; his brief opening addresses as Speaker of the Reichstag are barked rather than spoken. Nor is he master of parliamentary procedure. Once he forgot to close a Reichstag meeting, and it was only after the members had begun to rise and go out that I heard a low "The meeting is adjourned" from the chair.

Now and then Goering has intervened in foreign policy. He always stood ready to act as an envoy extraordinary to Poland. It is generally held that Goering has been friendly to Sweden also, and some people like to think that he is responsible for many decisions made in Sweden's favor. There is, however, less question about his friendly attitude than there is about his ability to influence Hitler in foreign affairs. He gives advice, but it isn't always followed.

Heinrich Himmler, the new Minister of the Interior, "Reichs Leader of the SS and Chief of the German Police," is perhaps the Nazi leader least known to the public. Apparently he considers this fact to be an asset; at any rate he has refused to authorize any publicity about himself and has even directly forbidden the SS organization to issue the customary propaganda about their chief. But even though he has tried to keep in the background, his work and position are of a type that seems to guarantee his name a place in history.

For a foreign observer, who must be on his guard not to come into contact with Himmler, it is hard to say how much the general idea of him as the incarnation of the modern police system, as *der Himmler*—in the Middle Ages, the one who hoisted people, that is to say, the hangman—corresponds to actual facts. Some regard him as merely a tool, first for Heydrich, now dead, and later for others, including Hitler himself. But there is unmistakable evidence that Heinrich Himmler is a man of independence who, with determination and energy, has built up an organization so complete that he is able to keep an eye on everybody, the Führer not excepted. In secret files Himmler has everything one needs to know about the escapades of Goering and Goebbels. Some people claim the organization has gone so far that there is even a fat folder with the label "Heinrich Himmler." The least one can say is that the

German Chief of Police has extraordinary powers, not only through his command over the Gestapo but also through his knowledge about the public and private lives of the Nazi leaders.

He is no less dangerous because he seems to tower above the usual Nazi scramble for wealth and decorations. In his attitude toward his associates he is said to be modest, friendly and helpful. He looks like a timid German official in a subordinate position. Only the cold, hard glance makes you conscious that the greatly feared head of the Gestapo is at hand.

Just before I departed I had a chance to study his features in the back of a mirror of my car. It was on a bright May day when I passed a big limousine with an ordinary license number and discovered to my horror that Himmler and his adjutant were the two passengers. I slowed down to the required 25 miles per hour, and the law-abiding Chief of Police also kept down to 25 in his big Mercedes. Himmler seemed jovial. He waved to children, who in turn waved to the big car; he chatted with his adjutant and laughed long and often. After fifteen minutes, during which I felt like a rat with the cat on his tail, I turned off the main highway and escaped.

What is the ambition of the newly named Minister of the Interior? Many hold that he aspires to be Number One in Germany and that his new post is a step on the ladder. Others say that Hitler offered him the Ministry of the Interior years ago, but that Himmler refused because of his great unpopularity. Nothing in his career seems to suggest ambition in the ordinary sense. But, what is far more dangerous, he has a demonic lust for power, which seems to be his strongest incentive. He also has one advantage in relation to most of his opponents in the struggle: he is relatively young. Himmler is only forty-two years old, and therefore ten years younger than the average for the other National Socialist leaders.

Martin Bormann, who is one of Germany's most powerful men, is almost entirely unknown outside his own country. The foreign correspondents in Berlin sometimes say that in fact if not in name he is the successor of Rudolf Hess. Bormann is Hitler's deputy and —like Hess—he is the chief of the Party Chancellery; in short he is Hitler's right-hand man in everything that concerns internal affairs. Whereas Hess was a modest and retiring man, Bormann is a master of intrigue. Whereas Hess used to be known as an impartial arbiter of clashes within the Party, Bormann never judges one of these quarrels without taking the opportunity to improve his own position. He has strengthened that position all the more with the help of persons he could trust in government circles and in the High Command. Bormann today is Germany's "Gray Eminence."

One great interest of his is ecclesiastical matters. After Kerrl, the Minister of Cults, died in Paris in a compromising situation, to put the case mildly, there was no one officially responsible for church policy. Bormann has taken over that task, to the great dismay of German churchmen. It is directly because of his orders that pastors and priests have been arrested, that church buildings have been closed or converted into granaries and warehouses for theatrical properties, and that religion has been frowned upon to such a degree that sometimes Christianity and not Bolshevism seemed to be the principal enemy.

Typical of his attitude is a letter from Bormann published during August 1942 in *Svenska Dagbladet*. In it one reads that National Socialism and the Christian point of view are two incompatible concepts and that the people must be vigorously separated from churches and pastors. "Just as the state puts an end to the injurious influences emanating from astrologers, fortune tellers and other swindlers, so too must it destroy any possibility that the doctrines of the Church will make themselves felt. Not until this has been done can the government exercise full control over the individual citizens." Bormann, who speaks for the government, regards the churches as rivals.

Dr. Joseph Goebbels, Minister of Propaganda, controls the minds of the German people like an orchestra director on his podium. He has a fine sense of what ought to be said and at what moment. He can either rouse the people to action or else, even more skillfully, he can put them into a lethargic state and keep them there. The strain on his nerves, however, has left traces on his face. The air of cynicism and perversity has become more marked than before, as his contempt for mankind has become more apparent and his hatred of the bourgeois community more intense. As a speaker, Goebbels is perhaps the best in all Germany. Nobody else has the same talent for playing on the psychology of the masses as if it were a musical instrument. The Minister of Propaganda is a far better speaker than his Führer, but it is the latter who has carried the German people with him. Instead of being a leader of the masses, Goebbels is unpopular and even hated. The leader has to be something more than an orator. I have a strong feeling that the Germans instinctively recognize the cynicism behind Goebbels' speeches; that the brains of his hearers are doubtless bewitched by his biting and vigorous words, but that their hearts remain cold.

Nevertheless, his political power last year was greater than ever. The reason why attacks on Goebbels have always failed is that Hitler cannot do without him. The greater necessity there is for propaganda to save the situation, the stronger his influence becomes. At the beginning of 1943 he received carte blanche from Hitler to organize the total mobilization. The campaign was only a partial success, and the result was that he lost some of his prestige, but he is still very strong. I should rank him fifth among the Nazi leaders.

When the history of this war is written, no words of praise will be wasted on Joachim von Ribbentrop, Germany's Foreign Minister. He is an example of the many energetic but completely unscrupulous personalities brought to the surface by Nazism. Originally a champagne salesman—hence his nickname, Joachim "Extra Dry"—Ribbentrop was adopted by a relative, therewith acquiring the coveted "von" in his name.

By keeping as close as possible to Hitler and giving him constant advice on foreign affairs, Ribbentrop came to exercise great influence. The advice he gave was pleasing to Hitler's ears, for Ribbentrop represented the clenched-fist policy, as opposed to Neurath, who had the thankless job of trying to persuade Hitler to be moderate. Ribbentrop also built up his personal organization, *Dienststelle Ribbentrop*, consisting of young, capable and ambitious members, which rivaled the official diplomatic service.

His big chance came when he was appointed ambassador in London. This was during the time when Hitler seemed to be interested in establishing close relations with Britain, the program he had announced in *Mein Kampf*. Joachim von Ribbentrop's mission to London was, however, a complete fiasco. The new ambassador greeted the English King with the Nazi salute, and made himself generally obnoxious. This did not affect his favored position with Hitler, since Ribbentrop succeeded in giving the impression that it was not the ambassador but the English who were to blame for his failure. After his return to Germany he became Hitler's special expert on England and, from 1938, his Foreign Minister.

The theory on which his policy was based is well known by now. It was his notion that the degenerate democracy of England would never cause Germany any trouble worth mentioning but would, at all costs, avoid getting involved in the coming conflict.

Many Germans believe that he is even more responsible for Nazi aggression than Hitler himself. Germany's foreign policy has borne his characteristic stamp. There seems to be a solid foundation for a belief one often hears expressed: that if Ribbentrop had not insisted that Britain would yield, and if he had not advised Hitler to force the Polish-German conflict to a climax, there might not have been a world war in 1939. Still it would have come sooner or later.

The Foreign Minister is an eloquent speaker and women find that he has an attractive face. Nevertheless he is disliked and even despised by the German people. You often hear it said that he is Hitler's evil spirit and has driven him to war. It is also said—probably with full justice—that Ribbentrop is conceited and snobbish. Many stories circulate about his extravagance and that of his wife.

But the most unpopular of the Nazi leaders is probably Dr. Robert Ley. He is corpulent, with a triple chin and hoops of fat around his neck; he has a hoarse, asthmatic voice and a bullying Nazi manner. He makes a spectacle of himself at official ceremonies, especially Reichstag meetings, as he shambles forward with an anxious look to greet those of higher rank than himself, always with a side glance at the photographers. Not even Field Marshal Keitel, nicknamed "La Keitel" because he is so willing to prostitute himself to anyone in power, can hide his disgust at the sight of the fat little cabinet minister.

Hitler, on the other hand, regards Ley as one of his few personal friends. The little doctor is a simple soul, always filled with gushing admiration for his Führer. It is this admiration that ensured his political success and made him leader of the Labor Front. Besides deciding the fate of German workers, Ley also finds time to eulogize the Führer several times weekly in the editorials he writes for *Der Angriff*—editorials that are masterpieces of sublime drivel. A foreigner reading them gets the impression that their author is possessed by some kind of primitive ecstasy. As a matter of fact, Ley was once a revivalist, and he still speaks with the same mystical fervor. It may sound like blasphemy, but those who have read or heard Ley cannot escape the impression that this simple man worships Hitler as a god. He himself says that on leaving the Führer he always feels his faith strengthened and is like a new person.

His new religion hasn't improved his personal morals. Many moderate Nazis have tried to drive him from public life, knowing that he has always been a center of corruption in the Party. They had no trouble in finding evidence of public drunkenness and large-scale peculation. Ley lives luxuriously in the great palace of the German Labor Front near the Fehrbelliner Platz. He owns considerable property (bought, of course, with what he saved from his official salary, or at least that is his story) and has so many country estates that there is one, near Berlin, which he hasn't even visited since 1938. Yet although his dishonesty is known even to the children in Berlin, there is no hope of getting rid of him so long as Hitler protects him.

One of the oldest champions of the Party and its renowned theorist is Alfred Rosenberg, who now holds the rank of Under Secretary. He was for many years editor-in-chief of the *Völkischer Beobachter* and he also had the special task of supervising the education of the German people in what the Nazis regard as their new world philosophy. His books, especially *The Myth of the Twentieth Century,* helped to provide an ideological basis for Nazism. But Rosenberg has also had a practical job and one that gave him considerable influence in the period from 1938 to 1941, when Nazi ideology had been pushed into the background.

Rosenberg is a German born in one of the Baltic states—Latvia—when it was under the Tsar; he was educated at a technical institute in Moscow, not being graduated till after the Bolshevik revolution. As a result of this background, he became Hitler's expert in Russian problems. In the fall of 1941, he was appointed Minister for the Occupied Territories in the East, an office that brought him into spirited rivalry with Ribbentrop. It is Rosenberg, however, who has succeeded in setting his stamp on the German policies toward the conquered populations.

In his secret instructions to officials in the East, Rosenberg demanded that they should have real ability for leadership, *echtes Führertum.* This meant, above all, the ability to make decisions—wrong decisions on the spot would be better than right decisions that came too late—and to command the Russians. "No explanations, no statements about our motives—the Russians want to see our men as leaders. Don't talk; act. You can never persuade or convince the Russians by talking to them. They know how to use words better than you do, because they are born dialecticians."

The reason why action alone impresses the Russians, Rosenberg continued, is that they are weak and sentimental in a feminine fashion. The Russians want to be a mass with somebody ruling over them. The German invasion will greatly please them today as it did in the time of Rurik a thousand years ago; the message they sent to him was, "Come and rule over us." Above all, don't relapse into weakness and sentimentality. "Keep the Russians at a distance, because they are not Germans but Slavs. Don't drink with the Russians. Under no circumstances allow yourselves to become involved with Russian women when supervising their work. You will lose your prestige with the Russians if you lower yourself to their level. After centuries of experience the Russian regards the German as a higher being. Take care to see that this German reputation is upheld."

And there was more in the same vein. Germans were to preserve their unity against the Russians. They had to defend other Germans even for their mistakes as long as Russians were present. "Poverty, hunger and contentment have been Russian characteristics for many centuries. The Russian's stomach is elastic; therefore have no false pity on him. Don't attempt to use the German standard of living as a gauge or to change the Russians into something better." These secret instructions, which have been followed by thousands of German officials in the East, help to explain why the Germans have aroused the undying hatred of the conquered population.

The Reichsleiter and Gauleiter—that is, the federal and district leaders—are the big men of the Party bureaucracy. Some of them have an extremely wide influence in their particular fields, but most of them play no great part in determining national policies.

Baldur von Schirach, the governor of Vienna, belongs to this category. He used to be the Nazi youth leader. Today he is middle-aged, but he still looks like a fat boy with expressionless features. He is a complete failure as an orator, for he reads from notes without showing any sparkle or spirit. At the Propaganda Ministry his photograph occupies a prominent place, but that is only because he is the son-in-law of Hoffman, the court photographer, who always manages to push his picture into the foreground. I have heard Baldur von Schirach accused of trying to advance his own interests at the expense of the Party, but this criticism is probably unfair. Nothing suggests that any strong will or ambition hides behind his weak and unprepossessing appearance. The one thing you can say for him is that, as governor of Vienna, he has shown some understanding of Viennese problems, this being a virtue not displayed by the other Nazi leaders. Hitler himself regards the Austrian capital with a mixture of love and hatred; sometimes he says that he wants to restore Vienna to its rank as a great city; at other times he calls it Gomorrah and wants to deprive it even of its imperial memories.

Robert Wagner, the Governor and Gauleiter of Alsace, occupies one of the most difficult positions in the German government. Time and again he has been forced to make threatening speeches not only to the Alsatians but also to lukewarm or self-seeking members of the Party. That speeches are not enough to keep the Alsatians content is shown by the many official reports of executions in Strassburg. Wagner is a former army officer, having retired after taking part in Hitler's Beer Hall Putsch in 1923. He is a fanatical apostle of Nazism, but undoubtedly a capable man, with more agreeable features than his colleagues.

Two of the administrative districts that include territory formerly belonging to Poland are governed by two of the most ruthless men in the Party. Danzig-Westpreussen is under Albert Forster, who is Germanizing his district with exceptional energy and brutality. Wartheland is under Arthur Greiser, who, besides showing the same energy, has become famous for his unlimited greed and passion for luxuries. He has erected a stone wall almost 50 feet high around his new palace in Posen. There he lives like a prince—or rather in the way Greiser thinks a prince should live.

When Josef Buerckel was Gauleiter of Vienna he was known as "Hitler's broom." He became so unpopular with the Viennese that he was transferred to Lorraine. When he left Vienna, a group of people at the station cried out, "Stay, Buerckel! Don't go, Buerckel!" Flattered, he asked where they lived. "We are from Lorraine," was their answer. Buerckel is now out of favor with Hitler, and I heard rumors last spring that he had been arrested.

Many of the Gauleiters have been given important posts in the conquered countries. The Gauleiter of Essen, Josef Terboven, is now the dictator of Norway. The Gauleiter of East Prussia, Koch, has been ruling over the Ukraine.

It must be remembered that there are two separate bureaucracies in Germany—that of the Party and that of the government. High government officials are often members of the Party without having any post in the Party bureaucracy; instead they are classed as civil servants. One of these men is Speer, who is Hitler's favorite architect; he designed the Chancellery in Berlin and many other monumental buildings. Perhaps he has not created any aesthetic masterpieces, but his designs are distinguished by a sober simplicity; they compare favorably with the gingerbread of the Kaiser Wilhelm period, as well as with the naked functionalism of architecture under the Weimar Republic.

When Major General Fritz Todt was killed, Speer succeeded him as head of the Todt Organization—in effect, the German Engineers' Corps. Germans in general thought that he was a good man for the job, since he was known to be friendly and honest, quite unlike most of the Nazi leaders. He has done his work well, perhaps even better than had been expected.

The Acting Minister of Agriculture, Backe, is another exceptionally able man, with a strong will and the ability to stand up for his ideas. He could not prevent the reckless increase in rations during the autumn of 1942, in spite of making lively protest, but otherwise Backe has been able to exercise great influence over the German food supply. He is reported to have an extremely wide theoretical and practical knowledge of agriculture. In this respect he is quite unlike Darré, his predecessor, who was a Nazi theorist out of touch with realities. Backe not only lays plans for solving agricultural problems but often makes an inspection trip and tells the farmers just what they should do to raise bigger crops. The farmers say that he is usually right.

The Police, the Party and the SS

The National Socialist regime rests on two solid pillars. One is the German police; the other is the Party with its various organizations, foremost of which is the Blackshirt Guard or SS.

As the invincible guarantee of the power of the Nazi Party over the population stands a police force consisting of at least 500,000 men. The departmental functions are handled by an intricate system of agents and cells. Within all social circles in Germany, Himmler has discrete observers and reporters who, without revealing their identities, keep the police informed of changes in the attitude of the German people. Naturally the police have effective assistance from the giant Party organization, but Himmler has also endeavored to enlist individuals outside the Party (by no means ignoring Jewish elements).

The police have at their disposal every kind of modern technical equipment. Prominent scientists are at their service as expert advisers, and special laboratories furnish drugs to compel even the most stubborn to talk. The police have developed to perfection a system of internal espionage and surveillance over foreigners which, from a technical point of view, it is difficult not to admire. Many foreigners have refused to believe that such a thing could be possible, and have later paid for their folly. They have discovered that people whom they regarded as their personal friends had reported in detail every word of confidential conversations. One of the greatest assets of Himmler's police is an enormous card system in which not only the whole German population is registered, but also nearly every person of importance in foreign countries. These dossiers are packed with the most intimate details of everyone's life.

The German police operate according to a carefully prepared system. Their cardinal principle is that every sort of crime must be prevented, but especially crimes against the Nazi regime. These crimes are the special province of the Gestapo, and its principal weapon against them is terror. The whole organization has an atmosphere of terror, of torture, that suggests the Middle Ages and the Spanish Inquisition. This atmosphere is deliberately maintained. Arrests are made at night or early in the morning; those who make the arrests are silent and grim; no explanation is offered, and the prisoner and his family are given the impression that he is going straight to the gallows. The victims may have to wait for weeks without even being questioned. They are packed together, as many as 40 in a small room, without ventilation, without a chance for unbroken sleep and with unbelievably foul sanitary conditions. Worst, perhaps, is the food, which is beyond description. Those who have been cooped up for three or four weeks are sometimes unrecognizable.

The Gestapo ignores completely the legal formalities that used to be observed in Europe. The following is a typical story from Vienna. Ex-king Ferdinand of Bulgaria has resided in Germany since 1918. The Weimar Republic respected him as a distinguished guest. The fact that his son, Boris III, entered into a close alliance with Germany should have been reason enough for the Germans to behave decently toward the old king, who since his abdication had taken no part in politics. A few years ago, however, one of King Ferdinand's German relations, the young Prince Dietrichstein, was arrested in the presence of the king. When King Ferdinand protested, he received the scornful answer: "Why should we care if you used to be a king?" The old monarch immediately informed his son of what had happened, and after a strong intervention from

Sofia, Dietrichstein was released. Apologies were extended to King Ferdinand; but it is quite unlikely that the Gestapo agent handling the arrest was demoted or even given a reprimand. For, as a person close to the Gestapo told me, "Such happenings instill terror in those who otherwise might think themselves protected by their position." This would apply especially to Vienna.

When terror doesn't work, the Gestapo incites people to rebellion, using the methods once followed by the Tsar's secret police, the Okhrana. When the German police chiefs hear that trouble is brewing in some corner of the country, they often send someone to organize a plot. When the faked plot has been "hatched," down comes the Gestapo to capture all the conspirators, except perhaps one or two.

In foreign countries there are two branches of German espionage, one military, under the jurisdiction of the three defense departments, and the other of political character, supervised by the Gestapo. One function of the latter is to keep an eye on Germans abroad, above all the German diplomats, who are under the strictest supervision. Very often one of their fellow workers or a domestic servant or a friendly foreigner may be reporting back to the Gestapo.

Despite its efficiency, the Gestapo is not infallible. It has often been fooled by people trained for that purpose. There are cases of German police officers, or women associated for years with chiefs of police, who in reality have been working all along for the British Intelligence Service. Himmler's practice of conscripting agents has also resulted in the employment of many unreliable people who, the moment they were safe from detection, have committed acts of sabotage

The National Socialist Party, the basis of the regime, is actually a giant organization parallel with the State. Each government authority and activity has its parallel within the Party. There are departments for both foreign and domestic policies, for racial questions, for public health and for political economy. The Party also has its military organ, in fact a complete army, the Waffen SS.

Many had expected that this perfect organization which Hitler had built up would perform government functions and would itself become the government. Such was not the case. The government retained its old structure, though key posts in the civil service were given to Party members. But alongside of it grew up a peculiar

counterpart of the government, that second government which is
the Nazi Party. Often this has led to impossible situations. New
measures are discussed simultaneously by government officials and
Party officials. Sometimes the two groups are in conflict; they may
even paralyze each other. In some cases Hitler himself, in his double
capacity as Party leader and Germany's chief executive, may have
to decide between them.

The Party administration is a burden not only to the German
government but also to the German society as a whole. On one side
stands the social and economic hierarchy of the government, which
regulates the relations between the director and a foreman in his
factory, between the owner of an estate and his hired man, or between the head of a German legation in a foreign country and his
porter. But if it happens that the foreman, the hired man or the
porter are "higher up in the Party," relations may be suddenly re-
versed and the boss himself has to take orders. Many have been
attracted by the idea that "the last shall be the first," but in its
German form it breeds incompetence to a degree unthinkable in
the democratic countries, so persistently criticized by the Nazis.
If a British or American official makes himself unbearable, it is
usually easy to have him removed; the people themselves take care
of that. But in Germany it is impossible to get rid of a Nazi who has
ingratiated himself with his superiors in the Party.

The system has other and greater disadvantages. It invites corruption and favoritism, striking at the base of the whole social
structure. A year ago I was told by an industrialist that his company
was always handing out large sums of money to the Party bosses
among the personnel. "It is cheaper," he said, "than to have them
always making trouble by denouncing the engineers for opposing
the Party and the managers for nonconformist views. Rather than
that, we would prefer the old union leaders. At least they understood that in order to prevent constant friction we had to have some
kind of understanding between management and labor. You can't
imagine one of them coming to my office during rush hours, seat-
ing himself on my desk, swinging his legs and discussing Party
politics."

The leading Nazis look upon Germany, and Europe, as their own
domain. They have recklessly used their power for personal profit.
They are not able and do not wish to distinguish between the
public property and their own. As far as the men in the highest
positions are concerned, the boundary is entirely obliterated. An

investigation into the fortunes amassed by key men in the Party would show that they have been no less greedy and dishonest than the Fascist bosses in Italy.

This does not apply only to those at the top. A foreigner often has reason to be amazed at the manner in which the Nazi leaders simply grab whatever they want. Among the most corrupt are those recruited from the Party for administrative work in the occupied territories. In the Wartheland and Danzig-Westpreussen territories seized from Poland, the administrators and their relatives are in possession of factories, warehouses and vast estates. Farther East it is even worse. Kube, the General Commissar at Minsk—who at one time was discharged for embezzlement—has sent home whole motor caravans of goods from his territory. One of his relatives was detained at the border because he had with him a suit-case full of jewels, some taken from churches in the district; but when it was learned that the delivery was being made for General Commissar Kube's account, the culprit was immediately released with profuse apologies. At most, Kube was advised to be a little more careful in the future.

Of course, the Party is not exclusively an office for corruption and immorality. Neither are all Party members corrupt. There are still tens of thousands of German men and women within the Party working unselfishly for what they believe to be right. Moderate Germans, opponents of the Party, are ready to admit that the huge machine has accomplished much in many fields, particularly through the *Nationalsozialistische Volkswohlfart* (NSV), the gigantic social-welfare organization devoted mainly to mothers and children. But an open door may tempt a saint, and Party members have many more opportunities for theft than ordinary German citizens. It is probably most difficult of all for Nazis to refrain from lining their own pockets from the various charity drives, a misuse of funds which is very common. A few are executed as an example, but mostly such offences are overlooked. People who give good leather gloves to soldiers often find them later on some district leader in the neighborhood. Another may see his fur cap on the head of a Party official.

The abuse of power and the corruption within the Party have aroused immense bitterness and disgust among the common people. The Party men are very much in the public eye, since they came into power, to a great extent, through loud criticism of corruption among their rivals—which, though it really existed, was nevertheless trivial compared with the present situation in the Third Reich.

A scandal which lately did enormous harm to the Party concerned Victor Lutze, the SA Chief of Staff. Early in May 1943, he took his family on a pleasure trip by automobile. On their way back to Berlin, with Lutze's son at the wheel, a pedestrian crossed the road and the son twisted the wheel to avoid hitting him. The car skidded and turned over—at 70 m.p.h. Lutze was fatally injured and died the following day. What annoyed people most was not that the pleasure trip was made in an official car, but that, after the accident, geese, hams, eggs and packages of butter were strewn along the highway.

Nothing is so hated by the Germans as the Party. There are endless stories to this effect. "One day things will be over; a better day is in sight," the German people sang, until it was forbidden, because the next line ran: "First falls the Führer, then the Party." The last story I heard was on the old theme of optimists and pessimists. It ran like this: The extreme optimist believes that the Germans will win the war and get rid of the Party; the conservative optimist thinks that they will lose the war and lose the Party. The moderate pessimist, however, is of the opinion that Germany will win the war and be forced to keep the Party, while the extreme pessimist foresees that Germany will lose the war and be left with the Party.

Of the Party's subsidiary organizations, two are of special significance: the SA and the SS.

The old Nazi organization for the protection of assemblies, the Storm Troopers (SA), gradually grew into a political militia. On June 30, 1934, however, it lost all its political importance and it is now little more than a uniformed guard at Party funerals. By the time war broke out most of its members had been conscripted. All that remains of the Storm Troopers' military organization is one regiment, the Feldherrnhalle, to perpetuate the tradition of the Beer Hall Putsch.

The progress of the SS has been quite the opposite. Originally it was a special élite guard within the SA, but on June 30, 1934, it separated from the parent organization, and quickly expanded until it became a garrisoned regiment, used for police duty.

The SS has come to be commonly identified with the police, but it was originally formed for other purposes. The idea was not only to establish a guard that would guarantee the personal safety of

Hitler and the other leaders, but also to form an élite organization which, by careful selection, would absorb the most capable, and form the nucleus for the choice of future leaders. As early as 1932 a decree was issued prohibiting SS-men from marrying without the permission of their superiors. The family histories of the men's prospective wives are minutely examined before marriage is permitted. The SS-wives are admitted into die Sippe, a word difficult to translate; the nearest equivalent is perhaps "kinship."

It is the special task of the SS to preserve the ties among all Germanic peoples. For a long time there were sincere elements in the SS that were serious about the idea of "Germanic unity" and even realized that such unity would be unthinkable without including the next largest group of Germanic people, the English. In the shaping of the Germanic policy, however, these elements were not able to exercise any influence. This was done by others who were prepared to bless their Germanic brothers with full-fledged rule by the Gestapo. Of this second policy, the SS has come to be the chief exponent.

At times, through conversations with SS men, the impression has been conveyed that they, in their simple-mindedness, hope to win over the small Germanic peoples to their side, even though they must realize that their policies are put into execution by the firing squads. Many of them even think, or claim to think, that they are being fair to the Dutch and Norwegians. "Of course we won't stand for any nonsense; those who are helping England are risking their necks. But we hope that the Dutch, Norwegian, Danish and Flemish peoples will learn to understand our policies and realize the necessity of fighting on our side for the West against the barbarians of the East." This is an argument I have heard many times in many different words. Quite often, of course, the argument has been purely cynical; but there are also times when the SS men really believed, in their one-sidedness and immaturity, that they were completely righteous in their severe but just treatment of the occupied countries. They regarded themselves as martyrs who, alone and misunderstood, were fighting for all the European peoples against the great threat from the East.

The SS organization has much to answer for. Their units have been used chiefly to drive the Jews out of Germany. Here they have shown an almost unbelievable brutality, although this appears to be nothing compared to what these same SS men have done in the East. How many Jewish, Polish and Russian lives they have on their conscience will perhaps never be known. The number of Jews executed will probably exceed two million, and at least a million Poles have been murdered. For the number of Russian prisoners of war and civilians who have been killed, I have no figures.

Of Lithuania's 250,000 Jews, only 25,000 were still alive in the fall of 1942. If any are alive today, I cannot say. Of the Ukrainian Jews, not many are left, though several hundred thousand remained last summer in the Government General and in Wartheland; in Litzmannstadt (formerly Lodz) alone, there were 150,000.

Many Jews have taken part in organized resistance and committed sabotage, but nothing they have done has furnished any justification whatever for the Nazi mass slaughter. The mass murders have been carried out in ways too revolting to describe. Sometimes men, women and children have been herded together, compelled to dig their own graves, and then machine-gunned. In other cases gas chambers or special trains have been employed, and sometimes the unfortunates to be executed have had to march in single file past a window, from which a soldier fired a shot into each head.

I should like to end here. It is repugnant for a Swede to describe these bestial actions in detail. But before going on to another subject I might give some idea how reports about the SS methods have leaked out.

SS soldiers forming the execution squads in the East are carefully chosen. They are recruited from the most brutal elements and are gradually trained to become harder and more ruthless. At first they may only have to take Jews out for street cleaning and snow shoveling. After a time they are assigned to perform single executions, with regular squads; only after this training is completed are they ordered to do mass executions.

Many have refused to take part in these and have been shot or, at best, sent home with circumstantial descriptions of what would happen to them and their relatives if they talked. Others have had nervous breakdowns and have been sent to asylums. Even the most hardened have at times caved in. Time and again physicians have been called to attend soldiers on leave who have had severe attacks of hysteria or prolonged insomnia or delirium tremens (soldiers in the firing squads often get intoxicated before executions, and may stay so continually). The story is always the same. "I can't stand it any longer—in my sleep I see nothing but blood," said a young Austrian soldier to his doctor. In many such cases the patients have collapsed and described their horrible experiences. But this is not all—there have been instances of outsiders chancing to witness executions and living to tell about them. And there are photographs in full detail.

The chief instrument for these ghastly practices is the SS. Sometimes it seems that the SS is driving the policy beyond the intention of the Party leaders. In any case, it is certain that the German public has little real knowledge of what is going on.

Finally, a word about the military aspect of the SS. At the beginning of this war, the Waffen SS was organized to guard the Nazi regime at home. Its nucleus was the trim and well-armed so-called *Verfügungstruppen, Leibstandarte Adolf Hitler, Germania* and *Der Führer*. It was augmented by volunteers, and the system of voluntary enlistments continues, although it is now only nominal. Most of the Waffen SS soldiers are graduates of the Hitler Youth.

Gradually the organization expanded and at present it constitutes a considerable fraction of the German army. It is not commanded, however, by the army generals but by its own officers, under the direct jurisdiction of Hitler. The Waffen SS has from the start been Hitler's special pet and has been pampered in every way. Many a time the SS regiments have been given the laurels while the regular army has done the rough work. Whenever the army generals had the opportunity to allocate SS troops according to their own plans, they did so, and in such cases these troops have sometimes suffered enormous losses. On the other hand, it cannot be denied that the SS troops have shown exceptional drive and initiative, and that their leaders, principally Sepp Dietrich and Theodor Eicke, have coped creditably with difficult tasks.

The SS men have considered themselves political soldiers—they have had to absorb into their ranks volunteers from various countries—and they have not concealed their attitude of superiority to the *Wehrmacht*. Their favored position has created bitterness within the regular army, which must have had an adverse influence on the conduct of the war.

Nazism and the German People

The Hitler movement is not merely an indirect result of Versailles; it is also an expression of certain characteristics in the German nature. Were this not the case, Nazism would never have come into power. But while the German national character undoubtedly has certain destructive features which have been brought to a head by Nazism, it also has constructive features which have, justifiably, placed the German people high among the civilized nations of the world.

The problem created by this dual nature of the German nation is not manifesting itself for the first time. The Germans are split into many factions; besides the haughty Prussian centralizing tendency, there is ample room for a particularism which, dormant now, is stirring under the surface. *Die Kleinstaaterei*—the system of small states—is thus a typical German institution.

It was perhaps a necessity, but surely a misfortune, that the focal point of a united Reich should be in northern Germany, in Berlin. No one can deny that the North Germans have exceptional ability and efficiency. But alongside these qualities they have others less laudable, above all their total inability to get along with foreigners. Seldom does a South German—a Bavarian, a Swabian or even a Rhinelander—on a visit abroad arouse the antipathy of his hosts as does a North German. Those from the West and South may not have the Prussian efficiency or the arrogant traditions of Frederick the Great, but they are endowed, instead, with more charm and warmth.

Nazism established its headquarters in Berlin, but even as late as 1934 Bavaria might have doomed the movement. The army in Bavaria wanted to strike before Nazism had infiltrated completely, and a revolt would have been supported by a great majority of the people. The Bavarians pinned their hopes on Crown Prince Rupprecht of the House of Wittelsbach. Knowing that such interference might jeopardize the national unity, the Crown Prince refused to act, and the idea of revolt was abandoned. Nazism won; its conquest was a victory for Berlin and a defeat for Munich, Stuttgart, Karlsruhe, yes, even for Dresden, Cologne and Hamburg.

From then on Hitler did everything possible to obliterate particularism; everything in the life of the nation that served to counterbalance Nazism was eliminated. The old President was shunted aside, the army and the Prussian Junkers were forced to accept Hitler; high finance and big business likewise. Civil rights were crushed, the Church was persecuted, community life was standardized, and labor organizations fell as ripe plums into the hands of the Nazis. Not only the bourgeois Germany of tradition but also the newer Social Democrats and Communists were silenced.

After a few years a united front had been created which has since become synonymous with the Third Reich.

It cannot be sufficiently emphasized that before Hitler took power only a handful had any idea of what Nazism really embodied. The majority accepted it as a strong nationalistic movement with an intensive social ideology which in changed circumstances would become progressive and abandon its revolutionary ideas. It must be admitted that Hitler and his henchmen thoroughly succeeded in camouflaging their real aims during the long years of their struggle for power. Nazism probably did not "show its true colors" until 1933, and then it reflected the real character of its leaders.

It is possible that some of Hitler's accomplishments will survive the fall of Nazism. His attempts to fuse nationalism with socialism will probably be tried again by others. The National Socialists' answers to a number of practical questions will also be recognized when passions and hatred have abated.

Nevertheless, despite the favorable aspects of the Nazi "philosophy," Adolf Hitler and his men will go down in history as the foremost nihilists, to use Rauschning's expression. The Nazis tried to change the whole foundation of German life. It is true that the German people were, to a great extent, secularists and that their indifference to religion had been growing rather than decreasing. But the moral foundation of social life was undoubtedly Christian, and even those indifferent to religion were markedly influenced by rules common to the civilized Christian world.

Hitler has tried to give the German people a new religion. This has never been openly declared; neither has it been followed through in the Nazi ideology. But looking back on Nazi policies of the last ten years it seems plain that intense efforts were made to destroy the Christianity of the German people, the last barricade against Nazi nihilism.

This has been accomplished by keeping German youth away from the churches and giving them something new to believe in. It is averred that Hitler considered himself a new Messiah, and that Hitler worship became a cult in many parts of the country. It was no more than superficial. What German youth has been inoculated with is, rather, nature-worship—a gospel of blood, power and Germanism.

A recent book, *God and People*, by an anonymous SS-soldier is an interesting echo of this new religion, this effort to create a substitute for Christianity. The young author writes, "Our faith is in Germany, which we love, not with the lukewarm, halfhearted love preached in the churches, but with a passionate, blind love that knows no bounds and no reserves. . . . Our road to God does not go through the Bible and Jerusalem; it leads through Germany." Church reform is futile. "We want a faith which has its source deep down in the German nature, in the German heart. A faith as befitting to the Germans as the Teutoburger forest, the North Sea and the quiet moor."

The German religion will be militant. "The fronts are fixed: one is Christ, the other Germany. It is not a question of weakening Catholicism by strengthening Protestantism. Our present task is to replace a religion alien to our spirit with a faith born in the soul of Germany itself." Christianity is an artificial religion, a cunning and coldly calculated invention of the priests, who exploit ignorance and innocence. It is the duty of fighters for the preservation of the German nation to abolish the cults, but not the belief in God. Away with all alien trumpery and dreams of celestial paradise! Return to earth! "Small difference whether we call the Highest God 'Light,' 'Providence' or 'Source'; all that is important is that we do not say 'Judah' or 'Rome,' but only 'Germany.' "

The suffering, pain-distorted figure of the Crucified must disappear, the writer says further. Our heroes shall again carry swords in their hands instead of crosses on their backs. We respect Christ. But we do not love Him and we do not want Him for our leader. Christianity cannot be the goal of the soldier. "The word 'Heathen' is therefore an honorable name. Moreover, it matters little if we are called heretics or heathens, so long as we are good Germans." If we are to have a Confession of Faith it should read: "I believe in a strong God and His eternal Germany."

A concluding chapter lists tasks of the disciples of the "German faith." We shall protect our youth from the religion of confession and educate our children as if there had been no Christianity. "We shall take them out of doors and show them the wonders of nature and God. We shall teach them our holy history and awaken in them a pride at being the sons of a great people."

What makes the book unique is its frank language. It states the aims of the Nazi youth movement candidly—perhaps in words too plain. For the Nazis themselves seldom speak openly about it; they prefer to act. The worship of strength and harshness emphasized by the young author is, however, typical of the bulk of German youth today.

Even the offspring of families that have done their best to give their children a philosophy of life different from that of the Party have been strongly influenced by this gospel of strength. Once I met a German lad who was a confirmed opponent of the Party and who discussed politics with an alarmingly precocious air. He explained to me that the opponents—they were many, because youth instinctively opposes—within the Hitler Youth and the labor service have only one weapon of defense. They must be even harder than the others, be extremely cautious, and work craftily and deceitfully. "You would be surprised," he said, "if you knew how the most fervent Hitler enthusiasts in my group are opposition leaders."——"How do you know that?" I asked. "Because I am one myself."

Unfortunately, I did not meet many boys and girls during my stay in Germany, chiefly because very few of them are left in Berlin. But on information gathered from various sources, I became quite convinced that the philosophy voiced by that young lad is common to the German youth today. What they really think about their country and its future, no outsider knows. During all these years they have been physically trained and fed propaganda. They know nothing, or practically nothing, about other nations' faiths and ideals, and they are unable to form any realistic picture of the world outside the German borders.

In the attitude of the German youth lies one of the greatest dangers of Germany and Europe. They cannot, of course, prevent the collapse of Nazism when the time becomes ripe. But what Hitler has sown others will have to reap. It may take generations before the seeds of Nazism can be dislodged.

Parallel with the creation of the new religion runs the systematic destruction of the old judicial system. Much has been said and written on this subject, yet it is difficult for outsiders to visualize the meaning of the new lawlessness introduced by the Nazis.

Does the world grasp that Germany is in a condition almost comparable to that which prevailed during the ill-famed Interregnum of the years from 1254 to 1275? That it is possible, both theoretically and in fact, for innocent and virtuous citizens to be arrested and immediately executed without any judgment or trial whatsoever? That not even a formal arrest is necessary—the person in question may be murdered in his own home? Can it be comprehended what this means to a people who have been considered one of the most cultured and civilized nations in the world?

In official as well as private life, brutality, servility, lying and corruption flourish. Honor exists no more; disloyalty and informing have replaced the aspiration to truth and honor.

Millions of Germans have reacted in the same manner as other Europeans against the manifestations of these Hitler policies but few have dared to make their protests vocal. This may perhaps be interpreted as evidence of the want of moral courage. That this is lacking where one would have expected to find it is a well-known and verified fact. But few outsiders are able to grasp fully the consequences of raising one's voice in a nation of the Nazi type. To show opposition is to risk not only one's own life, but the lives of one's family and relatives—and much more so in Germany itself than in the occupied countries. The frequent emphasis on this fact probably arises from a desire to encourage continued cowardice. There were, nevertheless, many who spoke out and in consequence went to concentration camps for many years, or ended their days in a police grave for prisoners "shot while attempting to escape."

The German people of today are afflicted. They have been subjected to ten years of the Nazi regime, with its systematic benumbing and segregation from the outer world. Thus it is most difficult to solve the problem of responsibility for Hitler's foreign policy, since it involves dealing with a pathological case. Nor must one forget that for a long time this illness has tended to be infectious. Of course, we may ask why the German people have not unburdened themselves of Hitler's regime instead of becoming intoxicated with triumphs and agreeing to pay the price—Nazism. Yet the primary question is whether there was actually a possibility of getting rid of Hitler and his men during the years when it must have become clear to all level-headed Germans what Nazism meant.

The Germans of today are in a frightful situation. Many realize that a German victory would be an intolerable straitjacket for them as well as for other peoples. It is something they cannot wholeheartedly desire. But the tragedy lies in the great conflict with conscience. It has been pounded into them with a thousand hammer blows that he who is without fanatical faith in the Führer is a traitor and that National Socialism is identical with Germany. Besides, those who lived through 1918 know what it means to be without arms and left to the pleasure of the enemy; after a new defeat it would be seven times worse. The people of Germany are beginning to feel the hate that smolders in the ashes of all Europe, the threat from that Europe which Nazism meant to integrate with Germany, but which it has unified against Germany. They also feel the pressure of the Slavs storming against them, and the latent menace of the millions of foreign workmen, the Trojan horse within Germany. They feel that they must run the race to the end. What other way out but to fight? The Allies have, as a matter of fact, given the German people no alternative except unconditional surrender. It is difficult to make a people accept such an outcome before a military catastrophe. *Actually this situation and Germany's enemies are whipping Germans together under the Swastika.* "Victory or Bolshevism" is the slogan that Goebbels screams out to the German people. For the Nazi leaders, it is literally a choice between victory and death.

The Opposition to Nazism

All opposition in Germany is revolutionary and has to remain underground. The difficulties to be overcome in solving the most elementary technical problems appear in what I have said about the Gestapo. An opponent of the Third Reich must constantly expect betrayal and arrest.

The prime requisite for an anti-Nazi group is to obtain facts about what is going on. Organizations which have access to official information agencies or to other authorized sources are in a good position to gain their end. Very important, too, is shadowing leaders in the government, for this provides excellent stuff for whispering campaigns.

A further problem is the maintenance of communications between members of the group. This is difficult because of mail and telephone censorship and the practically total restrictions on travel for civilians. The military are better off; officers sent abroad can easily convey oral and even written instructions, and the opposition uses the military courier post as a means of avoiding the Gestapo.

Propaganda calls for the most exact preparations; a petty slip may upset the applecart. Leaflets can be printed on hidden presses, but it is much simpler to produce them in an ordinary printing shop provided great care is exercised to avert the police scrutiny of everything that has to do with the printed word.

But the leaflets, when printed, have to be distributed. An obvious method is to stuff them into letterboxes, but that is not free from risk. The police are always setting traps. A common means of circulating leaflets is to slip them into newspapers or matchboxes which are then conveniently "forgotten."

More important than leaflets, however, is word-of-mouth propaganda against the regime. It has been well developed and in some places seems to have been organized systematically. Time after time malodorous secrets have spread over a whole town in a few hours. The private lives of the Party bosses provide inexhaustible fuel for the opposition's propaganda.

The radio is often used to good effect. There are quite a few secret transmitters in Germany and the occupied countries. The best known are Gustav Siegfried Eins and the so-called Wehrmachtssender (army radio), both of which let loose on the Party with subtle insults as well as with the heaviest artillery of the German language. The announcer for the latter station has shown himself to be particularly well informed about the most intimate details of the private lives of the Party bosses. Recently the Atlantik station has popped up, its objective being the U-boat crews.

Opposition stations come and go, reappearing on various wave lengths at unexpected hours. Their messages are generally brief, so as to make it difficult to locate their position. It is a mystery how they are able to exist at all. The most curious theories have been evolved. For instance, it was believed that one station was mounted in a barge, which slowly threaded the German canals. It seems likely that some stations are protected by the military or by other groups equally difficult of identification; there is no other explanation of their activity, which has extended over years.

Much that is happening in Germany just now would make foreigners gasp. In the autumn of 1942 it was estimated that 150,000 persons had "gone underground" and were living as outlaws. Today the number must be greater. Some of these are Jews, but the majority are anti-Nazi Germans. Harbored by friends or relatives, they live in a state of constant tension in the struggle to elude the Gestapo. Many of them are now favored by the chaos in the administrative machinery resulting from aerial bombing and evacuation. It is a mystery how these people manage to obtain food. Many of them must be without ration cards, but the black market is a partial explanation. There are some who have solved their problem by living on forged identity papers.

Foreign passports are not entirely impossible to obtain. Regular organizations for producing spurious passports exist, and the 12,000,000 foreigners employed at forced labor offer innumerable possibilities for clever and unscrupulous persons.

Sabotage in official circles is not unknown. Men of the opposition are everywhere—even with Herr Himmler. Dissatisfaction within the Party itself is a factor, partly in consequence of the changed situation. There are many who wish to secure their future by doing the opposition some service. How to dispose of the Nazis will be a difficult post-war problem. Hordes of members have been *Parteigenossen* only in name; many having been literally forced into the Party. But with the crack will come a curious phenomenon: nobody will be able to discover a man who admits to having been a really convinced Nazi!

As early as 1942 one would hear, "I was never really a Nazi," from persons who had been enthusiastic followers of Hitler both officially and privately in 1941. During 1943 hordes of Nazis have hedged in one way or another, but for the leaders there is no turning back. It would hardly help Goebbels, for instance, to go over to the Communists, although such a conversion would not in itself be unthinkable. Goebbels is a man with a pathological hate for the bourgeois way of life, a spiritual proletarian. The Germans differentiate in their language between the two conceptions of the poor man—the proletarian in the real sense of the word, *der Proletarier*, and the man who, so to speak, appears spiritually in rags, *der Prolet*. Goebbels belongs to the latter category.

But I reveal no secret when I say that all Nazi tricks will be vain. If there is anything those men have learned who, during these years, have stood aloof or actively opposed the regime, it is to separate the sheep from the goats. "We shall," said one of them to me, "present a questionnaire to every person of importance, and it will include: 'Were you ever in a concentration camp? If not, why not?'"

Nothing in Germany is so difficult to judge as the strength and character of the opposition to Nazism. The great mass of the people are anti-Nazi in feeling; they want to get rid of the Party and have peace and quiet. Only a minority know what they want in place of Hitler.

The real opposition, however, appears to fall into four large groups (in which there are hundreds of factions): monarchists, liberals, the moderate left (or the Social Democrats if you like) and finally the Communists. The boundary lines are not firmly fixed; inside each of the main groups are innumerable smaller groups, some of which operate independently.

It should be noted that there are three institutions of direct political importance which may be counted upon to survive the deluge: the churches, mainly the Roman Catholic; high finance, especially the Rhenish-Westphalian magnates; and the military.

The monarchists in Germany are relatively numerous. Their weakness lies in their failure to unite on a pretender. The ex-Crown Prince is not to be counted on, nor are other Hohenzollerns possibilities for a Fourth Reich. Duke Ernst of Brunswick is talked about but neither he nor other Protestant princes possess either the stature or the general esteem that would be requisite. The monarchists received a hard blow a year ago when Prince Wilhelm of Prussia was killed. Many who knew him think that he would have been a suitable candidate for the throne.

Of very special interest in the political scene is Bavaria's separatist attitude. There is a strong feeling for the house of Wittelsbach, and those who can assess opinion in the Bavarian towns and countryside point to development in the direction of monarchy. The Bavarians regard it as an advantage that their pretender is in relative safety; both Crown Prince-Regent Rupprecht and Prince Albrecht are said to be in Hungary. Thus the house of Wittelsbach may once again play a telling role in the history of Germany. It has supplied emperors before. The candidate and his heir presumptive are both highly regarded.

In this connection one may not ignore the foremost German ruling family, the Hapsburgs. Even though it is identified exclusively with Austria, and even though a revival of the Hapsburg-German emperor tradition in any form is unlikely, the possibility of a Germany with its center in the old imperial city of Vienna and with a Hapsburg on the throne cannot be utterly brushed aside. But the course of events indicates that the problem of Austria will be solved separately from that of Germany.

The question of a monarchy is further complicated by the difference of opinion among the monarchists themselves respecting the organization of the new state. All possible points of view are represented, with the principles of centralization and federalism conspicuously in opposition to each other. Generally speaking, the monarchists profess conservative views in domestic policy, but there are, besides, radical monarchists as well as conservative republicans.

The majority of the monarchists are to be found among those elements of the population which hold a certain conservative philosophy, such as independent businessmen, farmers, artisans and civil servants; but a considerable part of the intelligentsia, too, is monarchistically inclined. Many who seek stability and continuity for the new Germany lean in that direction.

Occasionally the thought is uttered that after the war a strong conservative party should be formed with a monarchist trend. The conservatism the intellectuals have in mind is much like that of the English; an active conservatism friendly to reform. "We don't want anything like the Hugenberg spirit," many people have said to me. Hugenberg, the most powerful and reactionary publisher of the days before Hitler, is now looked on as the gravedigger of conservatism in Germany.

The liberals do not take a definite stand on the question of the constitution of the state. They know that the Weimar Republic cannot be recreated, but they disagree as to whether the Fourth Reich should be a unified, national-liberal Germany administered from Berlin or a federated Germany. As to domestic policy, the liberals are for democratic methods as far as possible and for lightening the pressure of the state on the citizens. Liberals visualize the extreme opposite of the blind worship of the state which characterizes the present regime.

Chief among the liberal group are the urban middle class and the intellectuals. These represent Nazism's most dangerous enemies. The intelligentsia likes to use ridicule as a weapon, yet evidence of great personal courage is present. Six months ago a leading representative of German culture sent a memorandum to one of the Reichs ministries intended for Hitler's own eye. It challenged the Party's very right to exist; he termed the Party "a giant mutual-aid and insurance machine" and justified his stand by Hitler's own declaration of the sovereignty of the German people. In particular he assailed the Party for its use of the Gestapo to protect it against attacks with moral weapons and declared, in conclusion, that he looked for no improvement in the Nazi Party state but advanced his views, so that, "on the inescapable day when historical reality silences the raucous demands of the present state," it might not be said that there was no German to admonish the nation's leaders.

The Social Democrats are still numerous among industrial workers. Many German workers were favorably inclined, or at least not inimical to, the National Socialist regime. The Nazis' success in crippling the Social Democratic movement to a greater extent than the other political parties did away with almost all resistance among the workers. Certain Jews who had a marked influence on the Social Democratic party, although they never ruled it, were executed or tortured to death. What remained were mostly aging fighters who stood alone and, as time passed, discovered their futility. The great mistake of Social Democracy was that it failed to win over young workers and substitute them for old-timers in the party.

The millions of Social Democrats have not disappeared; their political credo survives, even if only among the older ones. It may even be that they have learned a certain wisdom from events. In any case, it is safe to regard many of the older workers and lower civil servants as Social Democrats, to say nothing of the considerable contingent that may be characterized as pink. It is to be conjectured that organizations have been set up, but such work is probably still only in the initial stage. Assistance might be forthcoming from the remnants of the trade-union movement, which would seem to have entrenched itself in sections of the Nazi Labor Front.

An estimate of working-class youth cannot easily be made. Like all youth it has been dominated by the Nazi doctrines of violence, and hence may have an intuitive sympathy for Communism rather than for the more tepid Social Democracy. But many of the young workers have tired of the "propaganda of action," and among these Social Democracy should perhaps be able to gain proselytes.

The Communists lead among those who aim not only to overthrow the Nazi system but to bring about a complete revolution in the social and economic spheres. It should be borne in mind that, with the march of events, the soil of the Third Reich has become receptive to extreme revolutionary movements. Hundreds of thousands have lost their all and have been driven to desperation by harsh police rule. Starvation threatens. Moreover, there are

12,000,000 foreigners within the land. The danger of anarchy cannot be disregarded.

It appears from the evidence that organized Communist groups exist. The German police have pursued them relentlessly with the frequent consequence of mass executions. As a rule the fact that they are Communist organizations, or "terror groups," as they are usually termed in the German press, is withheld, but there have been instances, especially in Alsace, where the judgments of the People's Courts have been reported publicly as a deterrent.

In Berlin I have seen Communist leaflets and have heard of occasional minor sabotage, but otherwise the Communists have shown scarcely any sign of existence. It would be incorrect to conclude from this fact that they are weak; they have fully adapted their methods to the actual conditions.

Thus, the Communists are extremely careful not to reveal their political home. They often pose as loyal National Socialists, only criticizing the "aberrations" of the system. Their leaflets stress the corruption within the Nazi Party and furnish instructions for practical propaganda. "Call attention to the old speeches of the Führer!" "Letters from the East do not lie; keep them circulating!" These were their slogans last spring

The Austrian opposition to Nazism has a character of its own and calls for separate treatment. The coming together of Reichs Germans and Austrians, as I have already pointed out, has not resulted pleasantly for Hitler. The Nazis sought to create a sense of German nationality in Austria, and in their day they were more successful than the Christian Socialists under Dollfuss and Schuschnigg, who wanted to create an Austrian national consciousness, but had nothing to back it up but the tiny post-war state.

A change has come over the spirit of their dream; five years of Nazi rule have caused a renaissance of Austrian patriotism. Many Austrians have pondered the problem: "Are we the same people as the Germans?" Their experience has inclined them to the opinion that language alone does not constitute a people.

This development is as yet only in embryo, but the supporters of an Austria liberated from the connection with Germany already appear to be in a considerable majority. The Nazis have perhaps 10 to 15 per cent of the population behind them. Another faction, possibly equally strong, is anti-Nazi yet not absolutely against the

Anschluss idea. The rest echo the cry, *"Los von Berlin,"* Break with Berlin! There does not seem to be any strong difference of opinion among the opposition regarding the form of the state. I have met Social Democrats who declared themselves monarchists, and asked me how the Swedish Social Democrats felt about it. The supporters of a republic are strongest in Vienna, once the Social Democratic stronghold. Former Mayor Seitz enjoys an exceptional reputation, and he as well as other former Social Democratic functionaries are allowed their liberty.

Monarchism finds its strongest support in the old upper class and among the younger officers who belong to that group. It has taken wide hold of the lower middle classes, especially the tradespeople. Then, too, there are many monarchists among the industrial workers and their womenfolk. There is at least one powerful and widespread monarchist organization, and possibly there are several. All opposition seems to gravitate toward monarchist thought, even though the progress is sometimes devious.

Much will naturally depend on the behavior of the pretender to the throne and on the political situation when the revolution occurs; but the latter is conceivable only as the corollary of a military collapse in Germany. Austrians have a kindlier feeling for Archduke Otto than formerly. In some circles horror is still expressed at the thought that Empress Zita might settle in Vienna, while others insist that the emperor-to-be will somehow keep his mother out of his capital city. The current propaganda for Otto is based on the notion that he has American support, an impression that is widely spread as a result of his radio speeches. It seemed to me that the substance of these was generally known.

One must assume that Social Democrats and Communists still occupy a very strong position in Vienna. Possibly more than 50 per cent of the population of the city belongs to those camps. This is balanced however by their relative weakness in the provinces.

The overwhelming majority of "the Reds," to use this inclusive but not altogether adequate expression, is made up of various Social Democratic groups which, contrary to what was the case in 1918, are considered fairly moderate. But now there is a stronger group of Communists than in 1918, and they are prepared for anything, being well organized and in a state of high exaltation. They are losing many of their best members, however, to the Nazi execution squads.

It is by no means impossible that the Communists in a given situ-

ation might gain control in Vienna and in the provinces. In all towns
and villages there are masses of foreign workers and prisoners of
war who may be expected to make common cause with them and
who are, besides, largely of Russian or other Slav nationality. The
hard conditions under which they live might drive them to take
bloody revenge.

Naturally there are factions within the Austrian opposition which
cannot be fitted into any of the three main groups. There are,
for instance, circles that are broadly liberal and desire some kind of
republic, but they are unorganized and get smaller response from
the masses than the monarchists, Social Democrats and Communists.
In the liberal camp, too, belong those who do not wish to break the
Anschluss but desire to be part of a national-liberal Germany organized on a federative basis.

It is baffling to try to determine what the Austrian opposition
thinks regarding the country's future. Almost all who declared
themselves against continued union with Germany stated emphatically that any return to the Austria created by the treaty of Saint
Germain would not be possible. "We must be part of a larger
group," they said. "One may call it a new monarchy or a Danubian
federation or anything at all—but isolation is unthinkable." But
when those who pleaded for a federation were asked to declare
more exactly how they would like to have it, they quickly reverted
to a new Danubian monarchy under the House of Hapsburg. In
their opinion that would be the only way of forming a superstruc-
ture that could hold the people of the Danubian lands together.

The clergy of the Protestant churches have shown great courage
and tenacity in the struggle for freedom of conscience. But the
Catholic Church has headed the struggle—that church which, according to traditional ideas in Sweden, is the source of spiritual
and political reaction. It has been easier for the Catholics to maintain their attitude because of their connections outside Germany,
and to a certain degree they have been able to influence German
policy through the Quirinal in Rome, which has several times intervened at the request of the Vatican. It has also been easier for the
Catholics to resist pressure because they are financially stronger
than their Protestant brothers, and because Catholicism has maintained a much stronger grip on its followers than Protestantism has
been able to do.

But one must not lay too much emphasis on the differences be-

tween Catholicism and Protestantism, for in the face of common
pressure many barriers have fallen. Catholic priests preach in
Protestant churches, and Protestant pastors expelled from their
parishes have enjoyed the support of funds which Nazism so far has
not been able to rob from the Roman Church.

It is undoubtedly the firm organization of the Catholic Church
that has thus far succeeded in saving much of German culture and
spiritual freedom from the predatory grasp of the National Socialist Party. It is also Catholicism which is reaping the main advantage
of the religious renaissance which has been noticeable throughout
Germany. In many cases, also, leading Protestants have drawn so
close to Catholicism as to suggest a general movement in that direction. The Catholic churches are filled, and people stand far out in
the streets to listen to mass.

Even from a purely political point of view the Church of Rome
has been able to acquire a good will that is certain to become an
important factor after this war. This is chiefly due to the outspoken,
daring attitude of many leaders of the Church. I have already referred to a number of examples of this. Copies of sermons delivered
by Graf von Galen, the Bishop of Münster, have been spread all
over Germany, passing from hand to hand, and the cathedral
in Münster has been packed with listeners whenever the Bishop
preached. In spite of the bold language of his sermons, the
Gestapo did not dare to interfere. Every morning during the period
when Count Galen's arrest seemed imminent, peasants came into
town in their carts and called for the Bishop to show himself at
his palace, so they could be certain he was there and not in a
concentration camp.

Innumerable are the legends which have been spread about this
man. The best known is that of the Nazi Party boss who stood
up in the church one Sunday and shouted out that those who did
not contribute to Germany's fight for existence with their own
or their children's flesh and blood should keep silence. The Bishop
answered quickly, in a ringing voice, "I forbid anyone in this
church, whoever it may be, to criticize the Führer!"

Such stories are told not only of Galen but of many other priests.
The whole of Germany knew, for instance, that Bishop Schulte of
Cologne had spoken of "the lie that limps through Germany."
When he was called before the Gestapo to explain what he meant
by referring in that way to Propaganda Minister Goebbels (who, as
is well known, limps slightly), he answered indignantly and in a

tone of amazement that he for his part had been thinking of the devil.

The Catholic bishop of Berlin, Count Konrad Preysing, is one of those who have boldly said what they think. Immediately after the outbreak of the German-Russian war a pastoral letter from him was read in all the churches of his diocese; it said that if the question of choice arose for the German Catholic between his country and his faith, faith must be his choice. In conclusion the Bishop pointed to a list of the official measures which he considered were an interference with the practice of the Catholic faith and a danger to it. Many of Bishop Preysing's sermons gave rise to demonstrations that could not be misunderstood. Eyewitnesses of the ceremony on June 28, 1942, at the now destroyed St. Hedwig's Church, on the occasion of the Pope's 25-year jubilee as bishop, will certainly not forget it easily. The church was packed, and outside were large crowds. When Bishop Preysing arrived in his carriage drawn by white horses, a threefold "Heil for our Bishop" rang out, and likewise one for the Holy Father in Rome.

In his sermon, to which the congregation listened in profound silence, the Bishop said that justice could rest only on foundations in the breast of humanity. The great foundation is "Therefore, all things whatsoever ye would that men should do to you, do ye even so to them." Life is holy, continued the Bishop, whether it is a matter of an unborn child or an elderly person no longer able to work. The justice that is of God can never be replaced by a justice that is of the state.

The Church will certainly play an important part when a new philosophy of life is called upon to replace National Socialism in the minds of the German people. The old class divisions have disappeared; the well-to-do share church pews with Social Democratic workers and perhaps even with Communists. But the political good will gained by the Catholic Church is a delicate matter, and how far it will expand after the war is difficult to estimate. It is, for instance, impossible to predict whether a new Center Party will ever represent the Church in politics.

It is equally difficult to determine what direct part German high finance will play. It has also fought its fight against the regime, but cannot escape its co-responsibility for the rise of the system. The form of reasoning put forward by Fritz Thyssen in his book is not unusual in the world of German business. Like Thyssen, most of the German financiers have chalked up their score against Nazism. But they remain prudently in their places without, for the moment, taking any political initiative. Omitting the question of responsibility here, it is reasonably certain that high finance is another factor which will survive Hitler. Many German businessmen still have their international connections; the various groups are firmly organized and support each other at home and will continue to exercise power after the collapse of the system. They have to be accepted as one of the most important organized stabilizing factors. They possess a remarkable information system, and are well orientated in all aspects of the utter confusion that is known in the Reich as war economy.

Another important factor is the army. Ever since the rise of Nazism there has been talk both within and without Germany of the army's part in a possible liquidation of Nazism. But the years have passed with no more than weak signs of political initiative by the German military leaders.

The armed forces, without doubt, *could* have overthrown Hitler for some years after 1933. But the officers did not wish to crush what appeared to be the only power that could carry out the rearmament of Germany determinedly and thoroughly, and they were reluctant to engage in the unfamiliar sphere of politics, even though the armed forces during the whole Weimar period played a certain *indirect* role, somewhat after the manner of a "fleet in being" kept back as a threat but never taking the high seas. Hitler knew what he was doing when he had Schleicher shot. He was a political general, but there were not many such. After Nazism had been at work for some time, there was none.

The German officers are known for their loyalty and sense of duty. It is pretty certain that many of them, especially the regular and reserve officers from monarchist families, have for years nurtured a bitter hate for the regime and especially its military branch, the Waffen SS. But they have never rebelled, perhaps no less because of the German officer's lack of political initiative than because of Himmler's skill in isolating and checking the most dangerous oppositional elements. Himmler has been especially careful to make certain—and Hitler has also used his own keen political sense to the same end—that no officer should become popular or powerful enough to raise the flag of revolt. At the first sign that anyone might rise to such a position, several less important generals were pushed forward. It was no accident that in 1940 a whole string of field marshals received their rank simultaneously.

Once it looked as if one man would receive a special position above all others—Field Marshal Erwin Rommel. But he is an out-and-out friend of the new regime, hence not so dangerous. He was, besides, in Africa. But Rommel had gained a grasp on his troops that had no parallels in the German armed forces, and the Africa Corps would certainly have followed its leader even if he had cried "On to Berlin!" As long as Rommel's star was at its zenith, Hitler was remarkably sparing with honors. When the star began to set, matters changed. It was also very significant that during the time when Rommel's reputation was at its height, the Germans shook their heads doubtfully and said with an obviously double meaning: "Let's hope nothing happens to him—for instance, that he gets sent to the eastern front."

Sometimes it looked as though another soldier would obtain a special position in the East: Field Marshal von Mannstein. Many wise and pentrating observers consider this man Germany's fore-most soldier. Frequently he has stepped in and saved apparently hopeless situations brought about by the orders of that military dilettante who holds the supreme command. But whether Mann-stein can and will take Germany's fate into his hands is something that nobody knows.

The German armed forces have not proved to be an instrument suitable for use in politics, though sometimes the generals have tried to avert the worst mistakes of German statesmen. But ad-mittedly a situation may arise in which the higher officers may feel it their duty to intervene directly. Perhaps that situation is already at hand.

What role the opposition in Germany may play, no one knows. During 1943 it has acquired much strength and has even obtained weapons, chiefly through deals with the men in the supply depots, who made no bones about reporting higher "losses" for the arms in their charge, so long as they were bribed with coffee and food-stuffs. But from a purely technical point of view the opposition is still hopelessly inferior to the regime. Only if the latter were shaken by outside events, or for some reason were to lose its most promi-nent figure or its unity, would the opposition be able to seize power.

THE THIRD REICH AND
THE WORLD

Nazi Foreign Policy

By this time, the workings of Hitler's foreign policy are fairly obvious. The perfect co-ordination of all the national resources; the ruthless juggling of foreign states and factions; the lack of all moral ideals; the disregard for traditional diplomatic forms and the use of Quislings as battering-rams—all this has carried the Third Reich forward from victory to victory.

However, it did not take long for other nations to discover the ruthless manner in which the Nazis employed any and all means to gain their ends. When the now censored incidents of this war are disclosed, many will be amazed at the daring displayed.

During the last months several incidents have been revealed which serve to emphasize this daring, although it is as yet impossible to prove these stories true. There is the perfectly plausible story of how the Germans in Godesberg lured Chamberlain into agreeing in principle with German expansion toward the East at the expense of Russia. In the following year, during the negotiations in Moscow for a Russo-German pact, these same Germans played the recordings of Chamberlain's voice made at Godesberg, and thus influenced the Russians toward an understanding with Germany. There is also the similar story of Molotoff's visit to Berlin in the fall of 1940, when he presented a number of demands which, if revealed to her present allies, would certainly make Russia's position awkward. These negotiations have been kept relatively secret, the reason being, so gossips say, that Molotoff, who was no stranger to the trick of recording conversations, took care that Germany also compromised herself— by offering Russia advantages at Japan's expense.

The Third Reich has always insisted that others keep their promises to the letter. But when a treaty has lost its value for Nazi Germany, she has not hesitated to break her bargain in the most cynical manner possible.

The whole procedure has had an air of shortsighted diplomacy which relied on Germany's strength to prevent an eventual reckoning for its too easily broken promises. The result is that Germany has not one true friend. She is the object of intense hatred, not only on the part of her enemies and the occupied nations, but also, and in just as great a degree, of her partners.

I once found myself in a highly cosmopolitan gathering in Berlin, when the conversation veered to the relations between other European nations and Nazi Germany. Individuals from a great number of different countries emphatically stated their opinion that their countries harbored not the slightest sympathy for this Germany. Gradually those present agreed that the Slovaks were probably the only friends of Germany in present-day Europe. Thereafter the conversation took another turn. In the meantime a practical joker had fetched a Slovak who lived in the neighborhood and was personally acquainted with most of the assembled guests. When he arrived he complained of the accusations directed against his country when no Slovak was present to refute them. Needless to say, the guests that evening were people one could trust; otherwise, such a discussion would not have been possible.

The reason for the Third Reich's moral isolation is naturally not to be found in its political duplicity alone but also in many amazing lapses from tact and consideration displayed in its diplomatic relations with other states, especially those outside the circle of the great powers. I know that convinced adherents of Ribbentrop's policies argue strongly against such an assertion and insist that no state is as correct as the Third Reich. Are not all questions concerning the domestic policy of foreign countries avoided at press conferences, they ask, and does not the German press maintain the most scrupulous reserve in such cases?

It is true that Germany in its official policy strives to maintain formal correctness. This is also true of the press, since it is the mouthpiece of that policy. Each important article is carefully scrutinized and checked both by Goebbels and von Ribbentrop, if it is not jointly formulated by them and their subordinates. But when the German government considers it suitable, the position of the press changes from correctness to the use of the most flagrant invective, usually with little or no provocation.

The policies announced at press conferences and pursued according to official forms are one thing; the real policies of the Third Reich are another. It might be that Dr. Schmidt at a press conference would emphasize the sovereignty of Denmark. On the same day, however, his colleague Dr. Best might present a new and brutal ultimatum to the Danish government. Which were we to credit, the word or the deed?

Furthermore, the Wilhelmstrasse in later years has suffered a coarsening in tone that would have greatly shocked Bismarck. Although his policies were characterized by a certain brutality and lack of consideration, they also possessed a flexibility and an understanding of the feelings of other nations that is totally lacking today in those who call themselves his followers.

Two circumstances, above all, have combined to deprive the Third Reich of all sympathy and trust. These are, first, the ruthless imperialism which it has displayed to one nation after another and, second, its system of establishing Quislings in the occupied and unoccupied countries.

The objectives of the Nazi foreign policies were long enveloped in darkness. In the beginning it was announced that the aim was to unite all Germans into one nation, and this idea invoked sympathy even among the Western Powers. But when it gradually became apparent that the aspirations of the Third Reich did not end there, anxiety rose both among Germany's neighbors and elsewhere in the world. Where would Hitler halt? Chamberlain's peace policy received its death blow when Hitler marched into Prague in the middle of March 1939, and yet the Third Reich seemed bent on proceeding further.

Not until after the war finally broke out and France was crushed, the Balkans purged and England isolated in the summer of 1940, did there appear any clear idea of what Germany really wanted. Many people had guessed it earlier, but now for the first time the official goal was proclaimed: the New Europe, the "New Order" under German leadership. Much still remained in the dark, but any doubt as to Germany's desire for complete domination of Europe was forever dispelled.

The question was, however, whether Hitler would be satisfied with even this. During those days, while the combs swelled on the Nazi cocks, there was talk of both South America and Africa.

In the German concept of uniting Europe's people, there was much that could have been made attractive to the small nations. But the Germans felt it was hardly worth while to preserve the illusion. In fact, they flatly stated there was no longer any point in small nations' maintaining expensive military organizations; instead, they could pay subsidy to the German military power. Foreign-trade policies could be arranged by Berlin. Much was also said about the "Herrenvolk"—a topic that caused even Germany's allies to raise their eyebrows. Those who wanted further proof of what to expect could consider the statements concerning Holland, which affirmed that this nation, as well as the Flemish-speaking districts of Belgium and France, would be incorporated into Germany, since both the Dutch and the Flemish were of "German stock."

That Germany had no intention of limiting her expansion to Holland, parts of Belgium, Northern France and Alsace-Lorraine became obvious when Hitler (who fancies himself heir to the Austro-Hungarian monarchy) offered the Hungarians all their confiscated lands if they would join the German Reich. They declined with thanks.

As for the eastern territories, it is not yet clear if the Third Reich, thinking itself fully capable of determining the map of Europe, had decided to break up Russia into a series of small states ("the natural constituents," as they were described by the Propaganda Ministry during the summer of 1941) or if it would be satisfied to place the Ukraine, Kuban and the Caucasus under German domination and organize a Russian state—under German control. This would comprise the remaining territory, probably after Siberia had been detached and organized as a separate state under a Japanese protectorate. Moreover, the eastern territories were to serve as an enormous slave reservoir for the "New Europe." Of that there was not the slightest doubt.

As far back as 1940, thoughtful observers in Berlin believed that Germany intended to dominate the Mediterranean—even if, on the surface, this power were accorded to Italy. But the whole of Mussolini's empire could exist only on Hitler's sufferance, and even if Hitler had a high personal regard for Il Duce, it is hardly possible that after victory he would have hesitated before the demands of *Realpolitik*.

The hate almost everywhere engendered by the Nazis has been enhanced tremendously by the use of Quislings.

During Hitler's first years in power, guarantees were widely circulated that National Socialism was not for export. Later, when the "New Europe" arose as a subject for discussion, this problem became an actuality. Between 1933 and 1939, strong support had been given all movements in Europe which sought to further anything similar to the Nazi system. At that time Europe was swept by a veritable wave of loathing for democracy; and the weakness evidenced by democratic regimes in regard to military questions created a fertile field for extra-parliamentary currents. These circumstances were fully utilized by the Nazi underground.

Although the Third Reich maintained a certain official aloofness, the situation changed the moment Germany openly declared that

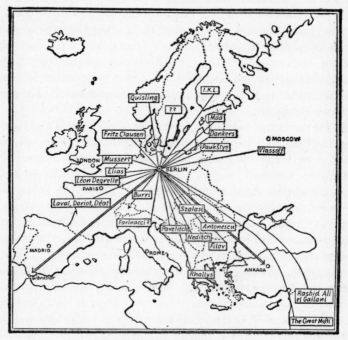

HITLER'S QUISLINGS

she was working for a "New Europe." Could a New Order exist without a common political denominator, an admission of those principles which the Nazis represented? To this Germany answered in the affirmative, at the same time using all her influence to spread the same political regime throughout Europe that existed in Germany. Soon all bars were down. The Quisling idea became the key to German foreign policies.

In France, Laval was supported while Marcel Deat and Doriot (once a Communist) were held in reserve. In Belgium it was more difficult to work with Quislings, chiefly because King Leopold was still on the throne. Agreements made with him hindered, for the time being, the establishment of that German civil administration which is the lifeblood of the Quislings. But Leon Degrelle, chief of the Rexists, would soon prove useful. Early in 1943, to the joy of the Germans, Degrelle declared himself for "German alliance." The chief of the Flemish Quislings (planted within the extremely nationalist organization "Vlaamsch National Verbond") was originally Staf de Clerque. At his death, Dr. Elias, strongly supported by the Germans, took over.

In Holland, Anton Aaron Mussert, had the honor to be received by Hitler as "Leader." But in spite of this, Mussert has been restrained. This is probably due in part to plans to incorporate Holland with Germany (a plan with which, in spite of everything, Mussert cannot agree), and partly to the exceedingly small regard in which the Dutch Quisling is held by his countrymen. A comic figure of no small proportions, he had the bad taste to marry his own aunt, who is 22 years his senior. She calls him "Toni." When Mussert appeared for a moment on the screen in a newsreel, a voice in the audience called out "Toni! Toni!" and immediately from across the theater came another voice: "Yes, Auntie?"

Among the Baltic peoples, the Germans have made spasmodic attempts to find suitable tools with which to further their policies. It is not quite clear if Dr. Mää of Estonia can be reckoned in this group. In Latvia, General Dankers has often been considered a possible chief of the Quislings. In Lithuania, Councilor General Paukstys is the Third Reich's most favored son. In Poland, however, the Germans have found it impossible to acquire a single Quisling.

As far as Russia is concerned, Germany has now managed to secure General Vlassoff as her man, but the Nazis have shown such hesitation on Russian and Ukrainian problems that the Quisling experiment there seems to be stillborn.

Less familiar to the general public is the fact that the Germans attempted to use Quislings even in Switzerland. In Germany, working with extreme discretion, is an organization which may be considered a Swiss Quisling movement. It is led by one Franz Burri, a journalist who otherwise commands little respect and who serves as correspondent for a news service in Vienna. When I heard the man speak some ten years ago, I was chiefly impressed by his incoherence. Burri has two accomplices, the former Major Ernst Leonhardt and Lieutenant Eduard Mange. The organization is known as the National Socialist Swiss Bund.

These Swiss Nazis argue that the Swiss are "a part of the German people." They greet one another with "Heil Hitler," declaring this salute to be an acknowledgment of "the leader of all Germans." Local differences, their pamphlets claim, will disappear. "We are proud," they boast, "to be called the fifth column."

Judging by statements from these sources, it becomes increasingly clear that the Swiss National Socialists intend a union with Germany of all Switzerland save the canton of Tessin (Ticino), which would become Italian, and the canton of Geneva, which they acknowledge to be French. The inhabitants of the remaining portions of French-speaking Switzerland are, according to their viewpoint, of German extraction, that is to say, Teutons.

In addition to the members of Burri's organization, there are also in Germany other Swiss who may be regarded as National Socialists, although they do not subscribe to this extreme opinion. To this group belongs the banished Dr. Wechlin, who lives in Berlin. What part the influential SS man, Dr. Franz Riedweg, also a Swiss, plays in this connection I do not know.

It is not the Quisling policy alone which has influenced European sentiment. The Germans in occupied countries have naturally increased hatred for themselves by their arbitrariness and total lack of justice. How can anyone at the present time ignore the ruthless plundering of nations? Like a swarm of locusts the Nazis have devoured everything of value. The result has been poverty similar to that which followed the Thirty Years' War.

Once Germany decided upon this tyranny, she had to continue, at an increasing rate, her executions, deportations and confiscations. And with each passing day old sympathies for Germany disappear. With each year of war Germany steadily becomes more isolated.

This may not have been a disadvantage so long as Germany was victorious. Hitler could repeat with Caligula, "Let them threaten me, if only they fear me." But when the situation changed, the dangerous consequences of Germany's ruthless piracy, of her broken promises, were at once apparent. Today, hardly a soul believes Germany's word, and her intentions are distrusted as much by her allies as by her enemies.

The German system of alliances is now like a sinking ship which the rats have decided to leave. The Berlin-Rome-Tokyo Axis belongs to history. But many changes are yet to be made. One of the

German Foreign Office's most important tasks has been to prevent the total collapse of the German system of alliances. Aside from this negative task, the first duty of the German Foreign Office has been to make peace for the Third Reich. That it will succeed in this is dubious. Peace may come to Germany, but not to the Third Reich.

Hitler and The North

The concept of The North as a unit does not exist in the future plans of the Third Reich. From the beginning, its policies have revealed a desire to split the northern states and, mindful of the phrase, "Divide and rule," prevent the formation of any coalition that could place the Scandinavians in a position to pursue independent policies.

Since Sweden is the power with the greatest resources, and because her geographical position would naturally make her the crystallization point of a northern union, it follows logically that the Nazis in all the other northern states have vigorously fostered a spirit hostile to Sweden. In Finland the Germans, with all the means at their disposal, have encouraged the strivings of the Pure Finns and have sought to bring about dissension between the Finnish and the Swedish elements in the country. In Denmark, Germany's henchman, Fritz Clausen, has shown open hostility toward the Swedes, and in Norway the Germans have supported Quisling agitations against Sweden.

The Nazi conception of Sweden is by now fairly well known. According to it the Swedes are "biologically weak," prematurely old and dying. They have had no history since Charles XII and they are governed by a regime which in effectiveness belongs in the eighteenth century. By means of agitation within the Party, this conception has been spread among the masses of German people. But there still remains on various sides a sincere sympathy for the country, and in German military circles a growing respect for Sweden's military forces. Among Party members, Sweden is extremely unpopular. Their view is that the country is nothing but a European beauty spot. It is no secret that Foreign Minister von Ribbentrop is definitely anti-Swedish, a fact that has been overwhelmingly confirmed by his faithful exponent, Dr. Schmidt. Even Goebbels is anti-Swedish. As for Hitler himself, I don't know. Ac-

cording to popular opinion within Berlin's political circles, the
Führer is said to entertain a high regard for King Gustav, with
considerably less esteem for the Swedish people themselves.
Goering's friendliness toward Sweden, however, caused great bitterness in the Party.

Sweden's independent policy, which has preserved the country's
integrity and prevented more extensive economic commitments in
the shape of credits, has aroused intense Nazi anger. Naturally there
was, and is, much in Sweden's foreign policy, as could be observed
from close range in Berlin, that incites difference of opinion. Swedes
on the spot would often have liked to see a less pliant attitude—
compliance not being the method to use in dealing with the Nazis.
But in general the Swedish stand has remained pretty firm. More
than once we wondered why Nazi Germany did not reply to the
"challenges" (which is how the Nazis describe any political opposition) with their usual attack. Why did the whole of 1941 pass
without Germany taking one preventive act against Sweden? Why
were the Swedes spared in 1940?

I personally felt that the Germans really meant business. For a
long time the Swedes in Berlin had received hints that action
against Sweden was in the offing. At the beginning of February
1942, I received a tip from a source I considered reliable. The
following week of unbearable tension we spent preparing for a
temporary internment at the Kaiserhof Hotel while German
troops "protected Sweden from the threats of the United Nations."
We felt we could write almost word for word the speech that
Foreign Minister von Ribbentrop would deliver to our colleagues
in the Bundesratsaal.

Then came Sweden's swift mobilization and her careful concentration of troops near the great lakes, where they were stationed as a precaution against possible landings from the air. We in
Berlin drew a breath of relief, though we realized, of course, the
danger was not yet over. But if this was to be war, the Swedes were
at least prepared. Days passed and gradually it became apparent
that, if an attack against Sweden had been contemplated, the scheme
was abandoned for the time being.

Naturally, I cannot state definitely that a German attack on
Sweden was planned for February 1942. But according to a source
which I cannot disregard, everything pointed to the fact that Germany had prepared a coup against Sweden for fear that our country would submit to an Allied invasion of northern Scandinavia.

February was bitterly cold, and the Baltic was frozen over. But my informant persisted in his belief that this was an additional reason for the Germans to choose that moment to attack. If they had waited till March, he maintained, the ice would have melted and the expected Swedish mobilization would have taken place.

If an attack was contemplated for February, the question naturally arises why it never materialized. Some say it was prevented by the intervention of Finland. This is debatable. There is no doubt, on the other hand, that the swift Swedish mobilization had a decisive influence on a plan whose first premise was the relatively weak state of Swedish preparedness in January and February. Winter war with Sweden, even then, would have been a difficult task for the powerful German war machine. But to attack a *prepared* Sweden under weather conditions favoring that country would have been an act of sheer stupidity.

Some weeks after the February crisis I met an individual reputed to be a specialist on Scandinavian affairs. He voluntarily mentioned the Swedish-German affair and explained authoritatively that German leaders had no intentions against Sweden. If they had, he claimed, our country would long ago have been occupied by German troops. I replied that the Swedish war machine would be a hard nut to crack—harder still now that the Luftwaffe was so much weaker—and I added that not a man in Sweden would hesitate to take up arms if the King so ordered. The man in question, irritated by my intentionally confident tone, told me that I was not properly informed. It was true, he said, that Swedish opinion as a whole was against Germany, but he insisted Germany also had dependable Swedish friends. To my question as to whom he meant, he mentioned Per Engdahl and Dr. Rutger Essen. Even certain businessmen could "be persuaded." This had always been the case in other countries, pursued my informant, so why not in Sweden? It was only a matter of making satisfactory business deals. And what about the pro-German officers in the Swedish army? "Unfortunately," he finally admitted, "most of these have been retired."

I was convinced, I said, that all Swedish officers would obey commands whether in active or reserve service. "Yes," came the surprising answer, "but are you sure that officers will receive any commands?" He was immediately horrified for fear that he had said too much, and it was hours before I could bring him back to the subject. When I did, I learned that this man relied on alleged defeatists among Swedish leaders to acquire influence and by degrees inaugurate a pro-German government. More he would not say. When I insisted that he had misjudged the situation in Sweden and not given due credit to the prestige and responsibility of the Swedish royal house, he did not reply.

It should be pointed out that in Nazi Germany there are spellbinders whose business it is politically to bemuse foreigners. I am convinced that this man was one of them.

Germany's attitude toward Finland was of an entirely different type. None of Germany's confederates has been so praised for her achievements as has that country. It often looked as though this praise were penance for the stand taken by the Nazis during the Russo-Finnish War. But it may just as often have been inspired by a genuine admiration for the deeds of the Finnish warriors —deeds which have acquired added glory since the mighty German war machine encountered the same difficulties fighting through wooded terrain in winter as the Finns encountered when they won their victories.

But German admiration for Finnish military power has not compensated for the rage she felt against Finland for having refused to declare herself solidly behind the Third Reich and to join in the Tripartite Pact. Germany would gladly have sacrificed a couple of her other allies if she had been able to bring Finland to heel. But they have not succeeded. Finland may be Germany's "comrade in arms," but she conducts her own policies.

The Nazis have always wanted to strengthen political relations with Finland, not so much for actual gain as because they feel that the good will enjoyed by Finland throughout the world would enhance Germany's position both at home and abroad. But Finland fights her own war and can make her own peace. Naturally, the Germans are fully conscious of the limited power which the Finnish government has had in this direction. In the first place, the Germans have counted on the fact that the Russians would not offer any acceptable proposal, and in the second place Finland's dependence on the Third Reich for supplies has been so great that Germans could rest easy. Moreover, there are strong German troop concentrations in the country, and there have been innumerable warnings that Germany would not hesitate to use them.

Through I.K.L. (the National Patriotic Movement) the Third Reich has a form of political insurance in Finland. The collaboration between the Lappos and the Berlin Nazis has been pretty obvious. What Germany hopes to get from these allies in Finland has been revealed in several non-official comments. If the Finnish government sought to make a separate peace, then the Germans together with the Lappos would establish a new Finnish regime and so, they say, gain the support of at least part of the Finnish army. "We will simply occupy Finland if she tries to jump off the train," said a well-known German propagandist during the Finnish government crisis in the fall of 1942. It is apparent that Nazi Germany will never willingly allow Finland to quit. Germany has the greatest need of the Finns—not in a military sense, but morally. To the people of Germany, Finland is proof that the Third Reich does not stand entirely alone. Nor does Germany allow the world to forget it. "Look," they have said in effect, "look at Finland—a democratic state fighting on Germany's side. Isn't that proof enough that Germany doesn't force her form of government on other countries?"

The Germans have tried yet another means of insinuating themselves into the Finnish democracy, but this has been done with great secrecy. Whenever possible they have supported their friends, the Pure Finns. The Finnish name-forms, Helsinki, Turky, etc., have consistently been used in Berlin, and at the slightest opportunity, Nazis have joyfully dealt out anti-Swedish propaganda. Nor have the Nazis tired in their efforts to influence Finland's leading personality, Field Marshal Mannerheim, but they have apparently not been very successful. Newsreels made on the occasion of Hitler's visit to Finland revealed that Mannerheim was a grimly determined man.

The Third Reich's moderate attitude toward Denmark surprised many people. It is true that occupied Denmark's position in regard to Germany was, legally speaking, quite different from that of the other occupied countries, but as a rule this made no difference to the Nazis. Perhaps events in Norway, aided by Finnish pressure, were responsible. In any case, Dr. Best was instructed to win the Danes by gentle means. Not only was his personal standing with Hitler very strong, but he himself was a believer in moderation toward Denmark.

One reason why the German leaders chose a mild attitude was on account of the weakness of the Danish Quislings whose leader, Fritz Clausen, had a poor, and alcoholic, reputation. While the Danish Nazi Party was forced to mark time, it slowly but surely lost ground and was constantly being deserted by its followers. Since the last election, Fritz Clausen has made a desperate attempt to save the situation by adopting an anti-German policy, but it is too late. After the German attempts to win over the Danes with the usual SS tactics proved futile, the "Frikorps Danmark" invited no further efforts. In short, the Nazis had good reason to proceed with caution and not disturb activities in Germany's large granary.

One thing that was a constant thorn in the flesh of the Germans was the northern orientation of the Danes. In Denmark, the soil for anti-Swedish agitation has been considerably poorer than that in Norway and Finland, and no veiled threats can prevent the Danes from looking over to the bright side of the Öresund and thereby strengthening their hopes for a future as a free people. It was to no avail that the Germans at last forbade the Danish press to discuss the problem of The North.

By the end of August 1943, the situation in Denmark had become acute and the Germans had abandoned their attitude of caution. The restrictions then imposed placed Denmark in almost the same position as the other occupied countries, except that she has so far been spared a violent "quislingization." These restrictions are the result of increasing sabotage in Denmark and a growing German nervousness. The fact that Nazis have been firing on Swedish fishing craft along the Danish coast is an additional sign that Germany is on tenterhooks. But the people of Denmark will bear the new restrictions with the same dignity they have already shown in their bloodless battle for freedom. The Nazis will never be able to subjugate them.

Norway has been the proving ground of the Nazis' political experiments. While Mussert in Holland, at least in the beginning, was considered to have about 3 or 4 per cent of his countrymen behind him, no one has ever been able to prove that Vidkun Quisling had more than a scant 2 per cent. The Germans, moreover, have restrained Mussert while allowing Quisling a free rein.

The result of the experiment has horrified all sober-thinking Germans. But no one has been able to do anything about it. All attempts to remove Quisling have failed because of Hitler's gratitude to him for his services in the spring of 1940.

The German public knows little or nothing about events in Norway. They barely realize that a small Germanic nation is being ground down by the German heel. What little they do know comes entirely from soldiers home on leave. But bad news is not all that these men bring with them. Among other things, they return with Norwegian silver fox skins, which can be seen all over Berlin, with the result that the German public consoles itself by turning a deaf ear to the stories of conditions in Norway. "The Norwegians," they say, "are so cantankerous."

In political circles, of course, what is going on in Norway is perfectly clear. There is a desire to suppress at any cost the stubborn Norwegian resistance, since a defeat in Norway, the home of the Quisling concept, would be catastrophic for Germany's prestige. I have already mentioned, however, that many Germans could not conceal their personal contempt for the Quislings. "I could never shake hands with Quisling," a high German officer told me. But when I pointed out that there were propaganda pictures showing his Commander-in-Chief shaking Quisling's hand with obvious pleasure, the officer was painfully embarrassed. "It is the Party leaders who are inclined to do such things," he finally admitted.

Germany will certainly try to keep Quisling as long as possible. There is, however, no doubt that the stiff resistance in Norway has become one of Germany's most troublesome problems. Now that it can no longer be used as an offensive base against England and traffic through Sweden has been halted, Norway, in fact, has become something of a white elephant, and an expensive one at that. But an evacuation of Norway is quite unlikely for the time being; any reports to the contrary should be treated with skepticism.

Nazism and Its Allies

The Third Reich has gradually managed to secure a number of partners. These are Japan, who sought an alliance with the enemies of her Anglo-Saxon adversaries; Italy, who under Mussolini's leadership boldly gambled on a German victory; Hungary, who gave way before the threats of her mighty neighbor; Rumania, who in Germany sought protection from Soviet Russia and help to attain her territorial aspirations; Bulgaria, who with Germany's help hoped to revise Balkan boundaries; and finally Croatia and Slovakia, who arose under German suzerainty and saw a protector in the Third Reich.

Some solidarity between the authoritarian systems has played a telling role in Italy, Rumania, Slovakia and Croatia. But on the whole, the relations between the Third Reich and her partners have had only the character of *Realpolitik*. The Nazis have taken care to prevent any sentimental backing of the Tripartite Pact on the part of her associates. In many cases the German people have had anything but a favorable impression of their allies; the German public's attitude toward its enemies is much more respectful than its bearing toward, say, the Italians. This state of affairs has not passed unnoticed and mutual antipathies have steadily grown.

As the Third Reich's system of alliances has gradually dissolved, public opinion in the partner-states has played a major role. Although disintegration was inevitable, it increased in tempo the moment faith in Germany's victory began to disappear. By now, the partners' main concern is how best they can pull themselves out of the war. They live in fear of what will happen to them in the event of a German defeat.

Japan is undoubtedly the largest and most powerful of Germany's allies, and the two countries have exchanged innumerable expressions of friendship. The theory of their common political and military interests is one of the chief dogmas of Ribbentrop's foreign policy. Moreover, no German can deny that it has some truth, since the Island Empire in East Asia has undoubtedly relieved the pressure on Germany.

Nevertheless, a few weeks in Nazi Germany would suffice to reveal the simple truth that the Japanese are intensely disliked, while the Chinese, curiously enough, are very popular. This is due, in part, to the fact that the Germans have not forgotten Japan's attitude in the First World War. The Germans also have a feeling that perhaps Kaiser Wilhelm was not so mistaken when he kept warning Europe against the Yellow Peril.

Berlin's reactions to Japan's great victories in the spring of 1942 were very interesting to watch. At first, the Germans were enthusiastic and applauded vigorously. But as Japanese conquest continued and at last the Dutch East Indies fell, a profound depression settled over German political circles. Even very prominent Nazis let fall remarks such as, "It is Europe, the Germanic peoples, who are having to pay for the advance of the yellow races."

Although this belief did not last long, the German anti-Japanese sentiment persisted. Political circles, too, were extremely annoyed by the unwillingness of the Japanese to wage war according to the German plans and, above all, by their refusal to attack the

Soviet Union. The only thing Tokyo has consented to do for its ally has been to undertake negotiations for a separate peace between Germany and Russia. The Berlin-Tokyo Axis is simply a marriage of convenience in which neither party entertains the slightest qualms about sacrificing the other.

Worse still were Germany's relations with her former ally, Italy. What the Italians think of the Germans the world, of course, knows. Even in 1940, when it still seemed possible for Italy to gain something from co-operation with Germany, the Italian people were making no secret of their feelings. Before Italy's entry into the war, Luftwaffe officers, dressed in civilian clothes, were stationed in Sicily. The moment Italy declared war, they put on uniforms. One day some of these German aviators arrived in a small Sicilian town to find themselves surrounded by a cheering mob who offered them gifts and asked for their military buttons as souvenirs. The flyers (who understood almost no Italian) were flattered by their reception and not in the least embarrassed, until one of them observed that the mayor kept on repeating a certain phrase which, when translated, turned out to be: "We knew you would come." Only then did they realize that the townspeople thought the English had arrived.

The average German holds a profound contempt for the Italians because of their reputation as soldiers. Berliners call them Macaronis and mince no words about what they would like to do to their former allies. Many Germans, however, admire Italians for their accomplishments in non-military fields. Political circles, in fact, respect Italian diplomacy. "They work with stilettos while we brandish clumsy broadswords," a German diplomat once said to me. While contempt for the Italians as soldiers is certainly shared by German leaders and official circles, these groups have had to exercise an unusual self-control—a control often admirable simply as a technical accomplishment. Only the initiated really know the trouble the Third Reich had with its former brother-in-arms—and the initiated are those who have been obliged to lead the chorus of praise for Italy.

Naturally, in spite of the most minute control, stories of the German-Italian relationship have leaked out. One story that caused a great deal of amusement concerned a delegation of Bulgarian officers on a visit to Berlin. At a private reception at the Hotel Kaiserhof, where only Germans and Bulgarians were present, a number of distinguished officers of the German General Staff got drunk. Suddenly one of the drunken men climbed on a table and made a speech in which he asked the Bulgarians what they meant by skulking behind Germany's back and refusing to take part in the war against Bolshevism. There was a dead silence. Then, before any German officer was able to interfere, the leader of the Bulgarian delegation stood up. "My dear friend," he said, "there also has to be someone in the Balkans to kick the Italians out!" Everyone roared with laughter and the situation was saved.

The capitulation of Italy on September 3, 1943, brought with it at least one blessing for official Germany—at last they could openly express their feelings about the former ally. And the Nazis have certainly taken advantage of this opportunity. The "heroic" Italian people, who until recently were being praised to the skies, have suddenly been transformed into a nation of paltry traitors, too mean to deserve the leadership of the great Mussolini. That Mussolini still is an exception was demonstrated by Hitler's loud praise of that gentleman in his speech on September 10. Well-informed Germans, however, have certainly no illusions about Mussolini himself. The Foreign Office has not forgotten that it has in its possession a document from the Italian dictator's earlier career. This document proves that in 1914 Mussolini founded the newspaper *Popolo d'Italia* with the help of 1,250,000 lire received from the Russian Ambassador in Rome—for agitation against Germany.

As far as Hungary is concerned, it is an open secret that relations between Hitler and Admiral Horthy have always been extremely cool. Reasons for this may be psychological, for, after all, one man concerned turned his back on the Austrian Imperial Army, while the other, the victor of Otranto, proudly wears his Austro-Hungarian uniform to this day. On the other hand, whatever coolness there may be between the two men, it is no greater than that existing between lesser statesmen of the two nations. How, then, can we explain the fact that Hungary ever became Germany's ally?

After the Anschluss in 1938, the government in Budapest found itself in a precarious situation. The Third Reich was openly pushing its political center of gravity towards southeastern Europe, and Hungary lay right in the path of German expansion. Moreover, the 500,000 German-speaking people of Hungary had been subjected for a long time to intensive Nazi propaganda. German economic, political and military pressure on Hungary had increased every year. Politically, the country was isolated after Italy went over to the German side. Both England and France, uninterested in a tie-up with the Hungarians, were trying to keep the Czechs and Rumanians under arms. All Hungarian revisionist claims were rejected by the Western Powers, and revision of the boundaries established by the Treaty of Trianon was, and is, the Alpha and Omega of Hungarian policy.

It was not surprising, under such conditions, that Budapest chose to side with, rather than against, Germany. To oppose her militarily was out of the question at that time. It is therefore difficult to imagine how Hungary could have adopted any other attitude. The possibility of having part of her territorial demands accepted naturally clinched the argument in favor of her joining the German system of alliance.

In the light of recent events, however, it is quite understandable that the Hungarians are doing all they can to free themselves from the Third Reich. It should be remembered that in 1938 Hungarian opportunists (among them many army officers led by General Werth), believing in a German victory, took advantage of the situation. Last but not least came an extreme Rightist opposition of a Nazi character: the "Arrow Cross" men led by Szalasi, and a more moderate party under Imrédy. Against these pro-German factions, so far as I know, Hungary at that time had nothing to offer.

Since then, however, the Hungarians have done all they can to hold the forces of the country intact, to preserve their independence and to avoid identifying themselves with Nazi Germany. Tens of thousands of Polish refugees have been treated like friends, and 40,000 of those capable of bearing arms have been able to escape the country right under the nose of the Gestapo. In Hungary there is a Polish daily newspaper and a Polish high school with its own teachers. The Hungarian press has not joined in the German railings against England and the United States, nor against the neutral countries.

Even internal independence has been preserved. The Hungarian government has succeeded in blocking the countless German attempts to bring about a "quislingization" of the country. The Germans have spent millions ruthlessly exploiting Hungary's unfortunate social structure, and the last of many attempted Nazi coups occurred in April 1943; it failed like the others. The Hungarian Parliament has Jewish members and the Hungarian laws still allow the country's numerous Jews the possibility of existence, although many restrictions have been placed on them. The Social Democratic Party is tolerated and only one newspaper has been banned—the Nazi *Pesti Ujság*. Yes, in the summer of 1942, the Hungarian government actually permitted the publication of a speech by Count Stephen Bethlen, which assumed that adherents of the Fascist philosophy throughout the world were in the minority. The Hungarians are seriously preparing themselves for the post-war world.

Hungary's domestic and foreign policies have aroused a tempest of fury among leading Nazis in Berlin. Among the German people there is still sympathy for the Hungarians, but not in the Party. Dr. Schmidt hardly bothers to conceal his dislike for the Hungarians, and he is not the only one. The fact is that the German leaders have often considered a military attack upon Hungary, but for various reasons they have so far refrained from doing so. Nevertheless, the relations between Germany and Hungary are so tense that it is not at all certain the Hungarians will be able to preserve their independence until the end of the war.

For that matter, it is not certain that the Hungarians themselves intend to continue indefinitely their policy of avoiding direct conflict with Germany. The long-existing alliance between Hungary and Italy is not without interest in this connection. Actually, the fall of Mussolini has not destroyed this mutual sympathy, since even before his exit, Hungarian relations with the Quirinal and the Vatican were better than they were with the Palazzo Venezia. Now that Italy has quit the war by concluding an armistice with the Allies, it is not impossible that Budapest will follow suit, provided she is given guaranties that military resistance against a German attack would not be in vain. Since Budapest would presumably declare that the Tripartite Pact was no longer valid, and since no special agreements exist between Germany and Hungary, the Hungarian government would have an absolutely free hand. Moreover, it must not be forgotten that in the event of a change in the Hungarian government, it is quite probable that old Count Stephen Bethlen, the man most in favor of the Western Powers, would once again become Prime Minister.

As for Rumania, she has been just as popular in Berlin as Hungary has been unpopular. Hitler thinks very highly of Marshal Antonescu and on several occasions has offered to honor him by visiting Bucharest. Each time, however, Himmler has vetoed the idea, explaining that he could not be responsible for Hitler's safety.

Rumania's favor in Berlin is, of course, largely due to her ability to produce the vital necessity—oil. But the primary reason for her special position has been Rumania's political attitude. During the last part of his reign, King Carol threw himself into the arms of Germany and broke with the Western Allies. With Antonescu's accession to power, this development became more clearly marked. The country did everything in her power to please the Germans. In return she seems to have obtained a promise from them that she would receive the whole of Transylvania—something the generous Germans, for that matter, also promised the Hungarians.

Rumania continued to adjust herself to the policy of the Third Reich. After outrageous taxes had been imposed upon the Jews, thousands of them were transported to Poland. As late as May 1943, new demands were made upon what miserable resources they had left, while in the occupied territories in the Ukraine all Semitic elements were simply extinguished. The executions of Ukrainian Jews—which, according to official German figures, were 17,000 in a single day—were on almost the same scale as the SS executions further north. But the Rumanians, confident in German victory, went still further and treated the Ukrainian population, not only of Bessarabia and Bukovina, but also of the territories that had been Russian before 1939, with extreme brutality. As a reward for their efforts, the Rumanians hoped to keep the whole district between the Dniester and the Bug, where 90 to 95 per cent of the inhabitants are Ukrainian. This territory received the name of Transnistria. The Rumanians brought in their own civil officials, as well as Rumanian colonists. They printed extensive maps whose purpose was to prove that the region had belonged to them in ancient times and was still largely Rumanian in population. An entire "scientific" literature has grown up around this thesis.

Rumania's attachment to Germany of course found expression in the press, which was larded with the usual German propaganda. In the Wilhelmstrasse, the Rumanian journalists were and are the favorites of the Germans. Not all Rumanians, however, approved of this pro-German policy. Dissenting voices were heard, including those of Maniu, the old leader of the Peasants' Party, and of the groups around Bratianu and Tartarescu. But as long as things went well in Russia, the opposition was no serious problem for the Rumanian leader, Antonescu. Only when the chances for victory began to fade and the conquest of Odessa alone cost the Rumanians 30,000 dead, did signs of serious opposition begin to appear. Since the defeats in Russia, not even official Rumania seems to like the idea of the country's being one of Germany's most faithful allies. Various statements from Bucharest have suggested that Rumania should occupy the same position as Finland.

Even people around Marshal Antonescu are trying, very discreetly, to free their country from the German yoke. At the head of this group is the Marshal's namesake, Vice-President of the Council, Michael Antonescu. Then there is the Rumanian statesman Gafencu, who devotes his days in Geneva to the same cause. But, at the time of writing, there are still influential circles in the country that have not abandoned hope of a German victory, in which case they see Rumanian aspirations realized, especially at the cost of Hungary. Rumanian troops are still fighting in the East. Moreover, should Rumania decide to do an about-face—and the Italian capitulation seems to have given the Rumanians a real shock —the Germans are strong enough to put a stop to it. In contrast to Hungary, where there are almost no German troops, Rumania has large German forces within her borders.

As for Bulgaria, all Europe knows that since the outbreak of the Russo-German war, her position has been extremely delicate. A considerable majority of the Bulgarian people still see in Russia the liberator from the Turkish yoke. The alliance with Germany has been supported emotionally by only a small group. That Bulgaria, in spite of this, became the ally of the Third Reich was due primarily to the fact that Germany could restore to the country its lost territories and create a Bulgaria of approximately the same size as that of the Peace of San Stefano in 1878.

The pro-Axis policy was also supported by King Boris, whose death has completely changed the situation. The Italian capitulation, of course, has made matters even more complicated for the Germans. The prospects are that the Germans may be forced to act toward Bulgaria as they did toward Denmark. A change of government and the handing over of the post of Prime Minister to the leader of the opposition, Musyanov, should bring with it the same development as did Radoslavov's departure in 1918—in other words, capitulation to the Allies. The Bulgarian crisis is all the more of a blow to Germany since the Bulgarian leadership has consented to extend the zone of occupation and to replace, in part, the disarmed Italian divisions. Consequently, most of Serbia was occupied by Bulgarian troops at the end of August, and they had also taken over large portions of the former Italian zones in northern Greece, even down to Thessaly.

As far as the Croats are concerned, they and the Austrians have been in sympathy for a long time. By its support of the Ustachi movement, Nazism has succeeded in destroying every ounce of Croat sympathy for Germany.

It is difficult to determine what the great mass of the Croats think about their future. I hear from good sources that Dr. Matchek's Peasants' Party—the only political movement that enjoys the confidence of the Croatian people—wants to create a Croatian state having no connection with the Serbs and Belgrade. It is said to look rather toward Vienna, hoping to join a new Danubian union. But no one can tell what will really happen to the Croats. No one ever knows if a bloody settling of affairs between them and the Serbs can be avoided. What is universally known is the fact that the slaughter of tens of thousands of Serbs during the Pavelitch regime did not improve relations between the two peoples.

Slovakia has long been regarded as the Third Reich's only real friend. The Slovak state is also a creation of Germany, and Father Tiso's regime has Berlin to thank for its very existence. Nevertheless, it has been obvious for some time that even the Slovaks have begun to tire of their German protectors. This is partly due to the fact that recent events in Europe have made it easier for the opposition to raise its head than was the case last year. But it is also due to the behavior of the Germans in Slovakia, which has had to serve as the main larder for the Nazi bosses.

Today, both the ruling circles and the opposition are uneasy about the future of the country. Developments in London are closely followed. In the event of an Allied victory, the Slovaks know that Benes is likely to succeed in restoring some sort of Czechoslovakia, and neither the government nor the opposition wants that. However limited Slovakia's independence may have been during the years after 1939, the Slovaks have nevertheless become accustomed to ruling themselves, and no Slovak has the desire to return to the domination of Prague.

This should not be forgotten when observing the conflict that has arisen between President Benes and the leading Slovak émigrés, among whom are Hodza and Osusky. It is significant that Benes, during his tour of the United States, did not visit Pittsburgh, the center of the Slovaks of America. And it is upon the Slovaks in America that those at home are placing their hopes in the event of an Allied victory—an event which Slovaks in Europe are taking more and more into account. In August of this year a conference was held at which representatives of both government circles and the opposition discussed Slovakia's situation. They seem to have agreed to try to place the country's future in the hands of the American Slovaks, the idea being that no one could then say of them that they had acted under pressure from Hitler. This argument is directed against Benes, who wishes to establish the fact that the Slovaks cut themselves off from the Czechs as a result of German pressure. He has even explained in the Russian periodical *Slavyane*, organ of the Slavic Committee in Moscow, that the Slovakian problem is purely an administrative one. "A certain degree of respect for the national peculiarities of the Slovaks has been, and will be in the future," he wrote, "the only proper method of dealing with this matter."

It would be unjust to the Czechs to count them among Germany's allies. They take an in-between position as a "protected people" of the Third Reich.

After the German invasion, Bohemia and Moravia were isolated from the rest of Europe and had to work for the victory of their oppressors. Then came the German-Russian war. Hardly a soul imagined in the beginning that the German victories would not continue indefinitely. But when it became clear that the great Protector of the Czechs had at last met his match, the situation changed overnight, and the "wires" between London and Prague became intensely active.

The newly appointed Reichsprotector Heydrich put through punitive measures of appalling severity. At his side worked Under Secretary Frank, whose whole efforts were based on the total destruction of the Czech people or, if this were not possible, then their complete enslavement.

But Heydrich was intelligent enough to realize that the firing squads were not accomplishing their purpose. He therefore discontinued mass executions and began liquidating the potential leaders. At the same time he introduced a kind of conciliatory policy towards the Czechs. It was conciliatory, needless to say, in the National Socialist sense: after the people had been terrorized into submission, the German leadership began to work for their "best interests" by introducing a series of social reforms. Many Czechs are willing to admit that Heydrich really succeeded in solving many problems; but whether he himself believed that he could win the hearts of the Czechs by establishing vacation homes for workers and distributing to hospitals articles seized from profiteers, is certainly debatable. He was counting, however, on a certain easing of tension, and in this he succeeded.

When considering conditions in the Protectorate, one must not forget that the absolutely frantic hatred of the Germans was not inevitable from the beginning. The Czech political regime had suffered a moral defeat, perhaps greater than that suffered by any other of the governments set up at Versailles. Czech spokesmen have assured me that when the Protectorate was established, many people really wanted to reach a modus vivendi with the Germans on the basis of a somewhat milder form of Protectorate. Nor were the Czechs, with their realism, blind to the economic advantages of greater markets. As long as the Germans did not interfere with the basic conditions of their daily life, their salaries, their businesses and their pensions, the active opposition centered chiefly around the intellectuals.

But if conditions at the beginning were relatively favorable for the Germans, this does not mean that the Nazis had any better idea how to deal with the Czechs than how to deal with any other people. The opposition was given every justification for existence. After the Germans took advantage of the attack against Heydrich to direct new blows against leading Czechs, the situation was hopeless.

During the summer of 1943 disturbances broke out at several places in the Protectorate—in Beneschau, Jungbunzlau and Pribram, where Germans were evicting the Czechs and handing over their houses to German colonists.

The Czechs at home are unable to speak because of the Nazi terror and nobody knows how they contemplate their future. Travelers in the Protectorate last spring came back with widely divergent impressions. Most of them maintain that the opposition is in constant touch with London, but at the same time they insist that the exiled government has relatively little influence among its own people. I talked with one well-informed Czech who said that the exiles would be welcomed back to Prague but would not be permitted to take over the government. He expected that the new leaders would be wholly different people—men who had stayed at home and had given an example of courage and decency during the hard fight with the Germans.

When I asked this man, who belonged politically to the Czech Agrarians, what attitude he thought the Czech people might adopt towards a new Danubian monarchy, he answered that it was still too early to say, but that the Czechs by and large considered a repetition of the 1918-38 policy unthinkable.

Germany and Her Three Great Adversaries

The relationship of the Third Reich with its enemies is a complex and exhaustive study. I will limit myself to a few aspects of the problem which may be of some aid in interpreting events.

The Nazis regard Britain as the primary enemy. They feel about her as they once felt about their enemies at home: some violent, personal element is involved, a sense of inferiority, a feeling that England always wins the last battle. Just as under the Weimar Republic, the Germans today feel an instinctive admiration for the British. The most hardened Nazi could not help admiring British morale during the days of the blitz. "After all, the British are Germanic," was a common enough expression.

The Nazis naturally are aware of this and they have done their best to counteract such sentiments. Indeed, the propaganda carried on against England is unequalled even by the anti-Semitic campaigns. No opportunity is missed to stress the three so-called British attributes: baseness, cowardice and weakness.

From a political point of view, the Nazis have tried, above all, to present England as being on the verge of Bolshevism. Dr. Schmidt turned amazing somersaults to attain this end. Cripps' entry into the war cabinet he automatically presented as decisive evidence that it was only a question of time before England became a Soviet Republic. When Cripps left the cabinet, Schmidt had nothing to say about "Bolshevization."

Foreigners found little pleasure in watching the progress of German anti-British propaganda. Correspondents in Berlin will never forget the interview which Rommel gave in Goebbels' presence. The famous Field Marshal told them the British were cowardly and fought dishonorably. "We have beaten them," Rommel added, and he declared that the Germans would certainly conquer

Egypt. The interview took place a few weeks before Montgomery counterattacked at El Alamein.

The boasting made little impression, while the ridiculing of the English made an impression of the wrong sort. Most of the newspapermen contrasted it with the Englishman's admiration for Rommel. The respect which correspondents in Berlin held for the Field Marshal was canceled by that one interview. "He is a great soldier," they thought, "but certainly not a great man."

My German acquaintances were nonplussed when I told them what Rommel had said. One man who had been serving in Africa at the time of the interview remarked that no one there could understand what had come over Rommel. He tried to explain it, saying that it might be his bad health or his complete ignorance of politics. Goebbels, of course, had talked him into it. Or perhaps British sabotage had been the cause—for the Field Marshal has lost some good friends in the desert at the hands of the British patrols.

Even Major Sommerfeldt had received instructions to emphasize the cowardice of the English. On one occasion he delivered an entire lecture on the subject, stating that the British soldier was more base and cowardly than any other soldier the Germans had encountered. It made about the same impression on hearers as had the Rommel interview.

A week later, something unexpected happened. It was announced that a Captain Von der Heydte, if I remember correctly, holder of the Iron Cross and a soldier who had been through the conquest of Crete, was to lecture on the experiences of the parachute troopers.

He had come directly from his plane, so couldn't have received any instructions. Before a scarlet-faced Sommerfeldt and a delighted foreign press, this uninformed warrior stalwartly praised the enemy. "The Tommies," he said, "are the toughest and bravest opponents we Germans have met. They stormed our positions seventeen times. If they had charged once more, we would have had to yield. Ammunition was running low. But there wasn't an eighteenth time."

He gave additional examples of English courage. His talk made a crushing impression on the row of Propaganda Ministry officials. For this was a man who knew, who had "smelled powder," who had won his Iron Cross in the conquest of Canea. For weeks after, people talked about the magnificent blunder.

The Germans know next to nothing about events in England. But today the British are better informed than ever about conditions in Germany. Some British agents were there before the outbreak of war; some arrived later. They land from planes and leave in small boats from the French-Belgian-Dutch coast. Once out at sea, they are picked up by planes or submarines.

Czech saboteurs are dropped over the Protectorate. They are smuggled out from there and take jobs in factories all over Germany, where the man-power shortage is so acute that a thorough investigation of a worker is impossible.

Englishmen, Alsatians, German émigrés and Jews are used as agents. They are perfectly equipped. Captured British parachute agents, so Germans told me, carry a complete and correct outfit of papers: military passport, furlough papers and ration cards. Counterespionage seldom traps the British agent; chance, it turns out, is Nazi Germany's best detective.

One such "chance" was told me by an acquaintance. A lieutenant, a non-com and two privates stood in a subway. A girl came on, stumbled as the train started, stepped hard on the non-com's foot. He swore at her. The officer objected to this uncalled-for behavior, and demanded to see the non-com's credentials. The man stammered, finally showed his papers. They were in order; nevertheless the officer ordered the two privates to arrest him. More than likely, if the non-com had simply gone along, he would eventually have been released. Instead he tried to escape, and almost succeeded. But someone tripped him. He was instantly searched and on him were found telltale maps and photographs.

I have cited the bombing of Stettin as an instance of how well-informed the English are as to German military conditions. But a man in the know has revealed that they show an equally minute knowledge of conditions in the German airplane factories. Many times English bombers have paid precision calls just as finished planes were ready to be shipped out.

A good friend of this informant was on hand at one of the larger German plants when 180 fighter planes, completely assembled, were turned over to the Luftwaffe. According to schedule they were to fly the planes out the next morning. But that night the officer in charge had dark premonitions. Suddenly he decided to call in his pilots. In spite of the late hour, he ordered them to fly the assembled planes to nearby air fields. By ten o'clock the planes were out. A few hours later heavy bombers devastated the assembly halls.

The British Intelligence Service works all over Germany. When the war is over, records may reveal that for years prominent Nazis have been in the service of the British Intelligence.

The Nazis' attitude toward America is similar to that toward England. Germans are very sensitive on the subject of the United States. Most of them feel an instinctive warmth for America, mainly because millions of Germans went there; at the same time, they feel an instinctive awe because they remember America's role in the First World War. Respect for its material power is widespread.

Here, too, Nazi propaganda has systematically "corrected" German opinion. During the past years its method was to ridicule America's strength. Berliners were ironic about the "mania for figures," declared the "liberty system" a complete fiasco and said that the American armament industry was far below production levels claimed for it by Roosevelt.

Along with this basic approach, the Nazis did all they could to discredit America. But in 1942, when such propaganda was at its height, it seemed to me that Dr. Goebbels had failed to convince the German people that the United States was a weak or morally decadent nation.

In the meantime, both the Foreign Office and the Propaganda Ministry pursued a studiously thorough campaign against America. With routine monotony, representatives of the foreign press listened to endless discourses by a foaming Dr. Schmidt on the subject of Roosevelt.

But Schmidt made one blunder which for months became the talk of international circles in Berlin. One day—I think it was in the early fall of 1942—Schmidt enlisted no less a person than Envoy Thomsen, Germany's recent chargé d'affaires in Washington and current minister to Stockholm, to lecture at his *Stammtisch*. To the amazement of everyone present, Thomsen's ideas of America refuted at every point Schmidt's policies expressed daily at the conference table in the Wilhelmstrasse. The astounded host tried to pull the lecture back to a more orthodox channel, but he failed. Either Thomsen did not or he would not understand what Schmidt expected of him.

The Chief of the Press Division asked Thomsen whether the

American people were becoming aware of Roosevelt's treachery. Thomsen roundly answered that America's president was a great statesman and that he had the entire country behind him. "We must have no illusions," he declared. "When the American people get into this war, they will fight to the end." Some of Schmidt's closest associates then asked a leading question: Wasn't United States policy controlled by the Jews? Thomsen's answer, extraordinary for a Nazi and a shocker for the audience, made a distinction between Jews and American Jews who think and feel as Americans and not as Jews. The veins on Dr. Schmidt's forehead swelled. Nevertheless, Thomsen rejected all efforts to salvage the Schmidt propaganda line. The limit was reached when Thomsen soberly warned them that they were underestimating American armament. Schmidt was beside himself. It would have been interesting to have witnessed the meeting between the two gentlemen after the lecture. Thomsen's lecture had been so effective that several weeks went by before the topic of America was once again broached at a press conference, and then it was another story.

The old propaganda was no longer tenable. America's contribution to the war was becoming apparent even to the German people. Goebbels and von Ribbentrop had to find another way out. They came up with the idea that Britain and the United States could not achieve a decisive blow against Fortress Europe; consequently it was of paramount importance for Germany and her partners to hold until the Allies saw the pointlessness of continuing hostilities. Today, America is such a nightmare to the Nazis that the subject has become almost taboo. Considerably less was heard during the spring of 1943 of the once popular thesis that America is about to "take over" the British Empire; that a serious split exists between London and Washington. Even though there is always a grain of truth in such propaganda, the facts, in this instance, spoke too clearly to suit Nazi fancy.

The Third Reich's attitude toward its third great enemy, Russia, is far more complicated. I have already mentioned that in the fall of 1942 I seriously feared the Nazis would capitulate to Stalin. What I must emphasize here are the bonds that exist between Bolshevism and Nazism. Nothing so excites, bewilders or infuriates the orthodox Nazi as the contention that the two totalitarian systems of government have a good deal in common. On the other hand, he is the first to admit that in practice this is a fact. One need not waste too many words on the links between the Third Reich and the Soviet Union. Perhaps they are best characterized by a statement supposed to have been made by Hitler himself: "Stalin did the only proper thing when he ruthlessly liquidated all opposition. I, too, have wanted to do that, but my advisers prevented me."

It matters little whether this statement is authentic or not. The point is that, so far as domestic policy is concerned, there is no difference between the Nazi and the Soviet viewpoint. The ruthless concentration of power is characteristic of both Berlin and Moscow. Nor are their foreign policies so divergent. I have heard a well-known Nazi state at a social gathering not only that Russian foreign policy is handled extremely well, but that it is marked by the "realistic spirit of the age." Russia, he said, has "utilized the pact" to suit her own purposes. She has not hesitated to "trick the stupid democracies" by negotiating with them and with the Germans at the same time. This Nazi claimed that, during her 1940 campaign, Germany received excellent assistance from Russian reports regarding the plans of the British and French General Staffs. I cannot vouch for the truth of this, but Nazi respect for the "realism" of Russia's foreign policy is by no means small.

There are even people outside Party circles who take a relatively benevolent attitude toward Russia. Bismarck's line still has adherents. Some high-ranking Nazi officers follow in the footsteps of General von Seeckt, and believe that Germany should strive to bring about an alliance with the great continental power.

On the other hand, within the Nazi Party powerful forces oppose any idea of a new pact with Bolshevism. So far as one can make out, military circles insist that, in the East, Germany should never surrender; it is only to the Western Powers that she might conceivably capitulate.

In this connection, the significance of the contact between German and Russian soldiers should not be overlooked. As I have said, the German armies in Russia met an enemy with a mentality completely different from that of their earlier foes. The Germans were extremely bitter about the Russians' "base methods of waging war." To what degree this bitterness was justified is irrelevant here. What matters is that the different classes of German soldiers with whom I spoke all expressed horror and terror as their immediate reaction to the Soviet system. This system, they felt, constructed enormous government buildings, manufactured vast quantities of the most modern war matériel, and yet allowed the greater part of the population to live in indescribable misery. The cold, grim consistency of such Soviet policy horrified the German soldier and actually made him feel he was fighting for a better world against eastern barbarism. This impression may, in part, explain the German soldier's dogged endurance. But crowning this was their fear of what would happen to them if they fell into Russian hands. They insisted that massacred Germans were not an uncommon sight during the advance.

That was the German view of the matter. What the Russians thought about the Germans was something I could only guess from the little I heard in Berlin. They could most certainly be excused for hesitating to describe German methods of warfare as humane. Nobody in Berlin took the trouble to deny that the Germans began by executing a great many Russian prisoners of war. I have met many eyewitnesses of these deeds. They defended the execution on the grounds that no guards were available, that there was no food for the prisoners—and that death was administered painlessly, by gas. Despite such "defenses" the facts remain. It appears that German military leaders protested strongly against these murders of prisoners which, needless to say, were committed by the SS.

German propaganda in Russia, that is, in the conquered territories, has apparently had no success. True, the Nazis did acquire a Quisling, General Vlassoff, but the great mass of the population has remained hostile, a fact due mainly to Germany's amazingly awkward eastern policy. Hitler has played into Stalin's hand one trump card after the other. Nor have the Germans made any attempt to counter Communism. They have refrained, too, from introducing any idea of a re-established Tsarism, even though this notion would certainly have drawn response from some of the older Russians. It is true that the Nazis have talked of defending religion, but they have done nothing to help the Orthodox Church to its feet. Neither have they re-established private property which, admittedly, is a gigantic task, especially during wartime. It might have been worth trying, if only as an attempt to take a trick in the game against Stalin.

More serious has been the fact that the Nazis had no idea how to exploit Ukrainian nationalism. This was entirely the fault of the Party. The military leaders, on the other hand, had studied both Napoleon's campaign and Kaiser Wilhelm's war in the East and had concluded that it was imperative to win the Ukrainians for Germany against Moscow.

Under the leadership of Field Marshal von Brauchitsch, the German military had concluded an agreement with the Ukrainian émigrés (represented by the Organization of Ukrainian Nationalists), according to which a sovereign Ukrainian state with its own army and in alliance with Germany should be established in the event of a Russo-German conflict.

At first it looked as if the plan would work. It was reported that Ukrainians by the scores of thousands had deserted from the Soviet forces in order to join the National Ukrainian Army which, propaganda maintained, the Germans had set up. But to the great astonishment of the Kremlin, the plan never materialized.

On the contrary, most of the conquered Ukraine was put under German civil government and parceled out to the Party. At the head of it was Erich Koch, the Gauleiter from East Prussia, whose nickname was "the Hangman of the Ukraine."

To the jubilation of Moscow, Koch cleaned out the Ukrainian nationalists. An informed German explained this to me as follows: "Since we ourselves plan to take over the entire Ukrainian territory after the war," he said, "naturally no Ukrainian nationalism can be allowed to grow up." Under such conditions, it is readily understandable why German eastern policy was a fiasco. But that was not enough. The administration succeeded in whipping up among the Ukrainians a real hatred for Germany. Masses of Ukrainian nationalists were shot—after having been betrayed, it is said, by Russians whom the Germans had taken into their service. Among these men were former Ogpu agents.

It is significant that a large partisan force has sprung up in the Ukraine under the leadership of a Ukrainian officer calling himself Taras Bulba, who directs his activities against both Russians and Germans. But the Russians also have large partisan forces there. They have not been slow to exploit Nazi mistakes and the U.S.S.R. now presents itself as a liberator of the Ukrainian people from the German yoke.

FINAL PHASE OF THE WAR

Germany's Strength

THE German war machine still commands respect. At present it probably consists of some 295 divisions—all in all, about 11,000,000 men. Of this total, however, only half can be considered as the army proper. Nobody outside military circles knows the exact disposition of German forces, but since the public at large seems to entertain some erroneous ideas as to the proportions in the various armed services, it might be well to give a rough outline, with no other purpose than to indicate approximate proportions

270 infantry and light divisions of 15,000 men each..	4,050,000
25 armored-car and tank divisions, each of 8,000 men	200,000
Heavy artillery and special troops................	250,000
Reserve army (depots at home to fill losses)........	1,000,000
Anti-aircraft force (in addition to regular field units)	1,000,000
Police troops (in addition to the normal police force)	500,000
Non-combatant reservists	500,000
Air force.....................................	900,000
Navy	250,000
Coast artillery	150,000
Supply troops, labor service units...............	2,000,000
Total	10,800,000
Bulgarian army, 30 divisions with special troops....	650,000
Rumanian army, about 25 divisions (more than half of these are only being organized)..............	600,000
Slovakian army	100,000
Croatian troops	100,000
Italian Fascists	50,000
Volunteers from other countries.................	20,000
Total of the satellite troops..........	1,520,000

Undoubtedly the German units are a formidable striking force. It is true that the morale of the Wehrmacht has been deteriorating and that the authority of the commander-in-chief has suffered a precipitate decline, but no one can yet say that discipline has been shattered. The German officers still have control of their men. The German war machine is battered but still intact.

Losses in the best units, however, reached a dangerous point in 1942, and it seems likely that many divisions now consist in large part of hastily trained reservists, the last scrapings of the barrel. The quality of the so-called *Ersatzheer*, or substitute army, is said to be particularly low. This army, stationed at home, is under the command of Colonel General Fromm. His troops serve both as garrisons—an important task in view of the 12,000,000 foreigners in Germany—and as replacements for the field units; but they are replacements that come far from reaching the former German standards.

Not all the field divisions are organized in the same fashion or have the same strength, even disregarding their losses. The figure of 15,000 men to a division is only an average. The acute shortage of man power is reflected in the recent announcement that a special Hitler Youth Division, consisting largely of boys under eighteen, had been formed in the Waffen SS, the Blackshirt Guards fighting at the front.

The strong anti-aircraft force—1,000,000 men—will be a surprise to many. The fact is that this figure includes only the regularly enlisted personnel; if we added the Hitler Youth, Russian war prisoners and others who serve in the anti-aircraft force, it would perhaps be doubled. The enormous expansion of this force partly explains the man power shortage that afflicts the German war machine.

The police troops represent formidable combat strength and are one of the most important instruments for maintaining order in the occupied countries. They comprise all kinds of units and are specially trained in street fighting and counterrevolutionary tactics. They are largely motorized.

The supply troops are charged with the organization of supply areas, and therefore have no direct combat tasks. The same is true of the OT (Organization Todt), the well-known pioneer organization that builds everything behind and at the front, as well as of the labor service units that usually work further to the rear. Numbered with the supply troops are the transport troops, which take care of communications, particularly in occupied countries, where they also must be prepared to fight against partisans and saboteurs.

Also numbered with them are the special troops used to guard prison camps, bridges, railways, etc., and as garrisons in less threatened areas. They ordinarily consist of older reservists, home guards (*Landesschützen*), the lightly wounded and quickly trained "rejectees." In this way the Third Reich has tried to compensate for its losses. We can estimate that at least 3,500,000 men—dead, badly wounded, missing and prisoners—have been put out of action.

The strength of the air force has been considerably reduced, and Reichsmarshal Goering has been forced to release some of his personnel to the army. The Luftwaffe probably has no more than 10-12,000 first-line planes. Most of them are fighters, on which aircraft production has lately been concentrated. Ten or twelve thousand planes is a strong force, but when they are dispersed over a whole continent the greater part of which is threatened by air attacks, this number is absolutely insufficient. Furthermore, the German air force is handicapped by insufficient fuel supplies. In order to save gasoline, student pilots are given fewer hours in the air, and this has lowered the standard of the personnel. Even in 1941, when standards presumably were higher, there were 20,000 training accidents in the German air force.

Germany has an air force reserve of considerable strength, and I was told that 3,000 planes are standing by for action—when the time comes. This, however, is too small a margin for safety.

The German navy has not been appreciably improved, except in submarines. Even these have shown a conspicuous lack of activity during the past few months, largely as a result of new Allied countermeasures. A great many people believe—and I think with good reason—that Germany is holding back a U-boat reserve against the Allied invasion of the Continent. And it must not be forgotten that Germany still has several powerful surface craft, including three battleships, that can be used when the moment comes.

The coast artillery has been gradually improved to meet invasion threats. It is strongest along the English Channel, but heavy fortifications also dot the North Sea coast.

As for the satellite nations, the Germans cannot count on the Finnish or Hungarian armies. Neither of these can be persuaded to offer any contribution to the war, except in defense of its own soil. Finland is said to have 300,000 men under arms. The Hungarians could produce about 40 divisions, with considerable forces in reserve—in all more than 1,000,000 men.

The Rumanians have no great reputation as soldiers, but they have been fighting rather well in the East. They have suffered severe losses, however, and the greatly reduced Rumanian army cannot be counted on to any extent. As for the Bulgarians, their value is totally dependent on the political development in the country. I have ignored the Bulgarian units serving under General Vlassoff, the Russian Quisling, these being of doubtful value. The Slovenes cannot now be used outside the borders of their country; nor can the Croatian puppet army, although it might play a local role against the Allies when they invade the Balkans.

We cannot fully appreciate the German weakness in the present situation until we make an attempt to apportion Germany's armed forces over "Fortress Europe." For a rough and wholly amateur list of German and satellite forces in August 1943 see page 290.

This table shows how hard it has been for the Germans to arrange their forces so as to meet the simultaneous threats of invasion from the East, the West and the South. If they had retained superiority in the air, the problem would have been simplified. But with all their communication lines subject to air attacks and with the railways becoming more and more disorganized, the Germans can no longer utilize the great advantage they possess of operating on inner lines. The Wehrmacht has lost its greatest weapon—its mobility.

In appraising the military might of Germany today, several other factors must be considered in addition to mere numbers. One problem presents itself immediately: the matter of fuel. German experts have stated that the country needs 22,000,000 tons of oil and gasoline yearly for offensive warfare. On the other hand, the defensive tactics on which the Germans have concentrated since the autumn of 1942 may not have required more than 15,000,000 tons for a year's warfare.

Germany's production of synthetic gasoline in the spring of 1943 was reported by reliable sources in Berlin as proceeding at the rate of 6,000,000 tons a year. From Rumania, Germany counts on getting 4,500,000 tons in 1943, but the total Rumanian production is said to have fallen to 5,500,000 tons a year, even before the big American air attack on the Ploesti oil fields. In addition to these 10,500,000 tons, oil also flowed from sources within the Reich (Austria and Hanover, 1,000,000 tons a year), from Galicia (800,000 tons) and from Hungary (1,000,000 tons), carrying the estimated total production for 1943 to 13,300,000 tons. The Italians

Area	Number of infantry divisions German	Number of armored and tank divisions German	Police troops	Army units, anti-aircraft, noncombatant units	Coastal artillery	Total directly military German troops	Satellites
The East front	120	10	50,000	300,000	..	2,230,000	145,000
Supply area	15	..	150,000	260,000	15,000	650,000	50,000
Government General	3	..	50,000	130,000	..	225,000	..
Protectorate	3	..	40,000	35,000	..	120,000	..
Finland	6	..	..	20,000	..	110,000	..
Norway	12	1	20,000	45,000	20,000	273,000	..
Denmark	4	1	10,000	15,000	5,000	98,000	..
Western territories	50	6	60,000	290,000	75,000	1,223,000	..
Italy	25	4	25,000	60,000	..	492,000	50,000
Balkans	15	1	30,000	55,000	5,000	323,000	1,175,000
Slovakia	..	..	5,000	..	..	5,000	100,000
Germany	5	..	60,000	495,000	30,000	660,000	..
Strategic reserve	12	2	..	45,000	..	316,000	..
	270	25	500,000	1,750,000	150,000	6,725,000	1,520,000

NOTE: There is also in Germany the so-called *Ersatzheer* (substitute army) of 1,000,000 men. The supply area in the East comprises all occupied territories in the East (inclusive of the Baltic and Bessarabia) which lie 100 km. or more behind the front.

had oil wells in Albania, with a 1942 production of 300,000 tons, and these are now in German hands. On the other hand, Germany had been forced to supply Italy with oil and gasoline, and the result was that her own supplies were reduced, despite measures of economy. Her reserves probably do not now exceed 2,000,000 tons.

One could list many other problems that make it increasingly difficult for Germany to continue in the war much longer. Vital raw materials are becoming scarcer, the transport system is disorganized, the lack of fats is felt more and more. But while the whole German community is overworked and suffering from nervous exhaustion, no one should underrate its strength. Nazism is not going to fall like the walls of Jericho. The Third Reich still has reserves and cards that have not been played.

To such reserves belong the new weapons about which so much has been said. It would be a mistake to think that this is only propaganda. The promise of retaliation that Hitler made in his speech of September 10 must be fulfilled. It is wise to count on the probability that the Germans have technical means which are the Führer's last trump cards. When a foreign newspaperman in June 1943 referred to a semi-official statement about a possible "preventive action" against England, he casually said something of the utmost interest. The German action, he said, was to be carried out partly with long-range artillery.

In my opinion, this remark points in a definite direction. During the First World War, the Germans surprised the world with their 75-mile guns. The Allies were never able to capture one of these Big Berthas; they were melted down. Today there is nothing to prevent the Germans from using guns that will carry twice that distance. In order to have a decisive effect, such a gun must possess tremendous propulsive power or the projectile must have enormous weight. In the latter case, the rocket system is a possibility. Low accuracy in firing is not a fatal drawback when the projectile is the size of a small house.

If this gun has a firing range of 150 miles, which is not impossible, the Germans would be in a position to destroy great parts of London and seriously damage England from well-protected gun positions on the Continent. If this happened, it would, of course, considerably weaken an important link in the Allied chain around Europe—but would it lessen the British determination to continue the war to a victorious end? The chances are that England, the United States and Russia would answer with new weapons. Crush-

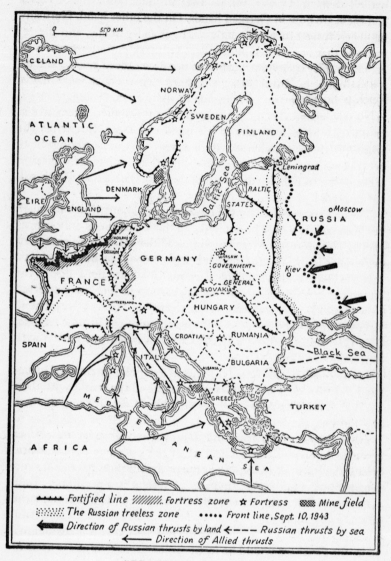

"FESTUNG EUROPA"

ing blows would be directed against Germany and against the area serving as base for these giant guns, from the parts of England that are beyond their range.

Germany's war power depends not only on the army but also on leadership. That brings us to the question: How strong is the Third Reich politically?

No one knows exactly what has transpired behind the scenes in Germany during the past few months. But it looks as though German military leaders have taken a hand in the political direction of the war, owing to pressure from the front. The generals are said to have been carrying on negotiations with the Nazi Party bosses. The story goes on to say that they told the Party to keep its hands off the Wehrmacht and the High Command, and devote its efforts exclusively to the home front and its pressing problems, including anti-aircraft defense and finding new homes for the civilian population.

Hitler himself has been pushed more and more into the background, and nobody knows whether he is playing an important political role at the present time. But Heinrich Himmler, who stands at the opposite pole from the Wehrmacht, is looking after his interests. There are persistent rumors that the generals claim Reichsmarshal Goering, Hitler's designated successor, as a member of their group. Both the Party and the High Command think that the Allies would be disposed to accept Goering as a negotiator in event of an armistice. This is one reason for his present strong position.

The capitulation of Italy must have made a crushing impression on the German public. Germans are inclined to draw parallels with the First World War, and Badoglio's surrender offers ground for comparisons. The word "1918" is beginning to have a more and more hypnotic effect on the German people as the Nazis are well aware. They fight vigorously against the notion that history will repeat itself. History never repeats itself, Under Secretary Karl Hermann Frank told the Czechs at the beginning of 1943. In talking about the impossibility of a new 1918, the Nazis never fail to mention the Gestapo.

And they have good reasons for doing so. As long as Himmler and the Wehrmacht work together, any attempt at revolt would be crushed in blood. The Gestapo has prepared defenses against internal enemies to the last detail. Machine-gun nests—camouflaged either as stone huts (for example, in the Wittenbergplatz in Berlin) or else as bomb shelters for personnel—have been installed in railway stations and traffic junctions in the big cities. SS men, armed with automatic weapons, occupy strategically important corner houses. As long as the friction between the Party and the police on one side and the Wehrmacht on the other side does not result in an open break, the home front will hold. But the relationship between Himmler and the generals is to a great extent affected by external developments.

Victors and Vanquished

During the summer of 1943, the military situation in Europe underwent radical changes. In the East, the Red Army started a summer offensive for the first time during the war and forced the Germans to surrender the most vital areas of the Ukraine. Meanwhile, developments in southern Europe forced the German military leaders to weaken their lines in Russia.

The losses have been very great on both sides. A war of attrition is being fought, and in August the Germans were still hoping to "pump the air" out of their Russian opponents. If they succeeded in this aim, the High Command would have gained a respite of four or five months in the East. But although certain signs of weariness have appeared on the Russian side, it seems clear that the Red Army is the one that has the greater reserves.

Numerically, the Russians are vastly superior. Germany's total available man power is probably 11,000,000 men, whereas Russia probably has 17,000,000 in spite of her much greater losses. But Russia, like Germany, needs troops elsewhere than on the principal front, and probably not more than 300 divisions can be used for operations in the West. This is, however, twice as many as the Germans have available at the present time in the East. It will therefore be very difficult for the Germans to halt the Russians, and a radical shortening of the front line may be necessary.

In the South, Germany suffered a catastrophic defeat in the surrender of Italy. From a purely military point of view, it might have been a good thing for Germany to get rid of her Italian partner. Merely to stop sending 40 or 50 coal trains daily over the Brenner Pass must have been a tremendous saving. But the Allied invasion of Italy opens extraordinarily serious perspectives for the Third

Reich. Crushing air attacks can now be directed against what used to be the fairly safe areas of South Germany, Austria, the Bohemian Protectorate and Silesia—yes, even German factories in Poland. The prospect of doing battle in northern Italy must also have given pause to the Germans, since their supply lines cross the Alps through easily bombed passes, and the Allies will probably have control of the air.

If the Germans can hold the Balkans for a few months longer, the situation will seem more hopeful for the Third Reich. But it is doubtful whether they have strength enough there for a successful defense, even if they shorten the Russian front. What Hungary does will be of the utmost importance. The 40 Hungarian divisions could, theoretically speaking, stabilize the situation for Germany in Southeast Europe for six months or even a whole year. But Berlin has hardly any hope of help from Hungary, and the help from Rumania is wholly insufficient. And if Bulgaria surrendered, which is not unlikely, the Germans would either have to rush more troops to the Balkans, thus using up their entire strategical reserve, or else make a speedy evacuation. Neither of these measures would offer more than a temporary solution of their difficulties.

Thus, in a very few days, the surrender of Italy completely changed the situation in southern Europe. It will also affect the situation in the West. The natural course for the Allies would be to capitalize their advantage by attacking southern France. The French Mediterranean coast can be taken from two sides. An Allied landing between La Rochelle and Biarritz would come simultaneously with a landing between Perpignan and Nice. If, in addition, the Allies dropped air-borne troops on a heretofore unprecedented scale in all of southern France, particularly on the high plateau of Auvergne, the situation could be made untenable for the Germans. The Allies have one more advantage in this area— that is, the help of an effective organization set up inside France while the country was still controlled by the Vichy government, *before* the Germans marched in. The members of this huge organization have so far kept under cover by order from London.

The Germans also have to meet other difficulties in defending southern France. The fortifications are not nearly so well made as those in the Occupied Zone and reinforcements to the fighting German forces can be sent only from one direction—from the North.

Although southern France is particularly vulnerable, the whole coast from the northernmost tip of Norway to the Spanish border is threatened by an Allied invasion. The Atlantic Wall covers only the most important points, except along the Channel coast. The fortifications along the entire coastline have been erected with the help of foreign workers, who have doubtless made detailed reports to the British Secret Service.

The Germans will undoubtedly try to hold France at all costs. Pernaps they will throw in their last reserves of planes and matériel, not to speak of their "secret weapons," in the battle for the Atlantic coast. But it is hard to see how a German defense in the West could be anything more than temporary.

The situation looks gloomy for the Germans. Is there any chance that the Third Reich can avoid defeat? Leading Nazis still think that there is. They point to the situation in 1762, toward the end of the Seven Years' War, when Frederick the Great was standing alone against two great empires, Austria and Russia, and it seemed that he was facing an absolutely certain catastrophe. But the Empress Elizabeth of Russia died and her successor, Peter III, offered Frederick a separate peace. This time again, rescue might come from Russia.

Germans in general would certainly prefer a settlement with the Allies, no matter at what cost, provided it did not require a complete capitulation. But the Nazis themselves prefer a separate peace with Russia, because it might mean that they were saving not only Germany itself but also perhaps some added portions of the Third Reich. If the Nazis were forced to capitulate, they would much rather surrender to Stalin than to Churchill and Roosevelt.

For the past half year, German diplomacy has been working frantically for peace. In Kuibyshev and later in Moscow, representatives of Japan have toiled uninterruptedly in behalf of their European ally. The task is difficult, perhaps impossible, but the problem has been occupying the attention of the world for months. No one can deny that Germany and Russia have many interests in common. The Russians, too, might feel that their security would be endangered if England and the United States became too powerful. There is a community of interests among the continental powers as against the naval powers. The Germans play on these chords and apparently dream of creating a "continental triangle"— Moscow-Berlin-Paris.

As regards territorial questions, Germany can offer Russia more than the Allies can give. The Third Reich has not tied its hands in regard to the smaller nations. It would again sacrifice Finland as remorselessly as it did in 1939-40. Nor would it permit any "sentimental regard" for Rumania to stand in the way if the great objective could be reached.

The Germans are also counting heavily on an actual split between the Allies and Russia. In Berlin, everything has been done to magnify the differences; for example, the affair of the 10,000 slaughtered Polish officers was an effective means of creating disunity. Berliners have also noted with satisfaction certain events in Moscow that have deepened the gulf between Russia and the Allies—for example, the creation of the Free Germany Committee.

To dispassionate observers, it seems a bit hard to believe, however, that Russia should grasp Hitler's outstretched hand. A German-Russian separate peace would not end the war. The Allies are sufficiently strong to bring the Germans to their knees, even if they effected some kind of peace in the East. For the Soviet Union, the only way out of the dilemma would then be to support Germany against her enemies, and the resulting situation would resemble the Russian shift that saved Frederick the Great after the death of the Empress Elizabeth.

A situation of this kind is perhaps conceivable, but it is most unlikely. In any case, a German-Russian combination would suffer from grave military disadvantages. The Allies would still be masters of the air. Without access to outside food supplies, the position of the continental combination would be precarious.

A direct capitulation to Stalin by the Nazis, which in my opinion was a possibility in the fall of 1942, is now out of the question. If the Russians should seem willing to make peace with Germany, there are forces in Germany that would refuse to follow Hitler. The position of the Nazi regime is considerably weaker than in 1942. Besides, the Allies are in Italy and would not passively stand by.

Germany's hope of a separate peace, therefore, seems faint and kept alive by wishful thinking. But this does not mean that Germany is unable to play one enemy against another and thereby weaken both.

Today the German question is the greatest of all those standing between Russia and her allies. The permanence of the Anglo-Russian coalition will depend on its solution.

Certainly there is no point in putting false emphasis on the creation of the Free Germany Committee in Moscow. But there are other signs that the Russian policy toward Germany differs in important respects from that of her allies. Naturally, Stalin holds that Nazism must disappear. Russia is as unlikely to sign a separate agreement with the Third Reich as are the Western Allies. Stalin believes that the Germans must surrender the occupied territories and that they must do reconstruction work in Russia. But what if Stalin declares himself willing to let the German military machine remain intact, and what if he seeks the sort of an understanding with the German generals that would not constitute a break between himself and the Allies, but would, on the other hand, give Russia a deciding voice in German foreign policy? The British and the Americans have demanded unconditional surrender. The Russians have let it be understood that they are prepared to accept the existence of the German war machine. Thus, the Russians can offer the German generals far more advantageous terms than unconditional surrender. Furthermore they are fighting on their own soil, whereas the British and Americans have carried the war to Germany and, by their bombings, have provoked a popular resentment that might easily be utilized to justify an agreement with Russia.

Judging from all signs, a race for German favor is about to begin. The vanquished may find themselves courted by the victors. The present Allies may bid against one another, for any nation with Germany on its side can dominate all Europe. The Russians so far have the upper hand, since they are not bound by a demand for "unconditional surrender." [1]

It must not be forgotten that there is another side to the problem—Japan. The Anglo-Saxon powers seem determined not to compromise, but to continue the war in the Far East until absolute victory has been achieved and Japanese military power permanently crushed. But it is within Russia's power either to hasten or to delay this outcome. Perhaps a situation will arise in which the Russians will show themselves just as cold to Allied pleas for a second front in Siberia as Great Britain and America were to Russian pleas for a second front in Europe.

It is clear to everybody who will be vanquished when this war is over. But who will be the victors? From a purely technical point of

---

[1] *This was written in August, when the conflict between the Russian and the Anglo-American policy toward Germany was at its height. Later, in the Moscow Pact, Stalin endorsed the demand for unconditional surrender.—Tr.*

view, the United States, Great Britain and Russia will be on the winning side. But even if the split between them is patched up, as seems likely, important differences will remain after the war. These must disappear—or lead to conflict. A new world war would be certain to create chaos, and there would be no victors afterwards; there would be only the vanquished.

The Responsibility of the Victors

What the last phase of the war will bring we still do not know. We are not even sure that general disintegration can be averted. Want and misery have created havoc. Foreign workers deported to Germany may rise in a new Spartacus revolt on a scale heretofore unknown in history. Flaming hate in the occupied countries is waiting for a release.

Old Europe's machinery is worn out. Supplies of the type that remained after the last World War are nonexistent, and in many places the masses lack all essentials. Communication lines have been disorganized and permit only slow transit; ports have been destroyed and thousands of ships are now at the bottom of the sea. Millions of people have been killed at the front or behind it. No one is untouched by the changes. After this war, peace and welfare can be restored only by intensive efforts that must last, perhaps, for generations.

Should the war continue without compromise until the Third Reich is defeated—which is likely—the responsibility for reconstruction will rest on the three powers that now lead the coalition against Nazism—the United States, Great Britain and Russia.

First of all, they will have to solve such immediate tasks as the supply of food, medicine, other essential articles and—what may prove more difficult—the maintenance of law and order. Only afterwards can they take up such problems as punishing the Quislings and the Nazis, liberating political prisoners, restoring stolen property and the settlement of private claims. Thereafter the victors must decide on methods for the political reconstruction of Europe.

There has been some indication of how many Englishmen view this problem. According to them, Europe can best be reconstructed on the basis of regional federations. But in Moscow such ideas are considered a threat to Russian security. Russia has vetoed not only a

Northern confederation but also a Middle European confederation.

One is led to suspect that Russia desires a weak Europe with many small states, which could be dominated by Moscow; but it is easy to see that a Russian endeavor to dominate Europe would meet no less resistance than the German attempt at a New Order. Europe is a divided continent, consisting of numerous nations, religions and cultures. History has taught us that its peoples do not desire to be ruled by one power alone. On the other hand, there will be no hope of solving European problems on a grand scale unless the three great nations that won the war can adopt a common peace program, after clarifying various obscure problems in the relationships among themselves.

What Europe needs today and tomorrow is an organic order that offers stability. Out of the experiences of this war, all peoples will emerge with a strong desire for peace and quiet, for a daily life without bombs, terror and starvation. When the first passions have been spent, this tendency will prevail even in the lands now occupied.

It is impossible to reorganize all Europe according to one pre-scribed formula. The structures of the states are too different. But there already exists a path, vaguely discernible before the war, that can lead to stability and continuity. It consists in the revival of con-stitutional monarchy, a phenomenon of which there are increasing signs today.

People everywhere are coming to realize that the monarchical state is a remarkable source of national strength. What would Nor-way be without King Haakon, Holland without Queen Wilhel-mina, Belgium without King Leopold or Denmark without King Christian? A growing monarchical tendency can be traced in Spain and Portugal, in Germany and Austria. In our times the monarch is not only a symbol of the past, but also a great stabilizing force that can be called upon when the day of decision arrives. The monarchical idea could serve as a framework for the restoration of Europe, or at least for the reconstruction of those countries that still possess monarchical traditions; and it could also be combined with regional confederations of the smaller states.

Many in their democratic zeal will mistakenly identify the res-toration movements with "reaction." To them "democracy" has become identical with "republic." This is true even for certain circles in the land of His Britannic Majesty, especially when they look at *other* countries. But the most violent opponents of the monarchical idea are the exiled governments of the new states created by the Treaty of Versailles. These wish to regain their old positions, and to a certain extent, they can depend on support from Russia. But it would be fatal if Mr. Benes—to mention one name—was permitted to put his stamp on the reorganization of Middle Europe. "Czechoslovakia does not need to change her policy," he said in a recent statement. "She continues her endeavors with the same Slovak and democratic goals as before." That sounds as if he had learned nothing and forgotten everything.

It seems to be agreed in Allied quarters that a solution must be found that will restore Germany to Europe and give the Germans an opportunity to find their natural expression as a nation-state. The task is difficult. At a time when millions are crying for blood and revenge, when almost all European peoples have suffered under the Nazi heel, it is hard to retain common sense and balance or to make the necessary distinction between Germany and Nazism. But not to make this distinction would lead to psychological consequences that might be disastrous. We have seen many indications —among others the stand taken by the British Trade Union Congress—that this fact is recognized by the Allied nations. There is no doubt that the German people as a whole will have to pay for Hitler's ten-year regime, but it would be a real disaster if they were forced to give "an eye for an eye and a tooth for a tooth."

To solve the German question demands great prudence, generosity and farsightedness. The Allies have the opportunity, which perhaps occurs once in a hundred years, to determine the future attitude of a nation with 80,000,000 people. There are many paths to follow. To those, however, who view the problem with steady eyes, Germany is a historic necessity. She should, of course, lose Austria, but to dismember the rest of the country would bring only misfortune. Nor does a Weimar Republic suit the German mentality, a fact that we may lament but cannot change. To force on the Germans a copy of the English, American or Russian forms of government would be fatal—as fatal as if the German borders were thrown open and all the oppressed nations allowed to satisfy their thirst for revenge.

The victors will be forced to examine the idea of letting Germany adopt a monarchical form of government. Many will regard this as a threat comparable perhaps to Nazism, one that would automatically lead to a German attempt at revenge. Others believe that the love for democracy—or rather, for liberty—that is certain to follow this war will make a monarchical solution unthinkable.

Nobody knows what Germany will look like after the liquidation of the Third Reich, nor does anyone know what leaders will shape the destiny of the new Germany. There are men both inside and outside the Third Reich who are going to play important roles. Among them is former Reichschancellor Bruening. For years he has devoted himself to science, at an American university. He has kept silent and refrained from doing anything, directly or indirectly, against Germany. He is a good German, something that not even his angriest opponents can deny. It is also generally known that his hands are clean. He has been criticized for his indecision in the days before Hitler. But in the new Germany he may play a very important role, particularly because of the international confidence he enjoys. One of his assets is that he has been able to follow the entire development from the outside.

One of the main reasons for the fiasco of Versailles was undoubtedly the fact that it destroyed the unity of the old Danubian monarchy and replaced it with a number of small states hostile to one another. Even in 1919 farsighted observers among the victorious powers warned of the consequences which would follow. It did not take long for their predictions to come true.

Once again the Danubian countries are being dissolved in the crucible of war. Once again the old problem presents itself—unity or disunity? And once again the governments-in-exile are demanding the creation of a new Little Entente, this time expanded by the forcible inclusion of a weak Austria and a weakened Hungary. But is this the best solution? Those who have studied the problems of Central Europe feel that a repetition of Versailles would lead to the same results all over again.

The natural solution would be the restoration of a Danubian monarchy. Statesmen used to say that if Austria did not exist, it would have to be invented. That is still true 128 years after the Congress of Vienna. Nothing short of monarchy would restore the unity of the Danube Basin, without which there can be no economic or political health in Central Europe. This is a lesson that Austrians, Hungarians and Czechs have learned from the past. As for the objections raised by the Czech government-in-exile, they need not be decisive. The Czechs now in the Protectorate may prove to be favorably disposed toward a Danube monarchy in which their nation would play an equal role. The Hungarians would doubtless welcome it; and I have already mentioned that large circles in Austria are entertaining similar thoughts. Need has been a harsh teacher for the Danube peoples. More and more they are beginning to long for a restoration of their former union

No other nation has been subjected to such a harsh fate as Poland. Her leaders have either been murdered or driven into exile. The small middle class has been deprived of all opportunities for education or professional work and the bulk of the people are living like pariahs in Greater Germany. For four years the Nazis have attempted by various means to change the Poles into a submissive mass without hope for a future. They have been treated as inferior beings whose sole task is to serve their masters, the Germans.

Yet Governor General Frank has not succeeded in crushing the courage of the Polish nation. He has not even succeeded in suppressing the secret Polish government that still exists in the homeland and that has organized resistance down to the smallest detail. Secret print shops provide the public with quantities of illegal newspapers, using all kinds of tricks to distribute them. If you turn to page 2 of an innocent-looking copy of the *Völkischer Beobachter,* you may find that it has suddenly become the fighting organ of Polish patriots. The Catholic Church offers powerful support to the opposition, with the result that many of its priests have been martyred. Passive resistance has been developed to the full, and active resistance is not lacking; indeed, the whole Polish nation participates in what are now illegal activities. The Germans themselves have done away with the old class distinctions. Members of internationally known Polish families that played an important part in their country's history now make their living as coal dealers or farmers, since they can find no other work. Each in his own place labors to maintain the spirit of the nation.

Perhaps the work now being done will atone for many of the political mistakes committed by the Poles, particularly by their upper classes. A great moral debt is owed Poland by the Allies. Nevertheless, the Polish question will be extremely hard to solve, not only because of the border disputes with Russia, but also because of the devastation caused by the Germans. It will take a long time to rebuild Poland into a state.

Not only the future stand of the Great Powers but also the fate of the small nations will create problems at the peace conference.

The Swedes are particularly concerned with the destiny of their neighbors. That Norway and Denmark will regain their freedom is self-evident; they are heart and soul against Hitler. Finland has been dragged into the war on Germany's side, but everybody knows that she would never have fought against Russia in June 1941 had not Russia attacked her in November 1939. Besides, if the Russians had not opposed all plans for a defensive alliance of the Northern States, there would have been an additional guarantee against Finland's being involved in the war.

It serves no purpose, however, to recall the past. Instead the question is: Has Finland any prospect of receiving an honorable peace? The difficulties are many. Nobody knows what terms the Russians are willing to offer. Does Stalin wish to reach an agreement that would mean a definitive solution of an age-old dispute? If that question can be answered in the affirmative, prospects should be bright for the Finns. Should the answer be negative, it would indicate the existence of a tendency in Russian policy that will not only be fatal to Finland, but will also create disturbing questions for other nations, including Russia's allies.

There are many obstacles on the road toward a United North, which is Sweden's peace aim. But The North will remain a political reality in spite of everything. A conviction that has such deep roots in the northern peoples themselves will sooner or later be realized. It is in line with the general trend toward the association of the smaller nations into groups that are held together by a spirit of mutual collaboration.

There is another question that Swedes regard as one of the most tragic political problems of northern Europe. After only twenty years of freedom, Latvia, Estonia and Lithuania have perished in the struggle between two great powers, Germany and Russia. Many things indicate that Moscow is not inclined to permit their restoration after a German defeat. Latvians, Estonians and Lithuanians are completely defenseless. Their fate is not connected with the fortunes of the victorious powers. Their eventual hopes of regaining freedom can not be founded on political factors of a realistic nature; they are mere pawns in the game. Nevertheless, they are not forgotten either by the neutrals or by the belligerents. All through the North there is a warm desire that Estonians, Latvians and Lithuanians should again be permitted to shape their own destinies. In the United States, with its millions of Baltic immigrants, the same desire is widely prevalent. It is too early, however, to judge whether international sympathy for the three small countries will be of any political importance in the peace settlement.

A Europe that is organized on a monarchical basis has every prospect of becoming a stable and peaceful Europe. There are, however, certain conditions that will have to be fulfilled. Its organizers will have to show strength and farsightedness. Even the vanquished must be heard, and they must exert some influence on the process of reorganization. There must also be an unbiased approach by all those outside Europe who will help to determine the terms of peace.

Will the Americans, who are different in many respects from Europeans, realize that Europe cannot be changed into an imitation of America, and that the choice is between an organic solution and renewed chaos? Realizing the ignorance of Europeans regarding America, one is often tempted to fear the worst if a corresponding ignorance prevails in the United States. But the healthy and unconventional attitude toward life that is prevalent among Americans can help them to understand European problems. Much has happened during this war to contribute to bringing the two continents closer to each other.

It may be too early now to discuss the problems of peace, but we can discern signs that the end may come earlier than we think. Already it is clear that this war has brought about the greatest changes in modern history. At some time in the future, when present events are far behind us, we shall perhaps look upon Hitler as a tool of destiny, but of a wholly different destiny from the one that he envisaged in his eagle's nest at Berchtesgaden, as he pondered over his world-embracing mission. Because of his tyrannical regime, freedom became a flesh-and-blood reality and a precious ideal, even for citizens of countries with long traditions of freedom. Perhaps history will judge that *this* was Hitler's mission.

As time goes on, we gain a different perspective on today's events. There is much that is now kept in the background by the fury of war. Most important, perhaps, is the fact that the European continent has undergone a profound transformation. It is no longer the center from which the world is directed. If Europe is to regain some of its former position and some of its old prestige, European nations will have to act in solidarity. No people can be missing from the linking chain.